For Roger &

Love,

Bob

JOHN DOS PASSOS

JOHN DOS PASSOS
POLITICS
and the
WRITER

by
Robert C. Rosen

UNIVERSITY OF NEBRASKA PRESS
Lincoln and London

Portions of Chapter 2, section XII, through Chapter 3, section V, have previously appeared, in somewhat different form, as "Dos Passos' Other Trilogy," *Modern Fiction Studies* 26 (Autumn 1980): 483–502.

The paper in this book meets the guidelines for permanence and durability of the Committee on Production Guidelines for Book Longevity of the Council on Library Resources.

Library of Congress Cataloging in Publication Data

Rosen, Robert C., 1947–
John Dos Passos, politics and the writer.

Bibliography: p.
Includes index.
1. Dos Passos, John, 1896–1970—Political and social views. 2. Politics in literature. 3. Politics and literature—United States. 4. Authors, American—20th century—Biography. I. Title.
PS3507.Q743Z79   813'.52   81–1928
ISBN O-8032-3860-6   AACR2

For my parents,
Beatrice and Morris Rosen

CONTENTS

CHAPTER ONE.
INDIVIDUALIST REBEL: 1896-1925

Uncertain Patrimony / 3; From Detachment to Involvement: *One Man's Initiation—1917* / 10; "Declassing Oneself" / 13; The Artist as Rebel: *Three Soldiers* / 15; The War at Home / 23; The Machine and the Garden: *Rosinante to the Road Again* / 26; Exotic Travels and "The Illusion of Geography" / 29; The Bohemian and the Radical / 32; Experimental Drama: *The Garbage Man* / 35; Eros and Civilized Society: *Streets of Night* / 38; Social Criticism and Literary Form: *Manhattan Transfer* / 41

CHAPTER TWO.
SOCIALISM AND DEMOCRACY: 1925-39

The New Masses I'd Like / 50; Writer and Martyrs: Sacco and Vanzetti / 52; Revolutionary Theater: *Airways, Inc.* / 56; On the Fence: Russia, 1928 / 61; The Role of the Middle-Class Writer / 64; Bloody Harlan / 67; Depression Politics / 69; Depression Drama: *Fortune Heights* / 72; Fascism, Communism, and Americanism / 74; The Individual in History: *U.S.A.* / 78; The Anatomy of Socialism / 91; The Civil War in Spain / 93; Despair and Defeat: *Adventures of a Young Man* / 96

CHAPTER THREE.
WORKING DOWN AT THE BOTTOM
OF A WELL: 1939-70

PREFACE

"Writing," Dos Passos once told an audience, "is like setting up milk bottles at fairs for people to throw baseballs at."[1] Indeed, Dos Passos, far more than most American writers, has repeatedly suffered partisan attacks for the political content of his fiction. A pacifist and a fiery socialist in his early years, a Goldwater supporter later, he always offended someone with his views, and his rightward drift left many early enthusiasts feeling resentful and betrayed. The intensity of these responses attests not only to the urgency of the questions his work raises, but also to the care required in interpreting and evaluating his literary contribution.

Many critics simply ignore or deny the essential political dimension of Dos Passos's work and life. Formalists focus rather narrowly on the subtle qualities of a "text" that seems to them to exist outside of history and biography. Some critics take due note of the charged political surface of Dos Passos's fiction, but see beneath that surface a politics that is "clearly non-political," or "essentially apolitical"— in other words, just a distraction, or a mannerism. Others admit that Dos Passos's fiction does indeed have serious political implications, but suggest, rather condescendingly, that Dos Passos himself wandered into a political arena where he (like all artists, presumably) did not belong, and ended up naïvely, and even embarrassingly, "parroting" the slogans and "uttering the cant" of various political groups. And still others dissolve Dos Passos's quite detailed social criticism into impossibly grand abstractions like "the human condition," or else simply find that criticism far less important than the deep-seated neuroses they are sure it manifests.[2]

But if Dos Passos's critics often lead us away from social issues, his work itself always leads us back to them. War, trade unions, the alienation of city life, the New Deal, American Communists, pseudopopulist demagogues, and, in *U.S.A.*, monopoly capitalism itself have been his subjects, not just background or metaphor for the examination of some presumably larger or more fundamental questions. Aesthetic purists notwithstanding, politics is not inimical to art, and for Dos Passos it is in fact its very essence, what makes his art possible. A criticism that fails or refuses seriously to engage itself with the political content of Dos Passos's work—and the point, of course, is not to pitch more baseballs at it—will miss what makes his fiction so often exciting and valuable.

Central to Dos Passos's achievement as a political novelist is the ambitiousness of his quest—to chronicle and analyze twentieth-century American society. Though broad in scope, his fiction is never abstract or mystifying. He persisted in trying to explain human conditions; he did not simply bemoan and reify their seeming irrationality. And he succeeded in dramatizing, often with extraordinary clarity and power, how great historical forces shape the lives of individuals. Further, the technical experimenting through which he sought to expand the scope of his fiction is not only exciting in itself, but also sheds much light on the complex relationship between political ideology and literary form.

A careful examination of Dos Passos's political thinking—expressed most unambiguously in his letters, diaries, journalism, historical writings, and the many causes he gave his name and time to—is obviously essential to a full understanding of his art. Moreover, his views, though not necessarily original, are themselves worth studying, for through them Dos Passos—as he becomes successively a youthful pacifist rebel, a libertarian socialist, a Jeffersonian democrat, and finally a conservative Republican—emerges as a sort of emblematic figure. The evolution (or, perhaps, devolution) of his ideas epitomizes, in many ways, the difficulties, the contradictions, and ultimately the fate of radical idealism in America; once he turns away from the left, he becomes one particularly articulate representative of a whole generation of ex-radicals. In addition, since he is an artist, a careful look at the entire range of Dos Passos's activities raises a whole series of still very important questions about the relationship between political passions and literary efforts.

This study examines Dos Passos's fiction in three interrelated contexts: his life, his political thought, and the history he lived through. My focus is primarily literary, and I treat all his novels and plays as the complex works of art that they are, not simply as documents of a life or of an era. But my aim is literary interpretation informed by biographical, political, and historical considerations. An intermittent commentary running through this study points out the general contours and the most important events of Dos Passos's life, for personal experiences often shaped his political views, and though his fiction creates a broad social panorama, he is in fact a rather autobiographical novelist. More important, I make extensive and detailed use of his writings as a journalist, historian, and correspondent—including unpublished material—in order to explain Dos Passos's troubled and often contradictory political views at each stage of his career, and do not rely, as many do, on his own convenient but misleading retrospective interpretation of those views in *The Theme Is Freedom* (1956). I also outline briefly the historical context of Dos Passos's personal experiences and changing political views, particularly those events—the "red scare" of 1919, the Sacco-Vanzetti case, the miners' strikes in Harlan County, and the Spanish civil war, to name only a few—that served as catalysts in his political development. Placing Dos Passos's fiction back into the personal, intellectual, and social contexts out of which it originally grew permits us to understand it more fully and greatly enriches its interest as literature.

The study emphasizes the complex relationship between Dos Passos's political thinking and his art, and it tries to answer such questions as the origins and characteristics of his early radicalism, its influence on his literary experimentation, the effects on his fiction—particularly *U.S.A.*—of his association with the organized left, the causes and exact nature of his later conservatism, and the connection if any between his rejection of his former views and the decline of his art.

Chapter 1 covers the first three decades of Dos Passos's life, through *Manhattan Transfer,* and traces the development of his rebelliousness and his intense individualism from a somewhat elitist aestheticism to a more political and democratic, but still contradictory radicalism. It discusses the way in which his war experiences, his travels, and his increasing discomfort with his own rather aristocratic class background helped determine the content and the form of his early fiction. Chapter 2 focuses on Dos Passos's continuing literary

xi

development in the context of his work for a variety of left-wing causes in the later 1920s and the depression decade, work which deepened and clarified his radical convictions and led him to seek—and to discover, in *U.S.A.*—a literary form more complex than that of *Manhattan Transfer*, one that could express those convictions more fully. Chapter 3 examines the last three decades of Dos Passos's life, in which he moved to the right politically, began reinterpreting his own past, and abandoned the expansive approach of *U.S.A.* for the rather narrow didacticism that mars his later novels. It also analyzes his new vocation as a historian and his bold but unsuccessful attempt in *Midcentury* to recapture the energy and excitement of *U.S.A.*

This study draws upon the invaluable biographical work of Melvin Landsberg and especially of Townsend Ludington. Ludington's recent authorized biography, *John Dos Passos: A Twentieth Century Odyssey*, is the first full biography of Dos Passos and it will, I hope, help bring Dos Passos the greater attention he deserves. My own study aims for something quite different from Ludington's. It is a work of literary criticism, while his is not, and it views Dos Passos as a more seriously, more essentially political being than does his. But it is much indebted to Ludington's lucid and thorough book.[3]

This study is meant to complement the valuable full-length literary studies that have explicated Dos Passos's fiction and established its literary importance. Its contribution is in considering the entire body of Dos Passos's writing and insisting on the importance to understanding his fiction of a detailed analysis of his evolving political thought. It takes Dos Passos's early radicalism quite seriously, rejecting the rather popular view of him as politically "a conservative who [finally] became what he always was," and it tries to emphasize the essentially political nature of all Dos Passos's fiction, without losing sight of its complexity as literature. Its focus is the very intersection of the political and the literary, for it is the melding of these two impulses that produced Dos Passos's best work and their divergence that produced his worst.[4]

Note on Dos Passos's Texts

Dos Passos's letters and diaries abound with errors of spelling and punctuation. In editing his selection of them, Townsend Ludington corrects spelling but not punctuation (including apostrophes), and I will follow his practice when quoting from unpublished material and will avoid the use of [*sic*].

Ellipses appear frequently in Dos Passos's published writing, and I will follow John Brantley's *The Fiction of John Dos Passos* and print Dos Passos's own ellipses *without* spaces between the dots (...), and my ellipses (indicating my deletions from the text) *with* spaces between the dots (. . .).

ACKNOWLEDGMENTS

I would like to thank the following people who read earlier versions of this study and offered valuable criticisms and suggestions: Barbra Apfelbaum, Barbara Foley, Donald B. Gibson, Louis Kampf, Richard Ohmann, Barry Phillips, Michael Reardon, Stephen R. Shalom, William Walling, and David R. Weimer.

I would also like to thank Townsend Ludington for kindly letting me read his biography of Dos Passos while it was still in manuscript, and Elizabeth H. Dos Passos for permission to quote from Dos Passos's papers.

ABBREVIATIONS

JDP   John Dos Passos (as author)
TFC   *The Fourteenth Chronicle: Letters and Diaries of John Dos Passos,* edited by Townsend Ludington (1973)
TCO   *John Dos Passos: A Twentieth Century Odyssey,* by Townsend Ludington (1980)

Works by Dos Passos:

AAL   "Against American Literature" (1916)
AI   *Airways, Inc.* (1928)
AYM   *Adventures of a Young Man* (1939)
BM   *The Big Money* (1936)
CC   *Chosen Country* (1951)
FM   "The Failure of Marxism" (1948)
FSP   *The 42nd Parallel* (1930)
FTC   *Facing the Chair: Story of the Americanization of Two Foreignborn Workmen* (1927)
GD   *The Grand Design* (1949)
GWSO   *The Ground We Stand On* (1941)
HP   "A Humble Protest" (1916)
IAC   *In All Countries* (1934)
MC   *Midcentury* (1961)
ML   *Most Likely to Succeed* (1954)
MT   *Manhattan Transfer* (1925)
NN   *1919* (1932)
NO   *Number One* (1943)

1

OE	*Orient Express* (1927)
OMI	*One Man's Initiation—1917* (1920)
PBU	*The Prospect Before Us* (1950)
RRA	*Rosinante to the Road Again* (1922)
SN	*State of the Nation* (1944)
SON	*Streets of Night* (1923)
TD	*Tour of Duty* (1946)
TF	*The Theme Is Freedom* (1956)
TGD	*The Great Days* (1958)
TJ	*The Head and Heart of Thomas Jefferson* (1954)
TP	*Three Plays* (1934)
TS	*Three Soldiers* (1921)
VHS	*The Villages Are the Heart of Spain* (1938)
YS	"Young Spain" (1917)

CHAPTER ONE
INDIVIDUALIST REBEL: 1896–1925

And what are we fit for when they turn us out of Harvard? We're too intelligent to be successful businessmen and we haven't the sand or the energy to be anything else—
Until Widener is blown up and A. Lawrence Lowell assassinated and the Business School destroyed and its site sowed with salt—no good will come out of Cambridge.

Dos Passos to Arthur K. McComb, *ca.* 1917[1]

Uncertain Patrimony

Bold, powerful, and confident, John Randolph Dos Passos, the writer's father, did little to prepare his son for the confusing and convulsive world he was to face as an adult. The elder Dos Passos, poor but ambitious son of a Portuguese immigrant, rose to the top of a rising class, from office boy to renowned Wall Street lawyer. For organizing the American Sugar Refining Company, successor to the 1887 Sugar Trust, he received the largest legal fee then on record. His thinking, ethical and rational, was conditioned by his place in the world; he defended American imperialism in the Philippines, and his most famous book, *The Anglo-Saxon Century* (1903), proclaimed the world-civilizing duties of the Anglo-Saxon race. By example as well as advice, John Randolph Dos Passos greatly influenced his son's intellectual development, endowing him with a somewhat contradictory mixture of intense individualism, political enthusiasm, moral fervor, and what Dos Passos himself later called "an eighteenth-century education."[2] His very wealth and social status—he owned a hundred-foot yacht and counted William McKinley among his friends—seemed to offer his son a secure sense of his place in the world.

John Dos Passos's place in his own family was insecure, however.

3

Only in 1912, when he was already sixteen, was he publicly acknowledged as a son and given his father's name. His mother—Lucy Madison, an aristocratic southern widow—and his father, who was unable to divorce his mentally ill wife, could pursue their love affair only fitfully; and young John Roderigo Madison grew up while living all over Europe and the United States. It was "a horrible childhood," a "hotel childhood," he later suggests in *Chosen Country;* the more so since he so infrequently saw his father. Some critics have attempted to interpret Dos Passos's literary and political expression primarily as the product of this early, painful relationship to an idolized but intimidating and often absent father.[3] He at least felt very much an outsider when young, and more than a little ambivalent about the world of financiers and politicians that his father moved in.

His years at college settled little for Dos Passos. After attending the Choate School and making a grand tour of Europe with a tutor, "Uncle Virgil" Jones, he began Harvard in September, 1912. Intellectual life there was bathed in what Dos Passos later called "the mauve afterglow"[4] of the 1890s. Those were the years of the Harvard Aesthetes, elite devotees of Walter Pater and Renaissance painting, sensitive young men, including Dos Passos, who felt trapped in a hopelessly vulgar and hostile world. It was also a time of great artistic excitement. Imagism, Eliot's early poems, the 1913 Armory Show come to Boston—there was much to stimulate Dos Passos and to educate him for his later experimenting with literary forms. He read widely—one recent critic has suggested that, except for Joyce, his range of reading "may be unmatched among novelists of this century"—and he eagerly pursued his other interests, which a 1915 letter to Rumsey Marvin, a younger friend, defined as food, travel, and Italy. A year later, however, his letters begin to reveal Dos Passos as a particularly rebellious sort of aesthete, more angry and alienated than most. Amidst French phrases and almost prissy literary affectation, we find pot shots at "stockbrokers," "hypocritical clergymen,"[5] snobbery, conventional notions of decency, and the deadness of middle-class life.

Dos Passos's writing for the *Harvard Monthly* reflects the ever more consciously political nature of his alienation, his divergence from the aesthetes, who ultimately felt more at one with the society they scorned than the illegitimate Dos Passos, with his "foreign accent" and "swarthy appearance," ever could. His generally lyrical and exotic early short stories gave way to more satirical ones,[6] and he soon

4

began writing polemical essays. He read Veblen, and he was exhilarated when John Reed—model aristocratic rebel, and activist intellectual—came to speak on "Life in the Trenches." After Reed's talk, Dos Passos later wrote, the world of Harvard seemed "frightfully petty." In two book reviews, he praised Reed's spirited reporting—on Mexico, and on the war in eastern Europe—foreshadowing his own lifetime of political and travel journalism.[7]

The big political issue at Harvard then, "preparedness" for war, centered around summer military camps for college students. In an unsigned editorial, July, 1915, Dos Passos saw the camps not as a step toward war, but simply as a much needed democratizing experience for Harvard men, who might return "with a little snobbery knocked out of them . . . [and] a smattering of slang to spice their conversation." But the following spring—sounding very much the elitist and the aesthete—he was attacking neutrality in a war that represented a "fundamental conflict between two ideas of civilization, the Latin ideal, the ideal of art and literature and the life of the spirit; and the Teutonic ideal, efficiency, material prosperity." Behind this lay only vague and contradictory ideas about what to do: three months later, he was urging, confusingly, "a policy of 'constructive pacifism' " against the "powers of darkness," a sensible middle course that would avoid "the Scylla of 'grape-juice' moralizing and the Charybdis of longhaired ultra-socialism."[8] Clarity would have to await direct experience in the war itself.

Around the time of his graduation from Harvard, Dos Passos wrote three long essays that reveal his troubled thinking as the minds of those around him were being mobilized for war. The first, "A Humble Protest," blasted "Industrialism and Mechanical Civilization"[9] as false gods and enslavers of mankind. The root of our problem, he wrote, was not science, but "that bastard of science" (HP, p. 119), the Industrial Revolution. Although he argued that uncritical worship had made science itself a "new supersitition" (HP, p. 119), Dos Passos's underlying assumptions remained, like his father's, humanist and rationalist: he called not for a retreat to a prescientific era, but rather —as he wrote Arthur McComb—for "a new Enlightenment."[10]

Despite its sure, often satirical tone, "A Humble Protest" reveals contradictions that were to characterize much of its author's later thought. While he sees the French Revolution as a great triumph over "superstition," and looks forward with hope to war-inspired discon-

5

tent "to sear away the old complacency" (HP, p. 117), he also gazes back wistfully at the more intense life, the greater art, and the profounder thought of Elizabethan England. The aesthete and the social critic remain at odds in Dos Passos, as do the elitist and the democrat: a tendency to judge a society primarily by its highest art, and some almost sneering references to "the mob" and "the crowd" (HP, pp. 115, 116) clash with genuine concern for the oppressed, the "three fourths of the world . . . bound in economic slavery that the other fourth may in turn be enslaved by the tentacular inessentials of civilization, for the production of which the lower classes have ground out their lives" (HP, p. 119). This essay represents not simply aesthetic displeasure with a vulgar modern world, or an aristocratic concern with the plight of the less fortunate, but rather a deep questioning—stimulated, no doubt, by the war's great technological destruction in Europe—of the value of industrial progress itself. It constitutes the not too humble beginning of a fundamental critique of society.

Dos Passos wrote "Against American Literature" on his father's Virginia farm the summer after he graduated, and he published it in the *New Republic*, which he found "the only live magazine in the country—though its not so radical as I should like it to be." This article—rather derivative of Van Wyck Brooks and others—criticizes American literature in order to criticize America, and in some ways complements "A Humble Protest." Dos Passos finds most American literature lacking in passion, mere "gentle satire,"[11] almost irrelevant. Like America, it is "rootless," unblessed with the organic connection to the past that characterizes European literature, which it feeds on without growing. The fault lies with industrialism, which has "broken down the old bridges leading to the past." Whitman alone, "our only poet" (AAL, pp. 270–271), successfully fought this sterile gentility by connecting with the future as a substitute for a past.

Equal to Dos Passos's celebration here of Whitman's "challenge to the future" is his own yearning for an agrarian past. But while our real loss, he writes, is "the lesson of the soil"—a theme Dos Passos would return to in his Jeffersonian thinking twenty-five years later—"our only course is to press on" (AAL, pp. 270–271). "Against American Literature" looks forward and backward at once, as it mourns the loss of old modes of life, but demands new literary forms.

Dos Passos found in Spain a nation that was not cut off from its own past. "Young Spain," based on his travels there late in 1916,

6

begins by describing a village baker and ends up expatiating on Spanish art, literature, politics, and national character. Dos Passos romanticizes the life of the baker of Almorox: his family, his beautiful countryside, his fulfilling work, and his pleasantly circumscribed world. "It was all so mellow, so strangely aloof from the modern world of feverish change . . . Everywhere roots striking into the infinite past."[12] Equally appealing for its contrast to the menacing trends described in "A Humble Protest" is the "intense individualism" (YS, p. 476) Dos Passos finds in Spain, individualism he attributes to a strong, isolated village life, spared centralization by topographical variety. Even Spain's immense social problems—"unbelievably corrupt" politicians, "wretchedly underpaid" labor, the "ignorant priest-ridden" aristocracy and peasantry (YS, p. 481), and impending famine—cannot destroy the charm Spain holds for him. Dos Passos sincerely cares about the lot of the oppressed, yet never completely abandons the aloof perspective his privileged position allows.

But two forces threaten to thrust the old Spain violently into the modern era: the war in Europe, and Spain's own revolutionaries. Dos Passos sympathizes deeply with the aims of "the revolutionary classes" (YS, p. 482), divided though they are, and praises the socialist vision of the writer Blasco Ibáñez; but he fears that revolution, like war, might unify Spain and destroy the vital individualism and richly varied art he finds in its separate regions. Once again, his aesthetic interests, his love of the past, and his class background mix uneasily with his growing interest in social change.

Away from Harvard, Dos Passos's world was expanding rapidly and his radicalization accelerating. To please his father, he had reluctantly gone to Spain to study architecture rather than to France to study the war. But his stay in Spain was cut short when John Randolph Dos Passos died in January, 1917. After disposing of his father's estate—the elder Dos Passos's extravagant spending left his heirs little—he moved to New York.

A growing atmosphere of repression in the United States helped intensify Dos Passos's dissatisfactions with the world around him. A week after the American declaration of war in early April, President Woodrow Wilson set up the Committee on Public Information, and its head, George Creel, launched what one historian has called "the biggest advertising campaign in American history." War hysteria mushroomed, the press censored itself, dissenters were attacked, and the postmaster general was soon empowered to deny use of the mail to the uncooperative. Less than three years later this was to culminate in the mass arrests and deportations chronicled in *1919*. In the spring of 1917, Dos Passos—eager to "think independently," not be herded like a sheep "with newspapers for watchdogs"—drifted around the edges of Socialist and Pacifist meetings, grew fond of "East Side Jews and . . . 'foreigners,' "[13] cursed the *New York Times*, and wondered how to make his life meaningful in a world that seemed to be going mad.

In this first year after graduation, Dos Passos's expressions of his rising political angers and enthusiasms were often highly self-conscious and defensively cheerful. In one letter to a friend, he derided "our sea-green, twaddling, rantling little agelet of greedy capitalists and sallow humanitarians," but then felt compelled to add, in self-mockery: "Isn't the lad fierce? for a pacifist too!" In another letter, he joked uneasily: "My only hope is in revolution—in wholesale assassination of all statesmen, capitalists, war-mongers, jingoists, inventors, scientists. . . . My only refuge from the deepest depression is in dreams of vengeful guillotines." But in more sober moments, the enormity of the war simply overwhelmed him: "Everything I do, everything I write seems so cheap and futile — If Europe is to senselessly destroy itself . . . I sort of lose my nerve when I think of it."[14]

Hopeful of escaping his paralysis, more than a little eager for adventure, and probably aware, as Townsend Ludington suggests, that as an aspiring writer he should not miss the war, Dos Passos sailed for France in late June, 1917, a "gentleman volunteer" with the Norton-Harjes Ambulance Service. Brutal days at the front alternated with pleasant or desperately rowdy days with fellow drivers, including several old college friends. Winter and spring, he served in Italy with the American Red Cross, but the pacifist letters he was writing— "mon premier succéss litéraire," he told E. E. Cummings sarcastically[15]—displeased its officials, and in June, 1918, he was denied reenlistment and charged with disloyalty. He appealed to higher authorities in Paris, but was told to return home or be deported. He left in August.

His year in Europe was a disturbing one for Dos Passos. From his training camp outside Paris, he wrote of taking comfort in total political despair: "the capitalists have the world so in their clutches . . . that I don't see how it can ever escape . . . I believe in nothing." He hid from the world in a "snailshell of hysterical laughter." But his first service at the front, five bloody days of an Allied offensive in August, cracked that shell, and his raw exposure to wholesale death and gore gave him what he later called "the horrors." His nervous joking over, he wrote, quite earnestly, that soldiers should "turn their guns" on their own officers. "I'm tired of wailing. I want to assassinate."[16]

Dos Passos had grown considerably angrier, but his diverse political ideas had hardly coalesced, and the detached observer, the aesthete, was still alive in him. Traveling through Italy in early 1918, he wrote blithely in his diary: "O for a revolution of laughter—couldn't all the world at once see the gigantic humor of the situation—and laughter shall untune the sky." His radical views fell neatly into none of the traditional categories—liberal, socialist, communist, anarchist —and his ideas about "revolution," something he saw primarily in individual rather than collective terms, still remained vague. Perhaps because he never suffered them, poverty and economic injustice concerned him only sporadically; rich and poor were often, in his eyes, equally enslaved—"to industry, to money, to the mammon of business, the great God of our times." As an intellectual, repeatedly offended by wartime lies; as an ambulance volunteer, spied on, harassed, and finally driven out of Europe by officials; and as a member of a privileged class, unaccustomed to taking orders, he found wartime discipline intolerable. The vague anarchistic feelings he had expressed earlier in his admiration for Spanish "individualism" were developing into an intense hatred for all authority.[17] Liberty stood far above equality and fraternity in his vision of a "new Enlightenment."

The war, finally, depressed Dos Passos. He rose occasionally to optimism and determination, but more often remained mired in despondency, with little real hope for a better world. He would settle, he decided, for being "a voice of one crying in the wilderness." Just before leaving home, Dos Passos had a final unnerving experience. As an emergency volunteer in a Paris hospital during an American offensive, he was assigned "to carry off buckets full of amputated arms and hands and legs from an operating room."[18] On the boat to New York he wrote a novel.

9

From Detachment to Involvement:
One Man's Initiation—1917

One Man's Initiation—1917, a loose episodic novel, records a young American ambulance driver's reactions to war.[19] Its autobiographical hero, Martin Howe, aloof aesthete at the start, is shocked by the war's brutality into an incipient political awareness and a genuine identification with his fellow human beings. Since we see through Martin's eyes, his shock is our shock; Martin Howe's initiation serves as an indictment of the war.

An early scene is typical: Martin sits at the sidewalk table of a restaurant, luxuriously soaking up the Paris scene, splashed with color. Leaning back in his chair, he looks "dreamily out through half-closed eyes, breathing deep now and then of the musty scent of Paris, that mingled with the melting freshness of the wild strawberries on the plate before him." A soldier sits down nearby, and suddenly Martin is staring at the man's face: "Between the pale-brown frightened eyes, where the nose should have been, was a triangular black patch that ended in some mechanical contrivance with shiny little black metal rods that took the place of the jaw" (*OMI*, p. 54). This sort of juxtaposition—repeated somewhat crudely throughout the novel—shoves the war down Martin's throat. The writing is less a "constant fluctuation between the poles of Walter Pater and Emile Zola," as one critic suggests, than a deliberate confrontation of those two worlds. And here and elsewhere, Dos Passos emphasizes both the unnatural and the terrifyingly technological qualities of the world Martin wakes up to.[20]

Dos Passos's prose, like Martin's early musing, is, in the words of one critic, "full of exotic overtones and lush images, complicated by a thousand romantic impressions and pseudo-impressions." Rimbaud—whom Dos Passos was reading in 1917—is only one of many writers he imitated badly. The almost cloying impressionistic style of much of *One Man's Initiation* also reflects the way Dos Passos himself tended, at times, to see wartime Europe: "Sopping up color-impressions," he wrote in his diary in early 1918, ". . . I fear I'm a mere sponge."[21]

But the writing in *One Man's Initiation* changes as the novel progresses, and the change itself dramatizes Martin Howe's developing awareness and constitutes a criticism of his and Dos Passos's own early aestheticism and passivity. The novel opens by a wharf, with "a scattering of khaki uniforms," "the noise of farewells," and "the trivial lilt" (*OMI*, p. 43) of a Hawaiian tune the band plays. Then, "Rosy yellow and drab purple, the buildings of New York slide together into a pyramid above brown smudges of smoke standing out in the water, linked to the land by the dark curves of bridges" (*OMI*, p. 43). Martin Howe, we learn, is standing in the stern of a departing ship. The third-person narrator describes the scene from Martin's very personal point of view. This almost solipsistic impressionism, though superficially judgmental—the music is "trivial," the farewells are "noise"—describes without explaining or interpreting. It neither expresses ideas about the world nor conveys any sense of a larger picture (where is the ship going? why?); rather, it simply communicates the moods, the reactions, of its real subject, Martin Howe. A certain leveling occurs, which tends to undercut the novel's social criticism: people become like other objects, mere collections of external sensory stimuli that impinge somehow on Martin's consciousness. This impressionism of style, particularly in its use of highly selective details and in its emphasis on color, never entirely disappears from *One Man's Initiation*. But as Martin's initiation proceeds, the style becomes simpler and more objective. Dialogue begins as snatches of talk Martin overhears, or occasional loose, short conversations he only half-heartedly participates in; but the novel climaxes in a long chapter which is virtually all dialogue, a political discussion in which Martin eagerly participates. The narrative voice in this chapter is only marginally more involved with Martin than with others, and the discussion itself elaborates analytic views of the world.

The war brings about the changes in Martin that the changing style expresses, and we observe those changes through his reactions to the war. Once off the boat, Martin rides the train to Paris; the beautiful scenery and the historic names of towns bring out his romantic view of war: "the floods of scarlet poppies seemed the blood of fighting men slaughtered through all time" (*OMI*, p. 52). Later, under shelling, he tries hard to see the sky in poetic terms, but soon gives up: "It might have beauty if he were far enough away to clear his nostrils of the stench of pain" (*OMI*, p. 71). More significant than Martin's abandonment of his early aestheticism, however, is his loss of detachment. At the start, he is very much the observer, set apart from the crowd. Sipping wine in a schoolmaster's garden, he watches soldiers pass by on their way to the front. He does not miss the significance of the scene—he sees the camions full of young men as "tumbrils"—but

11

still he scrutinizes them as *other*: "Through the gap in the trellis Martin stared at them, noting intelligent faces, beautiful faces, faces brutally gay, miserable faces like those of sobbing drunkards" (*OMI*, pp. 64–65). But gradually he comes to identify with common soldiers, dying or probably soon to die, in a series of scenes that culminates in his cathartic exertion to save a wounded German prisoner:

> . . . he clutched the wounded man tightly to him in the effort of carrying him towards the dugout. The effort gave Martin a strange contentment. It was as if his body were taking part in the agony of this man's body. At last they were washed out, all the hatreds, all the lies, in blood and sweat. Nothing was left but the quiet friendliness of beings alike in every part, eternally alike. . . .
> . . . It made him strangely happy. (*OMI*, p. 148)

During the political debate that swells a long chapter very near the end, Martin tries to sort out what his experiences have taught him. In an abandoned farmhouse, by candlelight, his French friends curse the war and advance various plans for radical social change. Martin shares their enthusiasms, but his own ideas remain vague. Still, he has progressed from mild skepticism about the war's goals, to a view of the war as "asinine" (*OMI*, p. 72) and "silly" (*OMI*, p. 85), and finally to fear and hatred of the "dark forces" whose "power to enslave our minds" (*OMI*, p. 159) has dragged his country into war. These unnamed forces rule the press and have spread the lies that blind us: "We are slaves of bought intellect, willing slaves" (*OMI*, p. 159). He eagerly drinks with the rest, rather confusingly, "To Revolution, to Anarchy, to the Socialist state" (*OMI*, p. 168). With people like these, he later tells fellow driver Tom Randolph, "we needn't despair of civilisation . . . the awakening may come soon" (*OMI*, p. 169). The next day the Frenchmen are killed in battle. This ending undercuts Martin's sudden optimism, but reinforces his and Dos Passos's condemnation of the war and the society that created it.[22]

However cloudy Martin's revolutionary ideas, the intensity of his commitment shines through. His first days at the front had made him want to "flee from all this stupidity . . . this cant of governments . . . this strangling hatred" (*OMI*, p. 81). He would spend long afternoons in an abandoned Gothic abbey, gazing back across the centuries through the stained glass windows, and dreaming he was a medieval monk. But his escape into the past cannot survive the pressures of the war's reality—the abbey itself, its cellar an ammunition dump, is soon blown up—and by the end Martin can no longer deny that he is of this world as well as in it. In a penultimate scene, carefully placed between the political debate and the deaths of the debaters, Martin comes upon an enterprising cobbler, whose gruesome but practical business is to cut up the rotten boots of dead soldiers into shoelaces. Martin does not turn up his nose, but buys a pair of laces; he takes up his share of guilt for the world's inhumanity and with it his responsibility to fight for a better world.

Dos Passos made things simpler and clearer for Martin Howe than he could for himself. Martin's early aestheticism, detachment, and love of the past are certainly versions (though exaggerated) of Dos Passos's own, as is the vagueness of Martin's passionately radical views at the end of the novel. But the rapidity and decisiveness of his transformation are a bit unreal. Dos Passos would not find it so easy to exorcise his own aristocratic values.

"Declassing Oneself"

Though the war had horrified him, Dos Passos was eager to get back to it. With help from his influential Aunt Mamie, he succeeded in joining the Medical Corps, despite his weak eyes and his suspicious record in the Red Cross. In September, 1918, he reported to Camp Crane in Pennsylvania, and on November 12—a day after the armistice—his section sailed for Europe. By March, still a soldier, he had enrolled at the Sorbonne. That summer, he slipped out of camp, found a sympathetic officer in another city willing to discharge him, and celebrated Bastille Day in Paris as a civilian.

Taking orders as a common soldier—a "sheep"—galled Dos Passos; it inflamed his hatred of authority, and intensified his concern with "the rights of the governed against the governors." "Organization is death," he told himself again and again at Camp Crane.[23] But he welcomed the chance to mix—as he had urged his Harvard classmates to do—with men of different social classes. "You cant imagine," he told McComb, "the simple and sublime amiability of the average American soldier—Here is the clay for almost any moulding. Who is to be the potter? That is the great question." The immediate answer confirmed his worst fears: he "could feel a wave of hatred go through the men" as they watched a propaganda film about villainous Huns. Still, as a mess hall officer on the ship to England, he was pleased to find a few men at least "stupidly truculent—I have more hopes of the U.S.A. since I've been in their damned army than I ever had before." The letters and diaries he wrote at Camp Crane express not only his characteristic fluctuations between hope and despair, but also tension between a certain condescending elitism and a genuine concern for "the average American soldier." Six months later he still wanted to learn "the mechanics of declassing oneself"; the army, he felt, had not done it for him.[24]

Once a civilian, Dos Passos left Paris for London (to secure publication of *One Man's Initiation*), and then joined friends to travel through Spain. A side trip took him to Lisbon to report for a British labor newspaper on a threatening antirepublican plot. Back in Spain, he spent a month in Granada, ill with rheumatic fever (one of several such attacks throughout his life), and then went on to Madrid, where he worked daily on what would become *Three Soldiers*. He finished the manuscript in Paris in late spring of 1920 and began searching for a publisher.

Dos Passos's radicalization was still proceeding rapidly. In an article on Portugal for the *Liberator,* he wrote sympathetically of peasant revolts, militant strikes, and vigorous syndicalist organizing: "in Portugal, as everywhere in the world, the giant stirs in his sleep. The story of Russia has spread among peasants and workmen." The Portuguese republic he found "entirely in the hands of the bourgeoisie"—having "done nothing to free the country from domestic or foreign capital, [it] has fulfilled none of its promises." In a didactic letter to Rumsey Marvin, he refused to "idealize" Russia, but found the soviets "a system of government based on the idea of 'pure democracy' . . . that every man shall take direct part in the government of the country." He further insisted that "*all* that is published" in the American press about bolshevism is "propaganda."[25]

Still, his deepest need was less to help build a collectivist world than to express his own individuality. Thoroughly a rebel himself, he quickly identified with anyone who attacked the established order; but his very cries of rebellion suggest that only uneasily did he link his aspirations and his destiny with those of the people most oppressed by capitalism. "We are too lively," he wrote Rumsey Marvin, "we have

14

too much curiosity, too many desperate desires for unimaginable things to let ourselves be driven down into the mud of common life. You and I and a few others and thousands of others we do not know." The context here is Dos Passos's effort to dissuade Marvin from entering the business world, but the elitist sentiment is clear enough. Dos Passos's political pronouncements were certainly no pose, but his radicalism was in part fired simply by a need to proclaim himself, to set himself apart, by rebelling. His sometimes apocalyptic fears, expressed in a letter from Madrid, reveal his ambivalent feelings about the very masses he hoped revolution would liberate:

> And this moment [February, 1920] is so on the brink of things. Over-population combined with a breakdown of food has wrecked the checks and balances of the industrialized world. In ten years we may be cavemen snatching the last bit of food from each others mouths amid the stinking ruins of our cities, or we may be slaving—antlike—in some utterly systematized world where the individual will be utterly crushed that the mob (or the princes) may live.[26]

The Artist as Rebel: *Three Soldiers*

Dos Passos expressed these and other contradictory feelings in his second novel, *Three Soldiers*.[27] John Andrews, its hero, voluntarily becomes one of "the mob" that the U.S. Army is trying to mold into a fighting unit, but his revulsion, unlike Martin Howe's, is not really against war but against the army itself. "What was the good of stopping the war," he wonders, "if the armies continued?" (*TS*, p. 259). War kills, but the army deadens, and in the world of *Three Soldiers*, this is far worse. As an institution, the army turns men into automatons, turns individuals into the faceless cogs of an inhuman mechanism. The metaphor of the machine[28]—suggestive of Dos Passos's earlier attack on industrialism in "A Humble Protest"—recurs throughout the novel and extends even to the titles of its six parts: "Making the Mould," "The Metal Cools," "Machines," "Rust," "The World Outside," and "Under the Wheels." Characters are judged and their fates determined by their relationships to the army machine. Most despicable are the YMCA or "Y" men, whose jingoistic sanctimony serves only to oil the machinery. Their efforts to rouse the soldiers—the kinds of men he had grown to like at Camp Crane—provoke the sort of sarcasm that Dos Passos was to develop fully in

15

U.S.A., as when one "Y" man sets out to help lead the soldiers in singing "Stand up, stand up for Jesus." "The men got to their feet," writes Dos Passos, "except for a few who had lost their legs"(*TS*, p. 234).

While Dos Passos narrowed his concern from the war in *One Man's Initiation* to its army in *Three Soldiers*, he made an effort to broaden his perspective. Instead of Martin Howe's limited, though developing, viewpoint, this second novel presents three points of view: those of Fuselli, Andrews, and Chrisfield, a schematically representative cross section of the United States, by class and by geographical region. Dos Passos seems to have wanted this triple perspective to shift the focus of the novel away from individuals and toward the institution of the army. When his friend McComb suggested he highlight the three distinct narrative points of view with typographical variations, Dos Passos rejected the idea, stating that he did not want "to emphasize personality too much."[29]

Dos Passos's effort to depict the army's destructive effect on different kinds of soldiers—thus on all soldiers—and not simply on an atypical, aristocratic one like Martin Howe, is not carried through, however; for Andrews's sensibilities and outlook come to dominate. More than half the novel—the latter part—is narrated from his point of view. In addition, Andrews is physically present in many other scenes, and the narrative voice has in his sections none of the distance from him that it has from Fuselli and Chrisfield in theirs. Artist, Harvard man, and outsider, Andrews is the most autobiographical of the three; and *Three Soldiers* comes to express above all, and without irony, the consciousness of this one soldier. Thus Dos Passos's attempt to write a novel that would embody more than one social perspective —a literary complement, perhaps, to his personal efforts to "declass" himself—is only partially successful.

Still, *Three Soldiers* represents a significant departure in formal terms from *One Man's Initiation*. Loose structure and crude juxtaposition have given way to a careful division into parts, each dominated by a character and a theme, and, more important, to a complex development of implicit comparisons between major characters. A plainer, less impressionistic style; greater use of dialogue; and a filtering of experience through sensibilities less aesthetic than Martin Howe's—all bring *Three Soldiers* firmly within the tradition of the realistic novel.

Three Soldiers begins attacking the army through its least compre-

16

hending victim. Fuselli, Italian-American optical supply clerk from San Francisco, is less an individual than a collection of visions, ambitions, and phrases from mass culture. His consciousness typifies the popular consciousness as Dos Passos saw it, or rather its lowest common denominator. Songs romanticizing war and patriotism play in his head, and he falls asleep at night "picturing to himself long movie reels of heroism" (*TS*, p.11). But in fact Fuselli is a coward and his real interest in the army is for a chance to get ahead, to become an officer. He hates the humiliating discipline, but swallows his pride and anger in his obsequious efforts to please his superiors. Of course, he fails; he never even makes corporal, and his final indignity is a court-martial for venereal disease, and permanent K.P. duty. Dos Passos treats Fuselli mercilessly—he might easily have been a character in *U.S.A.*—and his pitiful career serves as a vehicle for criticisms of the army and of the American Dream: Dos Passos makes Fuselli's belief in army myths ludicrous and repeatedly thwarts his second-generation aspirations for upward mobility.[30]

Indiana farmboy Chrisfield, the second soldier, personifies the anger and hatred Fuselli has repressed. He boils over with frustration and resentment at the army and strikes out in blind vengeance at whoever is closest—in particular, at a rather inoffensive Sergeant Anderson, whom he kills with impunity in the chaos of battle. It is through Chrisfield that we are shown some of the barbarity of war; he enjoys fighting and killing, and he embodies the kind of violence the army wants to arouse and channel. But Chrisfield gets out of control. Just before killing Anderson, "Chrisfield marched with his fists clenched; he wanted to fight somebody, to run his bayonet into a man as he ran it into a dummy in that everlasting bayonet drill, he wanted to strip himself naked, to squeeze the wrists of a girl until she screamed" (*TS*, p. 160). This is the underside of Fuselli's romantic dreams of "jolly soldiers in khaki marching into towns, pursuing terrified Huns across potato fields, saving Belgian milk-maids against picturesque backgrounds" (*TS*, p. 57).

Through John Andrews, the artist as soldier, Dos Passos proposes an alternative to Fuselli's servility and Chrisfield's confused and destructive fury. After an idyllic childhood in Virginia, study at Harvard, unsuccessful attempts at musical composition, and a stagnant stretch in New York writing mediocre music reviews, Andrews has joined the army to escape the burdens of freedom and of responsibility

17

for his own fate. However, the army proves worse, and he soon dreams of writing music to express its "dusty boredom, the harsh constriction of warm bodies full of gestures and attitudes and aspirations into moulds, like the moulds toy soldiers are cast in" (*TS*, p.18). He resents being told to salute officers whom he considers his inferiors and grows increasingly disgusted with himself for submitting to humiliating military discipline. During a long stay in the hospital, recuperating from leg wounds, he decides to desert; but that very day the war ends, and by flattering the right people, he gets himself assigned to a detachment of soldiers that are to study at the Sorbonne. Once in Paris, his enslavement to the army has become almost entirely symbolic; but his self-loathing, his shame, and his anger continue to grow. For leaving Paris without pass or dogtags, he is thrown by M.P.'s into a labor battalion, from which he escapes. He rejects an offer from influential friends to get him safely discharged—Dos Passos somewhat awkwardly inserts this scene to clarify the deliberate, principled nature of Andrews's desertion—and he travels to the countryside to visit the woman he thinks he loves and to work on his music. Eventually the M.P.'s find him, and as they drag him off to prison, his composition —"Soul and Body of John Brown"—is scattered by the wind.

The nature of Andrews's rebellion is complex. Fuselli's punishing life as a private drives him to servile efforts to become an officer, and the restless Chrisfield thrashes about in the army like a caged animal. But Andrews seems to be a free agent, neither driven nor trapped. In retrospect, he sees his desertion as a political act—an effort to loosen for all "the grip of the nightmare" (*TS*, p. 452)—or at least as a political gesture, the fulfillment of his earlier desire somehow to end "the hideous farce of making men into machines. Oh, if some gesture of his could only free them all for life and freedom and joy" (*TS*, p. 360). In truth, it is more an individual act of self-purification, to purge his self-hatred, and even an act of self-destruction, an effort in short—like his joining the army in the first place—to obliterate his own pained consciousness. Yet, his rebellion (rather like Dos Passos's own) becomes at the same time a powerful, though temporary, affirmation of his unique individuality: "He felt for a moment that he was the only living thing in a world of dead machines; the toad hopping across the road in front of a steam roller" (*TS*, p. 462).

Though he joins the army in part to escape the burdens of freedom, Andrews rebels in freedom's name. "Being free's the only thing that

18

matters" (*TS*, p. 427), he announces to his friend Henslowe. Besides escape from saluting and taking orders, Andrews yearns for free time to pursue his artistic work. But once in Paris, relatively free, he spends days and especially nights wandering the streets, glancing furtively and enviously at embracing couples, and mooning over women he passes. Though he never verbalizes it, central to the freedom he seeks is freedom from his own inhibitions. He wants his work to express his fellow soldiers' "thwarted lives, the miserable dullness of industrialized slaughter" (*TS*, p. 290), but he is in fact obsessed with a composition, "Queen of Sheba," which exudes sexuality. His abandonment of it for the "Soul and Body of John Brown" is not only a political act that caps his desertion, but also a symptom of his sexual frustration. Andrews's brief affair with Jeanne ends on a note of "passionate disgust" (*TS*, p. 361) for him, and the unsatisfying nature of his love for Geneviève Rod is best revealed in a dream in which she turns into a "wooden board" (*TS*, p. 398) as he kisses her. It is not just the army that imprisons Andrews; the tangled, often confused quality of his struggle for freedom, while it enriches the novel psychologically, undercuts much of its intended social criticism.

Three Soldiers, Malcolm Cowley argues, is really not social criticism at all, but an example of the "Art Novel." The Art Novel, he writes, portrays "two essential characters, two antagonists, the Poet and the World . . . [the Poet] tries to assert his individuality in despite of the World, which is stupid, unmanageable and usually victorious." Cowley concedes that *Three Soldiers*, like other early works by Dos Passsos, is not a "pure" example of the Art Novel, for the world was very real to Dos Passos, not simply the Poet's "shadowy opponent." He maintains, however, that Dos Passos subordinates detailed criticism of the World's institutions to sympathetic elaboration of the Poet's—that is, Andrews's—desperate plight. By the end of *Three Soldiers*, "we are made to feel that the destruction of this symphony, . . . dispersed in the wind, is the real tragedy of the War."[31]

Without Fuselli and Chrisfield, *Three Soldiers* might simply be an Art Novel. Andrews's most conscious urges are to express himself through his music, and trapped in the army he plays the role of what one reviewer called "the caged lark."[32] In one of his more self-indulgent moments he proclaims himself "one of those people who was not made to be contented" (*TS*, p. 366), and he feels that he, Andrews, lives "more acutely than the rest" (*TS*, p. 372). But Andrews has fellow victims: Fuselli and Chrisfield have not been assimilated into the World that oppresses the Poet, and their suffering, along with Andrews's, represents various facets of a generalized suffering under the rule of the army. Andrews certainly has the background of Cowley's "Poet," but life in the army erodes his isolation: "In a week [as a soldier] the great structure of his romantic world, so full of many colors and harmonies, that had survived school and college and the buffeting of making a living in New York, had fallen in dust about him" (*TS*, p. 29). Andrews's ivory tower (like Dos Passos's) is toppled, not merely encircled by Philistines as in Cowley's formulation. The novel seems divided against itself, as if Dos Passos had set out to attack the army as an institution through the eyes of three soldiers, but became absorbed in the pained sensibility of the soldier whose character was closest to his own self image. This division reflects the tensions in Dos Passos between social critic and aesthete, and between his radical views and his needs simply to assert his individuality. Much like the formal uncertainty of *Three Soldiers*—which begins as a sort of collectivist novel but gravitates to the fate of an individual hero—it reflects Dos Passos's only partial success in transcending his own background. For the Poet's perspective in the Art Novel is very much an upper-class perspective.

Ultimately, the novel's structural imbalance—the disproportionate weight given to Andrews—seems to tilt it in the direction of Cowley's category, the Art Novel. But unlike Cowley's Poet, John Andrews becomes aware of his relatively privileged position in the World he despises, and of the ways in which his ideas of freedom are conditioned by his class. At first, the sense of his own enslavement to the army—he is ordered to wash windows—preoccupies Andrews. Then he thinks of Fuselli, Chrisfield, and another soldier, Eisenstein, and suddenly realizes with amazement that they "seemed at home in this army life. They did not seem appalled by the loss of their liberty. But they had never lived in the glittering other world. Yet he could not feel the scorn of them he wanted to feel" (*TS*, p. 29). This benign condescension fades as Andrews learns that most other soldiers suffer as much as he but are simply resigned to their fate. By the time he has been thrown into the labor battalion, he has begun to think of his situation less in individual, more in social terms. Unloading heavy, dusty bags of cement from a boat, a "refrain" runs through his head: "People have spent their lives...doing only this. People have spent their lives doing only this" (*TS*, p. 401).

Andrews's understanding of his privileges and his growing desire to reject them—to "declass" himself—develop and are expressed through his relationships with two women. He falls in love first with Jeanne, who has lost her home and family in the war; whether she cares for Andrews or just needs the dinners he buys her is unclear. In a more effusive moment, he proclaims:

> "Jeanne, we must live very much, we who are free to make up for all the people who are still...bored."
> "A lot of good it'll do them," she cried laughing.
> "It's funny, Jeanne, I threw myself into the army. I was so sick of being free and not getting anywhere. Now I have learnt that life is to be used, not just held in the hand like a box of bonbons that nobody eats."
> She looked at him blankly.
> "I mean, I don't think I get enough out of life," he said. (*TS*, pp. 349–50)

To Jeanne, struggling merely to survive and to preserve a bit of dignity, Andrews's concerns about living his life to the fullest are incomprehensible.

Geneviève Rod also does not understand Andrews—and in this Cowley is correct: "the Poet is misunderstood by the World"—but she, unlike the impoverished Jeanne, has nothing to teach him. An aristocratic and dilettantish music lover, she enjoys this talented and impetuous composer's visits to her mother's summer home. Not surprisingly, when he deserts the army and rushes out to see her, she is cool to him; she refuses to acknowledge his desertion as an act of conscience. At a luncheon at her house, he suddenly feels out of place, though the other guests are the very sort of people he grew up among: "He had a crazy desire to jump to his feet and shout: 'Look at me; I'm a deserter. I'm under the wheels of your system. If your system doesn't succeed in killing me, it will be that much weaker, it will have less strength to kill others' " (*TS*, p. 455). By finally defining these upper-class people as *other*, and, soon after, by abandoning his love for Geneviève Rod, he consciously renounces the privileges of his class and understands for the first time the full political meaning of his act of desertion.

Nonetheless, Andrews never embraces explicitly revolutionary politics as we expect Martin Howe will. His hatred of the army does seem

21

at times to extend to the society that produced it and he once thinks of the war as not the "crumbling" but as the "fullest and most ultimate expression" of what he vaguely terms "civilization" (*TS*, p. 225). Visiting a deserters' hideout in Paris the first of May, he even responds enthusiastically to the news that the general strike has begun. But on the eve of his arrest, pessimism overwhelms him. He tells Geneviève: "human society has always been that, and perhaps will always be that: organizations growing and stifling individuals, and individuals revolting hopelessly against them, and at last forming new societies to crush the old societies and becoming slaves again in their turn...." (*TS*, p. 458). His rebellion seems to belie this despair— why rebel against so deterministic a world?—but in fact confirms it; he confesses at the end that he has done nothing to help others, that "he had not lived up to the name of John Brown" (*TS*, p. 469). He has achieved a certain understanding of himself and his society; he has fought for and won a few days of freedom; but he has left the army— and the world—unchanged.

Three Soldiers creates its meanings through the stories of Fuselli and Chrisfield, as well as that of Andrews. By the novel's end, all three men have in some sense been defeated. Andrews faces twenty years in prison; Fuselli's mobility has been only downward; and Chrisfield, convinced someone knows he killed Anderson, has become a paranoid deserter. The sense of frustration that pervades much of the book is countered, though unequally, by the optimism inherent in the long steady growth of Andrews's awareness and the psychologically liberating aspects of his doomed rebellion. This unbalanced tension reflects Dos Passos's own conflicting feelings of hope and despair, for he seems generally more at home with a pessimistic sense of his own and the world's situation. Oddly, *Three Soldiers* presents its clearest and most caustic social criticism through its character least capable of revolt, Fuselli, while its most active rebel, Andrews, tends to confuse the army's repression with his own inhibitions. This polarity, in a sense, between understanding and revolt may reflect a split in Dos Passos himself; for his radical critique of society is somewhat out of touch with the deepest psychic sources of his need to rebel, his angers never quite in tune with his social analysis. Still, the novel strongly expresses Dos Passos's hatred of the army, for the self-enclosed aspects of Andrews's rebellion do not undo the novel's indictment of the military machine he opposes and, by implication, its indictment of all repressive institutions. The message remains: "Organization is death."

The War at Home

Three Soldiers "burst like a bombshell into the postwar mood of disillusion"; for all its uncertainties, it provoked an intense and highly polarized critical response. Patriotic hysteria had peaked too recently for Dos Passos's antimilitary realism to be palatable to very many, but those who praised the novel did so enthusiastically. John Peale Bishop called its author "a genius" and was tempted to "go up and down the street with banners and drums" to celebrate it; the *Freeman*'s reviewer found its "workmanship" brilliant; and W. C. Blum, writing in the *Dial*, speculated that "if the book had ended with an appeal for contributions to get [Andrews] out of jail, contributions would have been forthcoming."[33]

But Andrews would have rotted in his cell if he had to depend on the editors of the *New York Times* for help. The *Times*'s assault on *Three Soldiers* consisted of the publication of two front-page book reviews, three editorials, four letters to the editor, and two additional articles. (To be sure, three letters defending Dos Passos also appeared, no doubt for some suggestion of balance.) The first review—"Insulting the Army," by Coningsby Dawson, a Canadian ex-soldier—denounced the novel's false picture of the army and "its unmanly intemperance both in language and in plot." It was "the kind of book," he wrote, presumably to show that the war was over, "one would have been arrested for writing while the war was yet in progress." The *Times* followed this up with two editorials: one reiterated Dawson's judgment that *Three Soldiers* was "slanderous"; the other, while listing Dawson's war experiences, worried that his review was open to the criticism that he was a Canadian, and promised a second review, "a like condemnation," from an American soldier. That soldier, Harold Norman Denny, grudgingly admitted that *Three Soldiers* was "brilliantly written," but focused on what he found to be its erroneous content. To Denny's "surprise," Dos Passos had a good army record; but he had not actually engaged in combat, and therefore simply "does not know what he is talking about." He added, snidely, that the

23

book's dust jacket was yellow. To prove that Sergeant Denny was not yellow, the *Times* printed his complete war record.[34]

Dos Passos learned of this critical salvo while in Beirut. He eventually replied, defending his novel simply as an effort to show "the effect of the army on the under dog in the army." The *Times* was unmoved: Dos Passos had sinned by suggesting that men like Andrews had "real grievances" and deserved "sympathy." His ultimate "obligation" in the book was somehow "to make clear his own appreciation of the men who fought the Germans and why they did it." Dos Passos, of course, had no such appreciation; he sympathized with the soldiers' suffering, but found the army itself and all the belligerent governments abhorrent. The *Times*, however, either failed to understand this pacifist position, or did not want to give it a place in public discussion of the war. It all must have confirmed Dos Passos's view, expressed four years earlier, that "half the ills of the country are caused by the fact that all educated and intelligent Americans believe the *New York Times* as if it were Direct Revelation."[35]

Despite the *Times*, *Three Soldiers* became a great critical success, and it eventually brought its author fame and money. But the *Times*'s attack was a symptom of what Dos Passos had called "the great docile sewer of canalized hate [that] was being turned away from the Germans against anyone who hoped, however vaguely, that the exploiting system of capital would not be eternal." In 1919, the public's fear of bolshevism and worry over a wave of bombings and strikes had been stimulated by the press, the American Legion, manufacturers' associations, and other groups, and had been exploited by many of these same groups in an effort to crush labor unions and the left generally. The assault had culminated in the deportation of about 250 leftists in December and in the Palmer Raids on 2 January 1920, in which the Department of Justice arrested over 4,000 accused Communists, many without warrants, often beating and starving the prisoners.[36] Thus were the twenties inaugurated.

Dos Passos had been abroad during this time, but he returned to the United States in time to vote for Eugene V. Debs—still in prison for having spoken against the war—in the 1920 presidential election. He rented a room in New York, wrote furiously, and renewed his friendship with E. E. Cummings, with whom he would sail for Lisbon five months later. An individualist, he bridled under pressures for conformity and resented those Americans who had succumbed to them.

24

The atmosphere he had found so disturbing at Camp Crane had spread to the nation as a whole, and his anger at the war and its supporters had not abated: "As for an intellectual class it can go f——— itself. Its merely less picturesque and less warmhearted than the hoi polloi and a damnsight eagerer to climb on the band wagon in time of need. The war's the example. Why they had to run special trains to get the intellectuals to Washington they were in such a hurry to run to cover. And those that didn't went into the spy service." He tended to worship action of any kind and found most of the postwar New York cultural scene effete. "Only do do do," he wrote Rumsey Marvin. "Down with esthetes littérateurs poet-tasters-genteel dog-, picture-, life-fanciers!"[37] Himself a 'littérateur," a member of the very "intellectual class" he despised, Dos Passos was once again awkwardly attempting to escape or at least deny his own privileged position in society. In addition, he was beginning to express the uncertainty about his role as a writer that would grow with his political radicalism.

Dos Passos voices his dissatisfaction with his country at length in "America and the Pursuit of Happiness," a *Nation* article in which he compares the repressive America of 1920 to its past promise and its possible future. Liberal intellectuals in Spain, he reports, had once looked to America as "a glittering *fata morgana* of imperishable beauty" and to Wilson's Fourteen Points as a source of hope for the future. But Wilson's dreams collapsed at Versailles, and the Spanish now see only hatred and repression here, "the fanatical worship of things established." In a few years, America has become "one of the most hated of militarist nations!" Opposition exists, to be sure, but its voice is overwhelmed by the patriotic press, by "the howling of the dervishes of militant capitalism." In an effort, then, to inspire and encourage nonconformity, Dos Passos reaches back into the American past, to before the post–Civil War era of "topheavy industrial organization." He invokes "the swaggering independence of our pioneers . . . the hardheaded individuality of our old Yankee skippers" and charges the public to recapture America's forgotten ideals. Dos Passos reveals in this essay some of the tensions of his developing postwar radicalism: he speaks like a patriot of American ideals, while denouncing his own country; and he takes up the language of a forward-looking, organized left, while waxing nostalgic over individualistic pioneers from the past who exemplify his ideas of rebellion.[38]

The Machine and the Garden:
Rosinante to the Road Again

It was to Spain that Dos Passos's thoughts often turned for an alternative to joyless, mechanized, repressive America, though his feelings
about Spain embody some of the same contradictions as his feelings
about his own country. Dos Passos had traveled to Spain several
times, spoke the language fluently, and had written on Spanish culture and politics. In the spring of 1921, he finished recasting his numerous articles on Spain into *Rosinante to the Road Again*,[39] a volume
which interweaves a series of essays on Spanish life with an episodic
tale of two friends—intense, serious Telemachus and hedonistic Lyaeus—who walk from Madrid to Toledo in search of "the soul of Spain"
(*RRA*, p. 233). The many characters Telemachus and Lyaeus meet
along the way express strong, often conflicting opinions on various social and political questions. The essays indirectly attempt to resolve
some of these conflicts, but often without success; the loose, composite
structure allows Dos Passos to leave some questions unanswered, some
tensions in abeyance.

The immediate inspiration for Telemachus's and Lyaeus's quest is
Pastora Imperio, the legendary dancer, whose precise and energetic
performance overpowers them. To Telemachus, the essence of Pastora's genius is a certain gesture, a gesture which epitomizes the Spanish
spirit and which he sets out to recapture and make "permanent." "I
must catch that gesture, formulate it, do it. It is tremendously, inconceivably, unendingly important to me" (*RRA*, p. 20), he announces.
Lyaeus, more sensibly, simply wants to drink to it.

Much of the light humor of the narrative sections of *Rosinante* derives from the unconscious or at least unacknowledged sexual aspect
of Telemachus's consuming interest in Pastora and her gesture. Near
the end, Lyaeus teasingly declares that he has found what they have
been looking for. As his friend describes a young woman he has met,
Telemachus, at first excited and envious, soon insists again on the
purely intellectual and aesthetic nature of their quest: "But I meant
something in line, movement, eternal, not that" (*RRA*, p. 232). The
source of Telemachus's inhibitions seems to be his mother, Penelope,
whose face or words appear ominously in his thoughts whenever they
begin to drift towards his less spiritual passions. Though he is a victim, we are still relieved when, in the novel's last scene, his pontifica-

tion on how he finally "felt the gesture" (*RRA*, p. 244) is cut short by a bucketful of cold water thrown on his head. Dos Passos seems eager to mock Telemachus, who embodies an aspect of himself about which he was no doubt very self-conscious as he traveled through Spain with Cummings and others, less shy and inhibited than he.[40]

The first-person narrator of the essays in *Rosinante*, the journalistic voice of Dos Passos, finds in rural Spain a soothing alternative to the grim industrialized world of Europe and America. As in "Young Spain" (1917), much of which he incorporated into *Rosinante*, Dos Passos tends to romanticize Spanish village life and sees as its essence the spirit of *lo flamenco*: life lived for its own sake, with style, "something that's neither work nor getting ready to work" (*RRA*, p. 30). He implicitly contrasts this with his own domination by the Protestant ethic and curses "that prig Christian" of *Pilgrim's Progress* "and his damned burden" (*RRA*, p. 46); in this respect, he is a wiser version of Telemachus. The rural Spaniard's enviable "unashamed joy" and "easy acceptance of life" (*RRA*, p. 70) are embodied in the figure of Sancho Panza, "to whom all the world was food for his belly" (*RRA*, p. 54).

But many bellies in Spain are empty, the narrator finds. Starving children with "fleshless limbs" (*RRA*, p. 85) haunt the cities' outskirts. And so Dos Passos also admires the spirit of Don Quixote, the idealist and fighter against injustice. Dos Passos seems to envy Quixote's selfless social commitment as well as Sancho Panza's unselfconscious hedonism, although he rejects Telemachus's dreamy abstraction and Lyaeus's social unawareness. Telemachus and Lyaeus are human, lesser versions of the pure types, Don Quixote and Sancho Panza. So while Telemachus may appear ludicrous, carefree Lyaeus can be cruelly insensitive. When the two travelers meet a pair of men along the road who look suspiciously like Panza and Quixote, and the thinner of the pair (who rides a horse named Rosinante) begins to discuss the plight of Spain's poor, Lyaeus callously replies that "the sensations of starving are very interesting—people have visions more vivid than life" (*RRA*, p. 74).

Liberal reformers hope to conquer poverty by industrializing Spain. The dilemma, as Dos Passos sees it, is that along with prosperity, modern industry would bring regimentation, a destruction of *lo flamenco*. Already, in large towns, "industrial life sits heavy on the neck" (*RRA*, p. 85) of the Spanish people. And vulgar commercialism would follow, as personified by the "universal agent" (*RRA*, p. 117), the importer-exporter that Telemachus and Lyaeus meet. He might have been a great man, the agent tells them, were his genius not stunted by dirty, backward Spain. But with proper development of Spain's resources, he insists, all could enjoy the culture of Paris and New York: "luxurious beds, coiffures . . . sumptuous automobiles, elegant ladies glittering with diamonds" (*RRA*, p. 118). Don Alonso, the man who rides Rosinante, suspects liberal intellectuals as well as universal agents of seeing in modernization a chance to enrich and to "unSpanish" themselves (*RRA*, p. 235).

Dos Passos sees more promise in the future envisioned by Spain's militant peasants and industrial workers. He outlines the history and significance of recent strikes by farm laborers and describes the land-owners' most potent weapon: starvation. But if the socialists and syndicalists succeed in politicizing the peasants' fight, Dos Passos can foresee the possibility of "a clean sweep of Spanish capitalism and Spanish feudalism together" (*RRA*, p. 113). Such a revolutionary transformation, if it spares Spain the curse of centralization and if it results from what he calls elsewhere a "thoroughly democratic system of collective action," could bring progress without destroying the nation's rich and varied local community life. This solution appeals to Dos Passos, no doubt, because it would dissolve the conflict between his love of the past and his desire for progressive social change. The key is the Spaniards' passionate individualism, their strong tradition of anarchism, for Dos Passos "an immensely valuable mental position" (*RRA*, p. 93).[41] Spain's political future would continue to preoccupy Dos Passos into the 1930s, in much the same terms, though by 1938 he would come to believe that Spain had no future at all.

The essays in *Rosinante* analyze literature as well as politics. Unsure of his own role as a writer, Dos Passos seems to be looking to Spanish writers as potential models. He finds the too prolific Blasco Ibáñez "An Inverted Midas" (*RRA*, p. 120), turning everything to common-place; and he objects "violently" to the "asceticism and death wor-ship" of Unamuno, though he identifies with him as a man "crying in the wilderness" (*RRA*, p. 225). But the novels of Pío Baroja represent "very near the highest sort of creation" (*RRA*, p. 99). Baroja writes sympathetically about Spain's most oppressed people and their strug-gles, but is "never a propagandist"; his "intense sense of reality" makes his work "natural history" (*RRA*, pp. 96, 100, 99). Especially

28

significant as a key to Dos Passos's future development, particularly through *Manhatttan Transfer* and *U.S.A.*, is his often cited description of Baroja's vision of the middle-class writer as revolutionary:

> He says in one of his books that the only part a man of the middle classes can play in the reorganization of society is destructive. He has not undergone the discipline, which can only come from common slavery in the industrial machine, necessary for a builder. His slavery has been an isolated slavery which has unfitted him forever from becoming truly part of a community. He can use the vast power of knowledge which training has given him only in one way. His great mission is to put the acid test to existing institutions, and to strip the veils off them. . . . it is certain that a profound sense of the evil of existing institutions lies behind every page [Baroja] has written, and that occasionally, only occasionally, he allows himself to hope that something better may come out of the turmoil of our age of transition. (*RRA*, pp. 93–94)

Rosinante itself is far from simply the "natural history" of a society. Somewhat at odds with its social and cultural analysis are the elements of picturesque travel literature in it; the aesthete's observations do not easily merge with those of the radical. Telemachus and Lyaeus behold, for example, "inexplicable shimmering plains of mist hemmed by mountains jagged like coals that as they looked began to smoulder with dawn" (*RRA*, p. 71)—such overwrought descriptive prose suggests an escapist impulse in Dos Passos. We suspect that he fears a modern, centralized Spain not only for the sake of the Spaniards, but because such change would destroy the charm rural Spain holds for him. But the perspective of the privileged tourist is a minor element in *Rosinante*. More significant is its implicit criticism of the United States. *Lo flamenco* serves as the antithesis of the deadness Dos Passos finds in his own country. Two views expressed in a conversation he observes sum up a major contradiction in American life: to a "beet-faced" bartender, America is where "people are very rich"; but to a donkey boy, whose simple life Dos Passos envies, people there "don't enjoy themselves" (*RRA*, pp. 28–29). In writing about Spain, Dos Passos was trying to clarify his attitudes toward his own country.

Exotic Travels and "The Illusion of Geography"

Dos Passos continued to travel and write about his travels, as he would for the rest of his life. In July, 1921, he arrived in Constantinople, where he began a journey through the Russian Caucasus, Persia, Iraq, and Syria, which included a thirty-nine day caravan trip across the desert from Baghdad to Damascus. Not just curiosity and desire for adventure motivated him; even more than Spain, the Near East promised an escape from the complex and disturbing industrialized world. Dos Passos enjoyed himself immensely in the desert and waxed cheerful and optimistic there: "It's an excellent little pippin after all, the world is," he told a friend.[42]

Escape was not always easy. With bitterness, he wrote McComb of his trip to Persia, of cholera and "people dying of typhus on mats along the edge of the railway track—and endless processions of ruined villages, troops, armored trains—all the apparatus of this century of enlightenment." By the time he reached Beirut in January, he had "destroyed the illusion of geography": politics, he had decided, was equally depressing everywhere, and he had tired of roaming "the government-encumbered globe." Articles for the *New York Tribune* and other periodicals helped finance his travels, but he soon grew weary of writing them: "Journalism is the business of fussing with bigbugs— and above anything on earth I detest bigbugs."[43] By February, 1922, he had returned to New York.

Dos Passos eventually worked his writings from the Near East, published and unpublished, into *Orient Express*,[44] a volume which included reproductions of paintings by the author. A first-person narrative, much of it is an impressionistic record of Dos Passos's travels through exotic lands. Its approach to the world of the Near East is rarely analytic, sometimes intuitive, and often simply a recording of details. Unlike *Rosinante to the Road Again*, it draws few conclusions; there is no search for the "soul" of the region, no detailed analysis of political forces. This is disappointing, perhaps, but not surprising, given the diverse and unfamiliar material *Orient Express* covers. However Dos Passos sometimes projects his own bewilderment onto the places and events themselves, writing not of his inability to understand but of their inscrutable nature. In a chapter derived from a 1921 article for the *New York Tribune*, he juxtaposes images of refugees living in "dazed and close-packed squalor" with those of "Greek millionaires and Syrian war-profiteers," only to wonder if "somewhere some day" he might discover "the key to decipher this intricate arabesque scrawled carelessly on a ground of sheer pain"(*OE*, p. 26). This is not mystery, but mystification.

Dos Passos's emotional response to the Near East is no more assured than his intellectual response. While he can dreamily enjoy the "extraordinary harmony of indolence" (*OE*, p. 96) in which middle-class Persians live, he cannot close his eyes to the appalling heritage of misery left by war and colonialism. Much of *Orient Express* is light, even humorous, as if Dos Passos, in the words of one reviewer, were "concealing his impotent pity under a shell of indifference"[45]—as in his first reactions at the front. Unable to find hope in lands that seem so vast and incomprehensible, how else could he respond to people dying in the streets, to "bundles of rags that writhe feverishly" (*OE*, p. 71)? He remains skeptical of change and argues at length against "the Sayyid," a Persian doctor he travels with, who believes machinery will bring his country the happiness and prosperity he finds in Europe.

Dos Passos tries to be optimistic about the very rapid changes the Russian Revolution had been forcing in the Soviet Caucasus. He finds great hope in the mass destruction of "Things" that war has brought, and he reports favorably on new schools and on a new theater program, "which might perhaps replace in people's hopes and lives the ruined dynasty of Things" (*OE*, p. 44). But he describes the headquarters of the Tcheka, the secret police commission, rather ominously, and thinking no doubt of America as well as the Soviet Union, he tells himself, sarcastically, that "the jail is the corner-stone of liberty" (*OE*, p. 59).

Dos Passos elaborates his views on the new Soviet Union more fully in a 1922 article in the *Liberator*, but his optimism remains tentative and qualified. He begins by warning his readers against believing him, because he speaks none of the languages of the Caucasus and has spent only three weeks there. The people, except for the peasants, he finds impoverished and terrified of the Tcheka. He blames the government's arbitrary methods for creating paralysis and thus contributing to the chaos created by war, revolution, and then civil war. But the Communist party, he feels, has nonetheless "done great constructive work and has indescribably cleared the air of the old brutalizing tyranny of the Church and the Grand Dukes." Despite "the new sort of tyranny," he has no doubt that "the mass of the people have infinitely more opportunities for leading vigorous and unstagnant lives than before the revolution." He sees the revolution as continuing, the Bolshevik methods he criticizes giving way to milder ones. He writes with hope that "communism in Russia is a dead shell in which new broader creeds are germinating."[46] But the revolution was not to fulfill its promise for Dos Passos; a second trip to Russia, in 1928, and involvement with bolshevism's American exponents, the CPUSA, would eventually transform his conception of the proper aims and methods of social change.

Close in subject and style to much of Dos Passos's travel writing, though less directly political, is his poetry, most of which he gathered into *A Pushcart at the Curb*, published in 1922. The majority of the poems are loosely constructed travel sketches, romantic impressions of various places he had visited the previous five or six years. The poems suggest a hunger for exotic scenes and a young man's mind cluttered with bookish allusions. Dos Passos sees with a painter's eye, and finds poetic inspiration in everyday street scenes—a scissors-grinder, women selling flowers—but his verse lacks the simplicity and directness that might best paint these scenes. Written in "a soft and outmoded vein," it seems to "show no awareness that a revolution in poetry [was] going on for the past ten years."[47] Dos Passos would prove a better poet in his novels.

In *A Pushcart at the Curb* Dos Passos writes most clearly when he writes of war: "Thicker hotter the blood drips / from the avenging lips / of the brass God." But he returns most often to the theme of his own isolation. His efforts to write sensual poetry are awkward; more powerful are his images of confused and thwarted sexual longing: "My mad desires / circle through the fields and sniff along the hedges, / hounds that have lost the scent." The fault lies with "the bitter blood of joyless generations" that has left him frustrated and alone, "to wander in solitary streets."[48] The burden of this puritan heritage would become the major concern of his novel *Streets of Night*.

The Bohemian and the Radical

Dos Passos was a traveler, not an expatriate. When he returned from the Near East early in 1922, he took an apartment in Greenwich Village, and did not go abroad for over a year. He wrote and painted — his interest in art, according to Ludington, was "thoroughly serious" —and he spent time with friends, E. E. Cummings, the F. Scott Fitzgeralds, John Peale Bishop, and Edmund Wilson among them. Even severe eye trouble and, later, rheumatic fever did not dampen his satiric enthusiasms. "I'm much better now," he wrote Robert Hillyer from the Midtown Hospital, "and am promised that the cutting out of certain ingrown tonsils where the tenement house conditions among the streptococci, were just disgraceful, my dear, and as for their morals well. . .will put me on my feet again."[49]

Greenwich Village—despite the war, repression, and, finally, the incursion of tourists—remained, in the early 1920s, something of the center of avant-garde art and left politics it had been before the war. It was losing many of its artists and intellectuals, as well as some poseurs, to Paris, but enough remained of the old Greenwich Village to influence Dos Passos. He searched for a position of his own between the two poles of Village nonconformity: bohemianism and radicalism.

The bohemians made middle-class values their enemies. They rejected tradition in art, puritanism in morality, and conservatism in personal behavior. Frederick J. Hoffman describes the bohemian movement as a rebellion against unrespected "authority," an attempt "to find the ideal life and the free one," and "a natural result of the defeat of respect and propriety that the war had caused." By itself bohemianism consituted no real threat to the social order it despised. The movement may even, as Malcolm Cowley argues, have helped satisfy the need in a changing economy for a shift from "a *production* ethic" to "a *consumption* ethic."[50] The radicals, of course, sought to overthrow the social order and replace it with a more just one.

Before the war and before the Russian Revolution, Greenwich Village bohemians and radicals were almost indistinguishable. What John P. Diggins calls the "Lyrical Left," and its best known literary-political magazine, the *Masses*, flourished during the 1910s. Floyd Dell later characterized the *Masses*, as well as its era, by eight animating passions: "fun, truth, beauty, realism, freedom, peace, feminism, revolution." The wartime and postwar antileft crusades made this combination very unstable: Village radicals, in Cowley's words, had to decide exactly "what kind of rebels they were: if they were merely rebels against puritanism they could continue to exist safely in Mr. Wilson's world. The political rebels had no place in it." The Russian Revolution itself suddenly made the abstract visions of "revolution" expressed in the *Masses* into something quite tangible; it created a millennial climate in which old parties and alliances split apart, again forcing people to choose sides. At the same time that political divisions were hardening, the mass working-class movements that had sustained, for example, the Socialist party, were being crushed. With no mass movement to support and be supported by, radical intellectuals in the early 1920s tended to become either passive and highly subjective critics of American society or to join the dogmatic, but still marginal Communist party.[51]

Some common ground did remain between the radicals and the bohemians. Many read the avant-garde *Dial* as well as the more political *Freeman* and *Liberator*. Radical activists continued to believe in the importance of art, and bohemian artists tended to link "capitalist oppression with middle-class stupidity."[52] The businessman became the enemy that united them: to capital, both art and labor were commodities. The images of the bloated plutocrat and of the vulgar Philistine merged easily. The vulgarity of the business ethic that dominated public opinion is perhaps best epitomized by Bruce Barton's *The Man Nobody Knows* (1925), a best seller for two years. Subtitled "A Discovery of the Real Jesus," it sees in Christ "the founder of modern business": "He picked up twelve men from the bottom ranks of business and forged them into an organization that conquered the world."[53]

Dos Passos was too reserved to become a bohemian—he seems to have been as inhibited as Telemachus in *Rosinante* and Andrews in *Three Soldiers*—and too much the individualist to join the Communist party. Though many years later, in *The Best Times* (1966), he disparaged "the tone of repudiation, the nose in the air attitude that always bored me about Bohemians," he seems to have had much in common with them: hatred of authority, alienation from middle-class society, an interest in experimental art, and an intense individualism. He attributed hostile reviews of Cummings's innovative novel, *The Enormous Room*, to public fear of anyone who did not conform, anyone who was "an individual, eternal and indissoluble"; the book's importance, he wrote, was "as a distinct conscious creation separate from anything else under heaven." Like the bohemians, he valued personal freedom very highly; and his unhappiness with the "straightjacket" of his inhibitions paralleled their aversion to a puritanical society.[54]

Still, Dos Passos preferred the *Freeman* to the *Dial*.[55] By the early 1920s, he had come to understand his country in terms of institutions as well as values and to feel that individual rebellion against the latter did not transform the former. He no longer sought freedom from society—his travels had disabused him of that bohemian ideal—but rather a society in which genuine freedom was possible.

Experimental Drama: *The Garbage Man*

While living in Greenwich Village, Dos Passos completed *The Garbage Man*, a play he had begun at least as early as 1918. It seems in many ways to be the work of a younger Dos Passos, the vestige of an earlier, less consciously political rebellion. Under an alternate title, *The Moon Is a Gong*, it was eventually produced by the Harvard Dramatic Club in 1925, and again, at the Cherry Lane Playhouse in New York, a year later. By then Dos Passos was describing the play, Edmund Wilson recorded in his notebook, as "'very infantile,' contain[ing] the remains of a very early idea."[56]

The Garbage Man combines vaudeville techniques, jazz, and traditional drama in an effort, as Dos Passos wrote in a production note, to bridge "*the horrible chasm between the 'serious' play that takes itself seriously and thinks that it's ART*"[57] and the Broadway show, which no one respects but thousands attend and respond to. The play's characters deliver their lines to the music of a jazz band, and often break into dance. Dos Passos uses the music and dancing both seriously and comically, sometimes to intensify the emotions a character expresses verbally, sometimes to undercut them. Although this technique often fails and hardly brought Dos Passos a Broadway-sized audience, *The Garbage Man* represents an important step towards that more successful experiment *Manhattan Transfer*.

Tom and Jane, the play's young protagonists, are estranged from their society; and Dos Passos's jazz-vaudeville methods express effectively the ludicrous, often grotesque nature of that society. Near the start of the third scene, the funeral of Jane's mother, we have the following stage direction: "[AUNT GEORGINA RIVERSON, a blond ample woman, floridly dressed in black enters gyrating to a tinkling waltz]" (*TP*, p. 12). Despite her affectations of mourning, Aunt Riverson thoroughly enjoys supervising the proceedings, as she waltzes around the house, fussing over the flowers and giving advice. Other relatives, some eager to see the will, dance and sing; their wailing chorus of "Boo hoo, boo hoo, boo hoo" (*TP*, p. 21) is the emptiest of rituals. When John, the black butler, who is genuinely grieved by the death of

35

Mrs. Carroll, spontaneously begins chanting a sermon—the music is now solemn—the hypocritical relatives denounce him as "Sacrilegious! Scandalous! Dreadful!" (*TP*, p. 25) and leave.

Dos Passos employs other expressionistic techniques, particularly fantasy and symbolism, to portray the world that imprisons Tom and Jane. A power plant hums loudly; a train is wrecked; characters appear who personify greed, conformity, and death; and Tom dreams of and finally succeeds in beating on the moon like a gong to escape it all. *The Garbage Man* is fragmented and chaotic; its violation of traditional dramatic conventions itself embodies much of the play's social criticism. Like expressionism generally, *The Garbage Man* transcends the naturalistic theater, "which assumes the ordinary bourgeois world to be solid," and uses symbol and fantasy to reveal "the estranged, self-divided psyches which 'normality' conceals."[58]

American normality—which only Tom, Jane, and a few others seem to find perverted—is a wasteland in *The Garbage Man*. Figures representing death—THE FAMILY PRACTITIONER, a MAN IN BLACK OVERALLS, the MAN IN THE STOVEPIPE HAT, and finally the GARBAGE MAN himself—stalk across the paths of Tom and Jane, giving advice, laughing, or making threats. All over the city, in factories, offices, homes, people endure what Jane calls "this humdrum slave existence" (*TP*, p. 28). She and Tom are among "the deadalive" (*TP*, p. 8), but unlike the rest, they want to change—to capture, in a sense, the spirit of *lo flamenco* Dos Passos had praised in *Rosinante*—and much of the play consists simply of their talking about their desires really "to live."

Frustrating their desire to live fully is a machine civilization, its symbol the power plant. The engines of the power plant, Jane tells Tom, "don't want us to be happy." She goes on: "They'd make us work until our hands couldn't feel and our faces were gray and our eyes were blank. Tom, the engine in the power plant; that's all people. The engines are made out of people pounded into steel. The power's stretched on the muscles of people, the light's sucked out of people's eyes" (*TP*, p. 5). Dos Passos uses the metaphor of the machine here more imaginatively and more penetratingly than in *Three Soldiers* and, implicitly, he is attacking capitalism itself. He had been reading *Capital*, and the passage echoes Marx's rather theatrical description of capital as "dead labour, that, vampire-like, only lives by sucking living labour."[59]

Most lives in the play are conditioned by their relationship to the

36

machine. The unemployed—the OLD BUM, the YOUNG BUM—remain free from it, but starve; the working-class characters—railroad workers, factory workers—are yoked to the machine through their jobs; and those from the middle class tie themselves to it through their often mad pursuit of wealth. The FAT MAN, to whom money lost is more important than the lives destroyed by a train wreck, and the REAL ESTATE AGENT, who chants rhythmically of money multiplying, are equally dehumanized. Tom sees such money-hungry people as both enslavers and enslaved:

> Their minds clicking like adding machines, their fingers itching for the round silver pieces, the crinkly green dollars.
> Walking lockstep.
> Shackled in Arrow Collar shackles.
> Crushing us.
> Making slaves of us.
> Making us walk lockstep. (*TP*, pp. 65–66)

Pressures to conform come from all sides. When Jane's mother dies, the Panglossian minister Mr. Brickstone, much like the NURSE before him, insists that in the end "everything from the larger angle is for the best" (*TP*, p. 24). As the police search for impoverished Tom, who has just helped rob a store, a "prosperity Parade" (*TP*, p. 64) marches by, and the VOICE OF THE RADIO denounces "dissenters, knockers, Reds, carping critics, nonchurchgoers, wearers of straw hats out of season, nonFordowners, loafers" (*TP*, p. 70). Conformity oils the very machine that produces it.

Jane has more ties to this world than Tom, and what little dramatic conflict can be found in *The Garbage Man* derives from Tom's efforts to persuade her to run off with him. Her mother's death frees her temporarily, but her mother's values soon reassert themselves in her mind, and she leaves Tom, an unambitious plumber's son, to pursue success. As the prospering actress, Janet Gwendolen, with many TEADRINKERS and HE and SHE INTELLECTUALS as friends—here Dos Passos goes to great lengths to satirize the effete side of Greenwich Village life—she finds no happiness. She asks Tom to "save" her (*TP*, p. 73), and together they decide to forget tomorrow's work and live for today. They plan to "dance with the skyscrapers and straddle the streetcars like hobby horses and weave the clotted colored lights into scarfs for [their] shoulders" (*TP*, pp. 73–74). In a last, brief scene they seem to be in outer space.

The Garbage Man mounts a sharp and often witty attack on conven-

37

tional notions of success, on myths of universal prosperity,[60] and on a dehumanized society obsessed with work and money and intolerant of dissent. But the play's values are less radical than bohemian, its criticisms more cultural than institutional, its rebelliousness more individualist than political. A fantasy, its resolution is effortless: Tom and Jane do not transform but magically transcend their world.

Eros and Civilized Society: *Streets of Night*

After a five-month trip through Europe, Dos Passos returned to New York in the late summer of 1923 and was greeted with the page proofs of *Streets of Night*, a novel he had been writing and rewriting since 1916. Even more than *The Garbage Man*, it reflects interests and anxieties of an earlier period of Dos Passos's life, though these interests and anxieties remained very much alive as he revised the novel in the early 1920s.

The conflict in *The Garbage Man* between Tom and his "deadalive" society is reproduced within the individual psyche of each major character of *Streets of Night*. While Tom—and, with his help, Jane— eventually triumph, the protagonists of *Streets*, self-conscious but powerless, lead dreary lives of futility and stagnation. Fanshaw, disdainful Harvard art instructor; Wenny, a minister's son frustrated in his attempts to conquer his inhibitions; and Nan, who uses her music career as an excuse to reject Wenny's love—these three friends whimper their way through three hundred pages of one of Dos Passos's least successful but psychologically most revealing novels.

Among the novel's protagonists, Fanshaw MacDougan, the aesthete, is the least self-critical, and the sections narrated from his viewpoint are the most ironic. Fanshaw finds the modern world unbearably vulgar and sordid, and he continually compares it to the nobler, purer, more poetic days of the Italian Renaissance he gazes at through paintings. "Cultivated people in this generation," he insists, are like foreigners in their own country. Inelegant eating, unrefined taste, even the sight of workers' coarse hands he finds frightful, and he virtually swoons at any open expression of sexuality: "civilized people don't let themselves think about those subjects," he tells a friend. Fanshaw, however, has his lower urges: as a freshman, he daydreams erotically about the untutored chorine Elise Montmorency, and his admiration for Wenny's physical and emotional vitality is thinly disguised sexual attraction. Dos Passos makes Fanshaw an easy satirical target—as if to exorcise the elements of Fanshaw in himself, qualities particularly apparent in his early letters to Rumsey Marvin. Fanshaw reflects Dos Passos's unhappiness with his own tendencies toward aestheticism and perhaps also his early doubts about his own "masculinity."[61]

David Wendell—Wenny—takes tea, takes walks, dines with Fanshaw and Nan, but rejects their world and hates himself for being "full of the genteel paralysis of culture" (*SON*, p. 102). He wants above all to be "alive" (*SON*, p. 181) and denounces Fanshaw's passion for Greek and Renaissance art: such culture, to Wenny, is "mummifying the corpse with scented preservatives" (*SON*, p. 185). Like Fanshaw, he fears his own sexuality, but where Fanshaw rationalizes, he rebels. He feels—more consciously than Andrews in *Three Soldiers*—caged by his own inhibitions, and he thrashes about madly. One day, clumsily and impulsively, he declares his love to Nan. When she rejects him, he shoots himself, eagerly embracing death instead. Too much the adolescent romantic, the whining rebel in the name of "life," Wenny fails to fill the proud and heroic role Dos Passos seems to have intended for him in what he called this "tragedy of impotence."[62]

If Wenny is meant to be tragic, and Fanshaw comic, Nancibel Taylor, Dos Passos's first major female character, is pitiable. While Nan shares some of Fanshaw's values, she understands Wenny's. She is spared from Fanshaw's ludicrous revulsion for anything bodily, but she is incapable of giving in to her intense sexual feelings for Wenny. When he proposed to her, she later remembers, "the flame of him had frozen her into a helpless clicking automaton" (SON, p. 250). She sublimates her desires and hides from them, by pursuing her musical career with a "ladies' orchestra" (*SON*, p. 32), the Fadettes. After Wenny's suicide, she continues to give stuffy tea parties and tries pathetically to communicate with him through a ouija board.

To blame for the unhappiness of all three characters is a puritanical society, and more specifically, its parental agents. Fanshaw's mother, Wenny's father, and Nan's Aunt M. have instilled crippling inhibitions in their young charges and are thus responsible for their adult paralysis. In somewhat mechanical fashion, Dos Passos has these authority figures appear in his characters' minds—like bad advisers in a morality play—at critical moments of decision. (Though Dos Passos uses Telemachus's recurring mental image of his overprotective mother to comic effect in *Rosinante to the Road Again*, he is quite serious here.) When Nan, for example, begins to imagine the contours of Wenny's muscles as she stands beside him, she hears a "little demon in her head," with "a voice like Aunt M's" hissing "Careful Nancibel, careful Nancibel" (*SON*, pp. 37–38). Sexual feelings trigger all three internal voices, though they warn against sexuality in different ways: Fanshaw's voice tells him not to abandon his mother, Wenny's talks of sin, and Nan's urges her to pursue her musical career. Dos Passos insists, through his hero Wenny, that puritanism is a social problem, but never succeeds in connecting these repressive pressures to society as a whole.[63]

Out of an odd mixture of bohemian and radical impulses, Dos Passos poses as the alternative to the sterile life of aristocratic and collegiate Bostonians the city's lower classes. Fanshaw disdains, Wenny idolizes, and Nan has mixed feelings about these people, usually immigrants, whom they pass in the street on their wanderings through Boston. When Nan is aroused by Wenny's muscular laborer's body and rough appearance, she squelches her feelings and quickly rejects him on the same terms: "Dirty little animal, said the voice in her" (*SON*, p. 40). A character's attitude toward the poor is a touchstone in *Streets of Night*: Fanshaw, who loathes them, is lifeless and unappealing; Wenny, the novel's hero, loves them; and the minor but symbolically important character Mabel Worthington, too alive to stay a Fadette, runs off with a handsome Italian laborer. Wenny seeks to live fully by trying to declass himself—much as Dos Passos had written of doing. As a boy, Wenny had envied poor, tougher boys—"muckers" (*SON*, p. 113)—and as an adult he envies Whitey, a hobo, whose life "sounds fun" (*SON*, p. 133). Dos Passos treats Wenny's ideas here without irony; he shows us nothing of the lives of the poor that would undercut these idealizations. This notion of America's dispossessed as its happiest and freest people rehearses an earlier, more romantic Dos Passos. Yet Dos Passos continued to accept the notion of the virtuous and vital lower classes, relatively untainted by effete culture and venal middle-class values: this notion appears in a different form in *Rosinante to the Road Again*, it lies somewhere behind the radicalism of

U.S.A., and it remains central to the increasingly right-wing populism of his writing after World War II.

Social Criticism and Literary Form:
Manhattan Transfer

By the time *Streets of Night* was published in November, 1923, Dos Passos had already begun his next novel, *Manhattan Transfer*. He worked on it while traveling through the South and to Europe in 1924, and completed it in New York during the late fall and winter. He quickly returned to Europe and remained abroad long enough to avoid the publicity surrounding the novel's publication in November, 1925. Despite his almost continual travel and his immersion in his writing, he managed to vote for the old Progressive, Robert M. La Follette, for president in 1924—a protest vote; his real sympathies lay with the militant IWW—and to find time to denounce, once again, "the liberal weeklies."[64] That same year, the Kamerny Theatre in Moscow asked him to come to Russia, all expenses paid, to help arrange a tour for Americans; the prospect excited him, but the plan eventually fell through.

Manhattan Transfer is the work of a very cosmopolitan writer. It reflects Dos Passos's continued cultivation of literary and artistic friendships in the early 1920s and his efforts to keep up with the many new developments in the arts. In New York, in Paris, and at the Cap d'Antibes villa of Gerald and Sara Murphy he spent time with celebrities such as Picasso, Gertrude Stein, and Ernest Hemingway. Aboard a ship crossing the Atlantic, he read *Ulysses*; in Paris, he helped paint scenery for a performance by the Ballet Russe. Dos Passos's retrospective discussions of the early influences on his writing are sometimes confusing, often imprecise, but he seems to have learned most from European artists, particularly the more innovative ones. "*The war had taught us Paris*," he remembered years later. Modernism in literature, cubism in art, and Eisenstein's film montage contributed to the making of *Manhattan Transfer*.[65]

The most striking aspect of *Manhattan Transfer* is its form. Dos Passos presents neither character nor plot whole, but rapidly shifts point of view and situation, to give the reader over one hundred discontinuous fragments of the lives of scores of characters. Metaphors abound,

41

often technological ones, as critics try to describe the novel's effect: a kaleidoscope, the cinema, a spotlight moving intermittently across the city. People and events are revealed "as if an aeroplane had swooped over New York, and turned X-ray eyes on the life under each roof."[66]

Although the novel can be seen as a further attempt by Dos Passos to broaden his perspective, a continuation of his efforts to "declass" himself in his writing, the structure of *Manhattan Transfer* represents more than a simple extension of the trisected viewpoint we find in *Three Soldiers* and in *Streets of Night*. The very quantity of narrative breaks brings qualitative changes, and the form itself—somewhat as in *The Garbage Man*—creates much of the novel's meaning. *Manhattan Transfer* dramatizes the isolation of individual lives and the fragmentation of individual psyches in the city; at the same time, its rapid tempo and incessant movement—"Brownian Motion," one critic calls it[67]—reproduce the chaos and frenetic pace of urban existence.

Manhattan Transfer begins to break down the traditional relation of character to society, and of reader to character. Dos Passos presents a broad cross section of characters, each receding to the background as the city itself emerges as the novel's protagonist. One critic describes it as "the first collective novel in American fiction." With its proliferation of people and disconnected events, its cubist multiplicity of perspectives, *Manhattan Transfer* makes identification with its characters difficult. The reader's involvement remains more intellectual than emotional, the experience a rather Brechtian one of thinking about the novel's action, trying to figure out its patterns and their implications.[68]

Manhattan Transfer, however, is a less than total break with traditional methods. Halfway through, two characters—one a descendent of Martin Howe, John Andrews, and Wenny—begin to develop into hero and heroine. By the end of *Manhattan Transfer*, Jimmy Herf and Ellen Thatcher have appeared in significantly more scenes than other characters, and the reader has probably begun to identify with them. Herf in particular, since he eventually pronounces many of the same judgments on the city that the novel as a whole does, seems like a vestige of an earlier stage in Dos Passos's technical development, a development that would culminate in *U.S.A.*, where the authorial representative, the "Camera Eye," is formally separated from the narrative sections. And just as Ellen comes to embody the city's values and il-

42

lustrate their hollowness, Jimmy Herf learns to reject those values and leaves the city at the end. Nonetheless, despite their centrality to the novel's meanings, the presence of these two major characters does not significantly undermine *Manhattan Transfer*'s social focus. The city, as the principal character, envelops them as well.

Dos Passos's methods of portraying characters—including, to some extent, Jimmy and Ellen—make much the same point as the novel's overall structure. What Blanche Gelfant calls the "impressionistic method of creating character," a "strict selection of isolated moments for dramatization," reveals disordered, alienated lives. Because Dos Passos shows us only disjointed fragments of a character's life, motives are often obscure or attenuated, feelings seem momentary and trivial. We rarely see thought preceding action; characters tend to respond to immediate stimuli. The dehumanizing nature of the city is revealed through the hollowness of its victims.[69]

Almost every section of *Manhattan Transfer* is narrated from a single character's viewpoint; the third-person narrator moves in and then out of that character's consciousness. Throughout, the emphasis is visual, and the visual perceptions themselves, often fragmentary, change rapidly. One segment opens as follows:

> A small bearded bandylegged man in a derby walked up Allen Street, up the sunstriped tunnel hung with skyblue and smokedsalmon and mustardyellow quilts, littered with second hand gingerbread-colored furniture. He walked with his cold hands clasped over the tails of his frockcoat, picking his way among packing boxes and scuttling children. He kept gnawing his lips and clasping and unclasping his hands. He walked without hearing the yells of the children or the annihilating clatter of the L trains overhead or smelling the rancid sweet huddled smell of packed tenements.[70]

This man seems, by virtue of Dos Passos's narrative method, to exist primarily in the superficial world of his senses, defined largely by what he sees and what he smells and hears (or fails to smell and hear). In this sensory world, people are objects among objects: the "packing boxes" and "scuttling children" have equal weight. The paratactical style—simple propositions strung together with little complexity of logic or syntax—reinforces the effect: the man's thinking, which might establish relations among people and things observed, is at a minimum. There is a suggestion—in the "clasping," "unclasping," "gnaw-

43

ing," the "picking," the repetition of "walked"—of subhuman existence, a world of automatic motor activity. Dos Passos gives most characters more internal life than this bandylegged man—he even writes several passages of very Joycean interior monologue—but he never abandons his efforts to demonstrate the city's inhumanity through the shallowness of the lives of its inhabitants.

Dos Passos's characters can only see, never truly touch each other. Their contacts with one another often resemble "mechanical toys bumping and going off in different directions again."[71] They are the "deadalive" of *The Garbage Man*, now in ceaseless motion. An old man on a stoop, moaning in despair, is ignored or avoided by strangers hurrying by. Bud Korpenning's suicide is simply an annoyance to the tugboat captain who fishes his body out of the river. People try to escape this world of alienation in fantasy, itself an isolating act. Dos Passos undermines their hopes relentlessly: characters are hit by a train, run over by a truck, burned while daydreaming.

As in the classical liberal version of society, these atomized individuals single-mindedly pursue their self-interest. But the result is hardly the maximum benefit for all that Adam Smith's "invisible hand" was to produce. In *Manhattan Transfer*, all scramble after success, many fail, and the chase degrades everyone involved. Ellen Thatcher uses her beauty to achieve wealth and fame; her glamorous life epitomizes success in Manhattan. But expedient marriages and the demands of her ambition deprive her of the capacity to feel anything; she becomes a hollow monument to the opportunities the city offers. Dos Passos dramatizes the deceptive allure of Manhattan by painting it as a world of moving colors and repeatedly contrasting its visual beauty with the impoverished lives that for him are its reality.

The city itself in part creates its citizens' obsession with success, as well as their stereotyped notions of what constitutes happiness and how to achieve it. Newspaper headlines, advertising, and the drastic contrast between the lives of the rich and the poor contribute as much as the actual sufferings of poverty to the desire to get ahead. A newspaper report of a bank robbery inspires jobless Dutch Robertson to begin holding up stores. The "bandylegged man," a Jewish immigrant, shaves his beard—to the horror of his wife—after seeing a razor advertisement showing a "highbrowed cleanshaven distinguished face . . . the face of a man who had money in the bank . . . the dollarproud eyes of King C. Gillette" (*MT*, p. 11). The city tends to homogenize aspirations; people differ mainly in the degree to which they realize them.

A gulf between virtue and success is central to Dos Passos's vision in *Manhattan Transfer*, as in his later novels. *Manhattan Transfer* swarms with the unpleasant rich; fat capitalists, their lawyers and politicians, and bons vivants who eat and drink too much appear in numerous scenes. But while some vomit their excess, others starve, for Dos Passos also peoples his novel with hungry tramps and underpaid workers, usually sympathetic characters, though he never romanticizes them as in *Streets of Night*. Repeated juxtaposition of scenes of wealth with scenes of poverty makes his point inescapable: the capitalist city does not deliver to all the prosperity it promises.

Success is highly sexualized in *Manhattan Transfer*. Many of the novel's down-and-out male characters want to be rich in order to pursue "classy dames," such as Ellen. The attraction of such women derives from their class: since rich men have chosen them, they must be the most desirable. Characters on the way up respond similarly. D. H. Lawrence saw sex as "the prime stimulus to business success" in *Manhattan Transfer*. In many ways, it becomes another form of consumption. Conversely, characters sell themselves in various ways to get ahead, or simply to survive. Anna Cohen dances with pawing men for their dance-checks; Emile courts Mme Rigaud, but really loves the shop she owns; and Ellen, fearful of offending Harry Goldweiser, who can help her acting career, must suffer "the hot determined pudginess of his hand" (*MT*, p. 203). Harry, a comic figure, feels he has worked hard, and now wants to enjoy the fruits of his labor: "All those ideels [*sic*] and beautiful things pushed down into myself when I was making my way in a man's world," he tells Ellen, "were like planting seed and you're their flower" (*MT*, p. 203). The critique here is now of a society that devalues sex, not of a sexually repressive society as in *Streets of Night*. This may reflect a change in Dos Passos as well as a change in America.[72]

Jimmy Herf is not immune to the city's enticements, and thus runs, like the others, in his "squirrelcage" (*MT*, p. 329). Early on, he rejects his Uncle Jeff's offer to help launch him on a career in business: he sees people leaving and entering an office building as "two endless tapes through the revolving doors out into Broadway, in off Broadway," and imagines those doors "grinding out his years like sausage meat" (*MT*, p. 120). While he is enough a nonconformist to repudiate

45

financial success, his still adolescent sexual needs fixate on Ellen, and through her he remains tied to the city's values. He eventually marries her and soon begins to feel the need to get rich. Only after she leaves him—the marriage had never been a happy one—is Herf able to free himself fully from Manhattan: at the end of the novel, in his first real gesture toward adult liberation, he quits his hated newspaper job and leaves. His sexual desires are no less frustrated now, but they will presumably develop in a healthier environment.

Herf's rebellion in no way promises change in the city he has come to hate. Unlike that of John Andrews in *Three Soldiers*, it is motivated by no specifically political feelings. Herf holds vaguely radical opinions, but his decision to leave New York bears no clear relation to them. It is a romantic act of nonconformity. Just before leaving, Herf becomes strangely elated when told about a man in Philadelphia who was killed on the street when he defended his wearing "a straw hat out of season" (*MT*, p. 401).[73] Herf sees in this man a martyr for individual liberty, his act of defiance a "golden legend" (*MT*, p. 402). While Herf's own action is also primarily symbolic, it is still a great act of affirmation in the context of *Manhattan Transfer*. He becomes the one person to break out of the seemingly closed world of the city; his departure implies an alternative, albeit unspecified, to the city's values. The truck driver who offers him a ride at the end asks how far he is going: "I dunno....Pretty far" (*MT*, p. 404).

The passivity of most characters in the novel, their domination by their environment, the widespread defeat and despair, and the repeated evocation of the city's unpleasant smells and sounds all seem—despite Herf's rebellion—to place *Manhattan Transfer* squarely in the naturalistic tradition. New Humanist Paul Elmer More, a foe of naturalism, found Dos Passos's novel sordid and denounced it as "an explosion in a cesspool." Certainly a sense of futility pervades the novel, and much of its imagery, as well as the form itself, suggests a mechanistic determinism.[74] Dos Passos begins with an epigraph that describes new immigrants landing in America: they "*press through the manure smelling wooden tunnel of the ferryhouse, crushed and jostling like apples fed down a chute into a press*" (*MT*, p. 3). Despite such imagery, the style of *Manhattan Transfer* is not naturalistic. Dos Passos uses language in expressionistic ways, selecting only a few, often subjective, details to sketch a scene or character—hardly the naturalist's exhaustively detailed attempt to reproduce reality objectively. Further, the very frag-

46

mentation of form that seems to deprive the characters of free will also tends to undermine the sense of causality in the novel, and causality is crucial to the naturalist aesthetic.

Manhattan Transfer does share the pessimism of the naturalistic novel. Most characters are passive and uncomprehending victims. Except for Herf and a few minor figures, the characters convey no hope that the world might be different. Nevertheless, the novel's pessimism need not be the author's. Early American naturalists like Norris, Dreiser, and London were reformers and radicals; they hoped, like Dos Passos, that an honest portrayal of intolerable social conditions would impel readers to work to change those conditions.

However, *Manhattan Transfer* has limitations as a social novel, as a novel that urges social change. Joseph Warren Beach found it paradoxical that in this putatively collectivist novel, "the social nexus is just what is lacking."[75] The fragmented form that dramatizes so well the absence of real emotional connections among characters also obscures their social connections. Superficially we see a cash nexus, as well as social encounters that have the impersonality of financial transactions; but deeper structural relationships are at best implicit. The reader wonders, for example, but never finds out, how the great wealth of the despicable financier, Phineas P. Blackhead, depends upon the poverty of Anna Cohen or the joblessness of Bud Korpenning. In shadowy scenes, Dos Passos hints at unsavory practices by Blackhead and his partner Densch, but these serve more to underscore the evil natures of these men than to explain their function in the city's institutions.

This vagueness on questions of causality and of how the various aspects of city life interact—central questions for the social novelist—derives in part from the rather unhistorical nature of *Manhattan Transfer*. Dos Passos tells us little about how Manhattan became the loathsome place he shows it to be. While the novel sweeps across roughly three decades and contains scattered references to specific historical events that locate several scenes precisely in time, it creates no sense of historical change.[76] The city seems unaltered from beginning to end—even the war changes little—and nothing in the novel suggests that it was ever different. This tends to undermine any hope that it might ever be different.

Manhattan Transfer is an angry novel, but the object of that anger is less apparent. Soviet critics welcomed it in 1927 as a "bitter criticism of capitalism," and one more recent French critic saw its author as "visibly influenced . . . by Marxism." Michael Millgate sees in it an implicit rejection of urban for rural life, a view that makes some sense in light of Dos Passos's later Jeffersonianism. One can also discover in *Manhattan Transfer* an attack on modern industrial life in general, a continuation of the debates in *Rosinante to the Road Again*. "Everybody in the city," Dos Passos told a reporter in 1926, "is part of the industrial mechanism." And to Edmund Wilson, "it was not merely New York, but humanity that came off badly."[77] The intensity of the indictment in *Manhattan Transfer* dissipates against its shadowy target, and the novel's elaborate structure remains at odds with its uncertain message.

Radicals within the novel—the anarchists Marco and Congo, Martin the socialist, Anna Cohen's Communist boyfriend—articulate organized criticisms of capitalist society. Dos Passos neither endorses these ideas explicitly nor shows them leading to productive action, but they are clearly grounded in the everyday lives of those who hold them. However, while Herf's rebellion is successful, though merely symbolic, their calls for revolution are concrete, but ineffectual. In the America of the early 1920s, Dos Passos found no left movement strong enough to pin his hopes on.

Neither carefully analytic, nor holding any prospect for change, *Manhattan Transfer* derives its great energy as social criticism from its intense indignation. The continual juxtaposition of the usually unsinning poor and the unvirtuous rich creates a dramatic moral landscape that, in one critic's words, becomes "a sermon on the Biblical text that money is the root of all evil."[78] While all are victims, some are villains as well, and Dos Passos often molds their corruption into their flesh. With the sagging faces and corpulent bodies of Densch, Blackhead, and others, aesthetic criticism almost begins to replace moral criticism, or rather, they merge.

The penultimate scene, followed only by Herf's departure, suggests that powerful combination of social analysis and moral denunciation that would characterize *U.S.A.* In this scene, Dos Passos condemns the insensitivity of the rich to those whose labor makes their wealth possible, and at the same time, with bitter irony, expresses despair at the impossibility of change. Having just agreed to marry rich George Baldwin, for whom she has no feelings, Ellen comes to Mme Soubrine's shop to try on an expensive dress. In the back room, Anna

Cohen, a seamstress, is dreaming of life after "the Revolution" (*MT*, p. 397)—a mixture of Hollywood images, political slogans, and popular songs. A fire breaks out, and Ellen, as instructed by Mme Soubrine, pacifies the other customers by telling them it is only "a pile of rubbish" (*MT*, p. 398). When she sees a badly burned Anna carried away on a stretcher, she is momentarily shaken, but minutes later appears at a dinner party, smiling charmingly.

Manhattan Transfer represented a technical breakthrough in Dos Passos's literary development. He had found a method for making society as a whole his subject, and for incorporating into his work the perspectives of characters from all social strata without sacrificing his own critical perspective. But *Manhattan Transfer* is not the "bitter criticism of capitalism" one might have expected, given the anticapitalist sentiments and the support for revolutionary movements Dos Passos often expressed in his letters, travel sketches, and journalism. In part, it was that the form of *Manhattan Transfer* did not easily allow Dos Passos to depict and thus attack a social *system*. But also, as we can see in the romantic, individualist, and ineffectual nature of his heroes' rebellions—Andrews's desertion and Wenny's suicide as well as Herf's leaving New York—Dos Passos's radical political views themselves remained uncertain and contradictory.

But within a year of the publication of *Manhattan Transfer*, Dos Passos had joined the executive board of the *New Masses* and had begun a long period of active involvement with left-wing causes—the New Playwrights Theatre and the Sacco-Vanzetti Defense Committee among them—that would deepen and clarify his radical convictions and lead him to search for new literary forms to express them more fully. The result would be *U.S.A.*

CHAPTER TWO
SOCIALISM AND DEMOCRACY:
1925–39

I'd like to see [the Communists] hang red ribbons on the liberty bell and take it away from the Chase National Bank.
—Dos Passos to Robert Cantwell, September, 1934[1]

The decade or so between *Manhattan Transfer* and Dos Passos's completion of the *U.S.A.* trilogy was not only a turbulent period in American history, but also, for Dos Passos, an extremely intense period of political journalism, activism, and thinking, perhaps the most intense in his life. The radicalism that produced *U.S.A.*—clearer, more democratic, less elitist and individualist, its anger more in tune with its social analysis—is quite different from the radicalism that lay behind *Manhattan Transfer*. A careful examination of Dos Passos's activities in the intervening years is essential to a full understanding of *U.S.A.* as a detailed, complex analysis and criticism—not without its contradictions—of American monopoly capitalism.

The New Masses I'd Like

Dos Passos spent the last days of 1925 traveling through small Moroccan villages, reporting on the rebellion of Berber tribesmen against European colonialism. This exotic research may have suited his contradictory needs for escape and for political involvement, but he soon considered returning home. He had decided, as he later recalled, that his real business "was to report the rebellions of the guys I'd known in the army."[2] By the following spring, he was on his way to Passaic,

50

New Jersey; his account of his trip to the scene of the textile strike appeared in the second issue of the *New Masses*.

In this brief narrative, Dos Passos reveals his self-consciousness and embarrassment at being a middle-class spectator at this drama of working-class hardship. His repeated references to "the people who had come from New York," and to their "taxis" and their "shiny sedans of various makes,"[3] suggest his discomfort with his own privilege as he rides past decaying tenements, deserted mills, and defeated people. He seems to feel no less powerless and out of place here than he had felt in Morocco.

Yet in "The New Masses I'd Like," despite his self-deprecation, Dos Passos expresses genuine optimism about the potential role of the middle-class writer in the battle against "the great imperial steamroller of American finance." Replying to Michael Gold, who called him a mere "bourgeois intellectual," Dos Passos argues that all writers, no matter how proletarian their origins or revolutionary their ideas, are members of the "great semi-parasitic class" of "word-slinging" individuals. Radical writers, Dos Passos continues—provided they shun abstract theories and imported ideologies—can nonetheless make themselves truly useful to "the masses" by exploring with an open mind the unexplored areas of American society and consciousness. Gold, a Communist, urged exploration with a "compass," but the *New Masses* Dos Passos wanted would be an expedition that would "find what it's not looking for."[4]

Dos Passos's concern for investigation unfettered by dogma reflected his uneasiness about organized political activity, a fear perhaps of losing his individuality in a group. Although he worked enthusiastically for the *New Masses* as a frequent contributor and a member of its executive board, he was often uncomfortable with the collective nature of the project and seems to have feared just a little for his intellectual autonomy. At an early meeting to organize the magazine, Malcolm Cowley reports, Dos Passos "self-derisively" declaimed: "Intellectual workers of the world unite, you have nothing to lose but your brains."[5]

The early *New Masses*, however, was an undogmatic, politically independent, and rather democratically run journal.[6] Dos Passos had, in fact, nothing at all to lose by joining. He eventually overcame much of his hesitation about working with organized political groups, and his association with the *New Masses* helped lead to his involve-

51

ment with other left-wing causes, an involvement that ultimately enriched his art.

Writer and Martyrs: Sacco and Vanzetti

The trial and execution of Sacco and Vanzetti accelerated Dos Passos's movement to the left. In Boston to cover the case for the *New Masses*, Dos Passos immediately felt great sympathy for the two men: they were anarchists, draft-dodgers, outsiders, martyrs, and individuals of deep integrity and sincerity. Their execution surprised and stunned him—he never really expected it to happen—and, most important, deepened even further the disillusionment with America that had begun when he saw his country go to war.

Dos Passos incorporated his *New Masses* article into *Facing the Chair*, a 127-page pamphlet he wrote for the Sacco-Vanzetti Defense Committee. It was published in the spring of 1927 and sold for fifty cents. Dos Passos studied the 3,900-page official transcript and interviewed key witnesses as well as the defendants themselves. Sacco found hope in the pamphlet's publication, calling it "a good bright piece of work, which will awaken all the intelligent human minds and the narrow minds of the race and cast[e] prejudice."[7] Dos Passos's sarcastic subtitle—*Story of the Americanization of Two Foreignborn Workmen* —suggests that, like Sacco, he was interested in the broader social and political implications of the case.

Facing the Chair opens with a brief narrative of events. Nicola Sacco, an edger in a shoe factory, and Bartolomeo Vanzetti, a fishpeddler, were active in Italian working-class organizations around Boston until their arrest in May, 1920. An unresolved payroll robbery and murder in South Braintree, the latest in a long series of hold ups, was embarrassing the police; following the only clues they had, they sought as suspects all Italians who had automobiles. Sacco and Vanzetti were carrying guns when arrested and lied to the police about their associates. They had just learned of an impending new crackdown on "reds" and were about to set out in a friend's car to warn their comrades when they were picked up. The police first took Vanzetti to Plymouth, where he was quickly convicted of an earlier attempted payroll robbery. He was then taken to Dedham and tried with Sacco for the South Braintree crimes. In a trial in which the prosecution successfully made the defendants' political views the major issue, they were convicted, on 14 July 1921, of first degree murder. Although significant new evidence was later uncovered, a long series of motions, including one before the Supreme Judicial Court of Massachusetts, failed to win them a new trial.

Dos Passos's analysis of the case proceeds on three levels: he debunks the prosecution's case by demonstrating the flimsiness of its evidence and by presenting detailed counterevidence; he attempts to prove that Justice Department operatives, long anxious to deport Sacco and Vanzetti as radicals, participated in a (possibly unconscious) frame-up; and in the most interesting sections of the pamphlet, he describes the social and political climate that made their conviction possible. Dos Passos's evidential arguments, though compelling, do not differ significantly from those usually advanced by defenders of Sacco and Vanzetti, then and now;[8] the case he makes for a frame-up, though less widely accepted, still reveals little about what it all meant to him personally. But his analysis of the historical context of the convictions of the two radicals tells a great deal about why their execution affected him so deeply.

The year of Sacco and Vanzetti's arrest, "the delirious year 1920" (*FTC*, p. 46), was the year of the Palmer Raids, the height of the "red scare" Dos Passos denounced in "America and the Pursuit of Happiness." Mass hysteria—"pretty consciously directed" (*FTC*, p. 47)— made foreign-born anarchists easy targets, Dos Passos argues, particularly in eastern Massachusetts, where old-line New Englanders as well as newly assimilated Irish Catholics felt threatened by successive waves of immigrants. Effectively, if hyperbolically, Dos Passos dramatizes this situation: "The January raids, the attitude of press and pulpit, howling about atrocities, civilization (which usually means bank accounts) endangered, women nationalized, put the average right-thinking citizen into such a state of mind that whenever he smelt garlic on a man's breath he walked past quickly for fear of being knifed" (*FTC*, p. 53).

Dos Passos opposes to this politics of fear and reaction a politics of hope: anarchism. He tries hard to make this philosophy less fearsome to his readers by characterizing it as abstractly utopian rather than revolutionary. Dos Passos describes anarchism as the product of a rural Mediterranean culture in which a vision of "the City of God" (*FTC*, p. 56) has survived from medieval times. Many Italians, disappointed to find that America was not the City, either "killed the perfect city in their hearts" (*FTC*, p. 57) or became anarchists. The ferocity with which New Englanders hated such dissidents, Dos Passos goes on to argue, derived from the intensity of their own repressed utopian desires.

Dos Passos is on firm ground when he describes the postwar reaction—he can document his assertions—but his venture into psychohistory is colored by his own preoccupations. As he describes it, the case of Sacco and Vanzetti seems to reenact the struggle between a vital immigrant lower class and a fearful, puritanical upper class he dramatizes in *Streets of Night*. In his pastoral depictions of its Mediterranean roots—"those scraggy hills in sight of that always blue sea" (*FTC*, p. 57)—the plight of Italian American anarchism echoes that of *lo flamenco*, the spirit of Spanish village life, which is threatened by the industrial world with extinction in *Rosinante to the Road Again*. None of this is central to the case Dos Passos makes for his protagonists' innocence, nor does it undermine his more objective arguments; but it renders *Facing the Chair* less persuasive to a skeptical reader.

In fact, Dos Passos seems to have had no clear conception of his audience, for he mixes liberal and radical appeals in perplexing ways. His long, detailed, evidential arguments are directed at "the average law-admiring, authority-respecting citizen" (*FTC*, p. 126). Yet he ties his legal brief to a radical interpretation of the postwar political climate and to an attack on the New England psyche that were bound to alienate this same "average" citizen. He mocks Judge Webster Thayer with heavy irony, and refers to the criminal world as "an apt cartoon of the world of legitimate business" (*FTC*, p. 24). More confusing, his final appeal seems aimed at the enlightened self-interest of those who ruled in Massachusetts, suggesting they spare Sacco and Vanzetti to forestall a threatening radicalization of the masses. For if these innocents die, he writes, "what little faith many millions of men have in the chance of Justice in this country will die with them" (*FTC*, p. 127).

More than haste or his inexperience at writing agitation literature, these contradictory pitches reflect unresolved questions in Dos Passos's own mind, tensions between reformist and revolutionary visions of social change, and uncertainty about just how rigid the barriers were between classes. Although his current sympathies were with the working class, his background after all was Choate and Harvard.

After the deaths of Sacco and Vanzetti he resigned himself to the ir-reconciliability of these two worlds and wrote, "all right we are two nations."[9]

Harvard became a symbol for Dos Passos of one of those nations, as the actions of its president, A. Lawrence Lowell, demonstrated that battle lines had indeed been drawn. In June, 1927, two months after Judge Thayer sentenced Sacco and Vanzetti to death, the governor of Massachusetts appointed an advisory committee, which included Lowell, to review the case. When the committee endorsed Thayer's verdict and sentence, Dos Passos published an open letter to Lowell in the *Nation*. Exhibiting some of the contradictory aims of *Facing the Chair*, Dos Passos's letter speaks of "the integrity of the legal system" and at the same time (in a mixed metaphor) deplores "the spiteful and soulless mechanism of the law." While it threatens Lowell, it also tries to persuade him. It is far angrier than *Facing the Chair*—a reflection, perhaps, of Dos Passos's continuing need to reject his own class background, which Harvard represented—and indeed it is almost ominous in tone. It calls Lowell "party to a judicial murder," labels him the enemy in "the world struggle between the capitalist class and the working class," and places with men of his position the decision whether "the coming struggle for the reorganization of society shall be . . . inconceivably bloody and destructive." Nine years later Dos Passos would urge a study of Lowell's "mental operations" as an example of "the incredible and destructive twists of men's minds" that have allowed fascism to triumph in Germany and Italy.[10]

The case of Sacco and Vanzetti had been a *cause célèbre* since their conviction in 1921. Crowds demonstrated and bombs exploded across Europe. In Montevideo, workers led a general strike and an attempted boycott of American goods. Protest came late to the United States, but eventually many thousands marched and went on strike. Dos Passos marched as well, and in August, 1927, he was arrested twice. During the final days of trying to stop the executions, as he wrote Edmund Wilson, he felt "virtually mad"; it was like "battering your head against a stone wall."[11]

The cause of Sacco and Vanzetti engaged Dos Passos so intensely in part because it was the cause of two individuals, not simply the cause of a class. The sympathetic biographical sections of *Facing the Chair* argue the defendants' innocence as effectively as the legal and historical parts. But theirs was a symbolic cause as well: "They are all the wops, hunkies, bohunks, factory fodder that hunger drives into the American mills through the painful sieve of Ellis Island. They are the dreams of a social order of those who can't stand the law of dawg eat dawg" (*FTC*, p. 45). Thus their defeat took on great importance for Dos Passos, and the night of their execution, "the death house in Charlestown suddenly swelled to become the whole world." A few months later, the public had already stopped talking about Sacco and Vanzetti, but Dos Passos was insisting that writers make it impossible ever to forget them. "We must have writing so fiery and accurate," he wrote, "that it will sear through the pall of numb imbecility that we are again swaddled in." By the following summer, he had begun "a very long and very difficult novel," *U.S.A.*[12]

Revolutionary Theater: *Airways, Inc.*

Dos Passos's continuing bitterness over the execution of Sacco and Vanzetti is reflected in *Airways, Inc.*, a play he wrote as a member of a New York radical and experimental repertory group, the New Playwrights Theatre. Early in 1926, Dos Passos had begun working with John Howard Lawson, Michael Gold, Francis Faragoh, and Em Jo Basshe to establish a theater company that would be both politically and aesthetically revolutionary; and as playwright, stage designer, scenery painter, publicist, and patient attender of meetings, he remained active in the group until shortly before its dissolution in 1929.[13]

Since the early 1920s, Dos Passos had been criticizing the New York theater as lifeless and irrelevant, out of touch with the daily existence and with the passions of the average New Yorker.[14] To survive, he wrote, the theater needed both effective "showmanship" and meaningful content, an end to "the idiotic schism between Highbrow and Lowbrow." The New Playwrights hoped to breathe left politics as well as life into the theater. As a manifesto stated, they would act as "a clearinghouse for ideas and a focus for social protest" and would pursue the "double work of innovation in method and ideas."[15] Such plans must have excited the author of both the polemical *Facing the Chair* and the experimental *Garbage Man*.

The New Playwrights' mix of dramatic experiment ("naturalism, expressionism, and vaudeville—cooked up together") and left politics

56

pleased few reviewers. Attacks by the "capitalist press" did not surprise Dos Passos. He understood, after all, the foolish "commonplace of American criticism that ART and PROPAGANDA are opposed and irreconcilable conceptions." Much of the radical press as well panned the productions of the New Playwrights, complaining that their form confused and their content deviated, sometimes to the right, sometimes to the left. Theatergoers themselves criticized each play by their absence. In letters and articles in the *New Masses* and the *Daily Worker*, Dos Passos came doggedly to the defense of his group's philosophy and productions. He conceded that not only critics, but "the whole drift of American cultural life" were against them. Still, he hoped eventually to create a significant audience of radicals, workers, and others for revolutionary theater. Such a theater, he wrote, must be big and flamboyant enough to compete with lavishly produced movies and with "the crafty skill in flattering the public of the smart realestate men who run Broadway." But it must also "draw its life and ideas from the conscious sections of the industrial and white collar working classes which are out to get control of the great flabby mass of capitalist society and mould it to their own purpose."[16]

Airways, Inc., the play Dos Passos contributed to this ambitious project, weaves two simultaneous plots through the lives of a disintegrating middle-class suburban family, the Turners. In one plot, Walter Goldberg, equally committed to Martha Turner and to the class struggle, leads a militant strike of textile workers at the Hartshorn Mills. By the time Martha can bring herself to put her desire for Walter above her self-imposed duty to keep house for Dad Turner and her brothers, the police have planted a gun on Walter and arrested him for murder. At the same time, unscrupulous men with ties to real estate interests want to use the well-known name of young Elmer Turner—an amiable but naïve aviator-inventor—to promote a new airline, All-American Airways, Inc. Drunk with fame and alcohol, Elmer innocently agrees to help a friend by flying over the striking workers and dropping Chamber of Commerce leaflets. He tries one too many stunts, and crashes, breaking his spine. In the last scene, after Walter (like Sacco and Vanzetti) has been electrocuted, Martha gives Elmer, now paralyzed, a drug to help him sleep, and then, in a final soliloquy, speaks her bereavement. The collective defeat of the mill workers, whose rally is brutally broken up by the police, is transformed into the personal loss of Martha, their leader's lover. The so-

57

cial exploitation and abuse of the technological achievements Elmer represents pale beside his poignant individual tragedy.

Despite this last-minute telescoping of social problems into individual ones—perhaps unavoidable for a dramatist, but also suggestive of a tendency in Dos Passos's politics—*Airways, Inc.* does attack capitalist institutions. Dos Passos is eager to show a reality greatly at odds with the inflated public optimism of the 1920s. While the police, the Chamber of Commerce, and a manipulated public opinion combine to defeat mill workers striking for a living wage, speculators like the blustering Jonathan P. Davis promise happiness and plenty for all: "once our great system of post-possession payments is in operation . . . No possible rational human wish [will be] unfulfilled" (*AI*, p. 29). And as Walter, Elmer, and Martha suffer their fates in the last act, we learn that All-American Airways is about to declare a 40 percent stock bonus. Corporations prosper while the individuals we care most about suffer and despair. The ironies, while heavy-handed, have unmistakable power.

Airways, Inc., according to Melvin Landsberg, is a satire on white collar employees for not understanding that they too are workers.[17] Claude Turner, older brother of Elmer and Martha, appears ludicrous as he bemoans his low wages as a Chamber of Commerce clerk while at the same time berating the strikers. Although *"Fifteen years of white-collar slavery have taken all the joy out of him"* (*AI*, p. 18), he identifies wholly with his employers and parrots their worries that the strike will destroy business confidence and lower real estate values. Martha and Walter, on the other hand, both understand who their enemies are, even though while Walter is out fighting them, Martha—tied to her family—is home entertaining them, as Davis and others made deals with Elmer. *Airways, Inc.* makes clear the moral virtue of opposing the capitalists—Martha and Walter are, after all, the two most sympathetic characters in the play—but it fails to demonstrate an identity of interest between the Turners and the strikers. The dramatic impact of the play is quite the opposite. Martha and Walter are punished, while Claude—shallow and unfeeling as he may be—eagerly shares in the growing corporate dividends. Claude's, therefore, is not a totally false consciousness.

This tension between moral imperatives and the logic of self-interest may reflect Dos Passos's own contradictory situation. Middle-class writers, members of a "semi-parasitic class,"[18] could become radical activists and support industrial workers because they feel they ought to or because they share Walter Goldberg's long-range passion for "a sane arrangement of society" (*AI*, p. 32), but hardly out of immediate economic self-interest. Class barriers are not so easily surmounted. When, with Walter dead, Martha wonders what to do with her life, she is perhaps echoing Dos Passos's own feelings upon the deaths of Sacco and Vanzetti: "If I was one of them [the strikers] my misery would all be melted into hate...I'd give all my life to working for the things he worked for, but it's not so easy as that..." (*AI*, p. 144).

Walter Goldberg is an appealing character largely *because* of his political views and actions. Martha, unmarried at thirty, possessed of "*a tired smiling bitter poise*" (*AI*, p. 14), feels "frozen" (*AI*, p. 81) without Walter. He brings her an energy and vitality he seems to derive from his contact with workers (an echo, perhaps, of Wenny's—and Dos Passos's—romanticizing of workers in *Streets of Night*). As Dos Passos's first major Communist character, Walter has none of the unpleasant traits with which Dos Passos would increasingly saddle his later fictional party members. Whatever doubts Dos Passos had about the CPUSA are suggested in the brief appearances of Eliza Donahue, Walter's comrade, a sour, suspicious, unhappy woman. Her main function in the play, it appears, is to make Walter feel guilty about the little time he steals from strike work to spend with Martha.

For all its militance, *Airways, Inc.* exudes the already characteristic Dos Passos despair, a political despair no doubt intensified by the executions of Sacco and Vanzetti. Aside from the depressing fates of Martha, Elmer, and Walter, we also have Dad Turner's. Once a famous inventor, Dad is now a bitter, self-pitying old man, no longer famous, creative, or even much appreciated by his children. He feels that society has used him up and thrown him on the trash heap. His companion, the Professor, with whom he has Pinteresque nonconversations, intensifies the present despair with his memories of past defeats. A radical in Vienna, he came to America after "the collapse of the shining socialist dream"(*AI*, p. 31). His moving reminiscences of lost youth and failed revolutions haunt the play. But while Dad Turner, defeated, hangs himself at the end of the first act, the Professor shows up at the strike rally that climaxes the second act. As the police kick and drag off Walter, the Professor intervenes: "In the name of humanity, I protest" (*AI*, p. 114). Dos Passos, now skeptical of the power of such humane protestations, continues: "*COP brings his club down on* PROFESSOR'S *skull. He falls limp to the porch steps"* (*AI*, p. 114).

Airways, Inc. exhibits much of the revolutionary content but little of the revolutionary form Dos Passos insisted was needed in the American theater. His earlier play, *The Garbage Man*, as well as most of the other New Playwrights Theatre productions, was considerably more experimental. The only technically daring moment in *Airways, Inc.* comes when Dos Passos juxtaposes rallying strikers with airline promoters who talk hypocritically of their "scientific and patriotic duty" (*AI*, p. 88) as they make deals. Fragments of the simple but eloquent speeches of the workers alternate with fragments of the self-serving, pompous talk of the promoters in a counterpoint that dramatizes the distance and the necessary antagonism between the two classes. Nonetheless, while Dos Passos makes much, in a "Production Note," of his elimination of "the pictureframe stage,"[19] the play remains conventionally realistic.

Airways, Inc. opened in February, 1929, and played for four weeks mainly to "empty seats." The critics, as Dos Passos wrote a friend, "guillotined" him. The *Herald Tribune* reviewer, Richard Watts, Jr., found the play "half-arresting, half-irritating . . . more moving in its intent than in its achievements." Brooks Atkinson panned it in the *New York Times*. The *Daily Worker*, for which there were three days of benefit performances, praised it—perhaps in part because its form was quite traditional—even though it was "hardly revolutionary drama." Most critics and reviewers agreed with Michael Gold's later assessment of the play as too ambitious: "There are as many buzzing themes in it as flies in a sugar bowl." Dos Passos perhaps had felt too much pressure from fellow New Playwrights to pack into it as much social criticism as possible. But the very exacting Edmund Wilson found *Airways, Inc.*, despite some reservations, "a remarkable play . . . one of the best-written things that Dos Passos has done so far." "Dos Passos has succeeded in producing the illusion that behind the little suburban street-corner of the Turners lies all the life of a great American city—all the confusion of America itself; and *Airways* made the meager stage of the bleak little Grove Street Theater seem as big as any stage I have ever seen."[20]

The New Playwrights Theatre folded soon after *Airways, Inc.* closed. Dos Passos left the group just before the end. He had been working late too many nights and spending too much of his own money in order to keep the show running. Internecine political battles were becoming wearisome. And, as Ludington suggests, he much preferred to "work alone as a writer." In his letter of resignation, he emphasized again the importance of the organized promotion of revolutionary theater, but argued that the group's members, from the start, "have not been sure of their aims or honest about them." He blamed no individuals—it was "a typically New York confusion of aims."[21] It was also not the most propitious moment in history to launch a radical theater company.

While the New Playwrights Theatre failed in many ways, the more successful workers' theaters of the 1930s owed much to its efforts. Dos Passos himself continued to urge the creation of revolutionary theater, a theater that would advocate "mass action" and serve as "a transformer for the deep high-tension currents of history," a theater that would "attract an audience and hammer into them some valuable truths." "The time for half way measures in ideas or methods," he wrote, "has gone, if indeed, it ever was."[22]

On the Fence: Russia, 1928

These years were busy ones for Dos Passos. Besides working with the Sacco-Vanzetti Defense Committee and the New Playwrights Theatre, he traveled to the West Indies, Mexico, and Russia; took walking tours through the Catskills and the Allegheny mountains; and shuttled to Provincetown and Key West from his base in New York. Stimulated by his various political involvements, he produced an explosion of radical articles and reviews for the *New Masses*. Among his targets were former President Wilson and "Oil Diplomacy"; an opportunist religious leader who soothed the troubled minds of bankers and war profiteers; and organized religion in general, a reactionary force that supports "any cheap nationalist or socially retrograde group that bids for [its] favor." In a book review, sounding a bit like Lenin, he lambasted diplomatic historians for interpreting events leading up to the war in isolation from "international finance" and other fundamental forces. In articles on Mexico, he praised revolutionary mural painters, Zapata, and the millions of oppressed peasants and workers who dared to stand up "against the Catholic Church, against the two world groups of petroleum interests, against

61

the inconceivably powerful financial bloody juggernaut of the Colossus of the North."[23]

Dos Passos's response to the Soviet Union, however, where the exploitative old order had been decisively overthrown, was less than totally enthusiastic. In midsummer, 1928, he arrived in Leningrad, and he toured the country until December. This, his second trip to the Soviet Union, provided an escape from the difficulties of the New Playwrights and a chance to observe the flourishing Russian theater.

Dos Passos's account of his journeys, like his travel reportage in *Orient Express* and in *Rosinante to the Road Again*, is informal and impressionistic. He takes the reader through an exciting but almost bewildering variety of experiences, and he introduces a succession of people who articulate a broad range of views on the revolution. The Russian section of *In All Countries*, Dos Passos's later collection of travel essays, presents a contradictory series of vignettes: inspiringly energetic theater and film people, and a depressed seaman, assigned to the smelly, confining Caspian sea; a newly literate young Kirghiz from the steppes of Central Asia, eagerly reading Gorki, and an old, cultivated critic, who had "missed the red train" (*IAC*, p. 32) and could no longer publish freely; young education students with boundless faith in bolshevism, and an older Englishman, terrified of midnight arrest because his Russian wife is of the old intelligentsia. Dos Passos was clearly not about to echo Lincoln Steffens's unambivalent endorsement of the Russian revolution: "I have been over into the future, and it works."[24]

Dos Passos's desire to see Communist society firsthand is repeatedly frustrated—much as in his 1921 trip—by difficulties with the intractable Russian language, a "maddening prismatic puzzle" (*IAC*, p. 72). But his language difficulties soon become something of a metaphor for a larger, almost epistemological problem: how is he, a foreigner, ever going to comprehend this vast, strange, complex land in a mere four or five months? The impressions he is gathering, he realizes, are about as valuable as "picture postalcards" (*IAC*, p. 57). Nor is collecting simple facts of much use. He is tempted to write home about the very factual stench of a "waterless closet" (*IAC*, p. 52) in a remote mountain village—and here Dos Passos seems less the political investigator than the finicky tourist—but he realizes the necessity of interpreting such a fact. What, if anything, does this stink imply about the revolution? He never is able to come to any conclusion.

Ultimately, Dos Passos decides that the one thing he can understand, and understand well, is the Russian theater. "Not knowing the language is hardly a barrier at all" (*IAC*, p. 57), he tells us blithely. He denounces the "gaudytawdry" New York stage as a mixture of "realestate speculation," exhibitionism, and vicarious participation in "sexual excitement, adventure, cocktails, money" (*IAC*, pp. 58–59); and he extols the vitality, diversity, and invigorating intensity of the Soviet theater, where people "feel part of the victorious march through history of the world proletariat" (*IAC*, p. 59). No doubt angry about the unpopularity of his own New Playwrights group, he mocks American detractors of the Soviet stage. Such critics, worried they are "hearing propaganda and will be converted to communism without knowing it" (*IAC*, p. 60), understand nothing at all.

Aside from a politically noncommital *New Masses* article in 1929, this pointed comparison of American and Soviet theater—which came out a year later in the *New Republic*—was Dos Passos's only public report on his trip until the publication of *In All Countries* in 1934. As such, it was in effect an endorsement of the Soviet government. A discussion with that terror-struck Englishman about Kronstadt—1921 scene of the brutal repression of dissident left-wing sailors—had originally left him shaken; at that moment, he wrote in his notebook, life seemed "too horrible to support." But no description of this discussion appeared until *In All Countries* was published. Dos Passos feared, he wrote much later, "*writing something that would be seized on by anti-Soviet propaganda in the West.*" But by 1934—when Stalin was more firmly entrenched, American intervention in Russian seemed more unlikely, and, most important, his own displeasure with American Communists was growing rapidly—he apparently felt different.[25]

Both socialists and antisocialists often looked to the Soviet Union as a testing ground for socialism in America, despite vast differences in culture, political history, and economic development between the two countries. Even Dos Passos, who had argued in "The New Masses I'd Like" that imported ideologies and methods were inappropriate for American radical movements, could not avoid such thinking and no doubt realized that others would read his reports on Soviet communism for hints of what to hope for—or fear—in the United States. The real drama of Dos Passos's full account of this trip derives from his efforts to discover which side he should be on. His repeated insistence on the difficulty of understanding Russia and its language are signs of his own political uncertainty. His description of his travels seems like a perpetually thwarted search for an epiphany, for some one aspect of Soviet life that might illuminate and help him judge it all. His puzzling series of vignettes draws the reader into this search. His decision to focus on the theater is evasive and his claim to understand it unconvincing, because the evils he alludes to in the rest of Soviet society raise many unanswered questions about the theater he celebrates.

Despite his reluctance to reduce his months of "braincudgelling impressions" (*IAC*, p. 51) to a single, total judgment, Dos Passos has no doubts about the great significance of the project the Russian people are engaged in and the magnitude of the difficulties confronting them. These final lines describe his return from a visit to a peasant village:

> The raw wind threw an occasional handful of sleet in my face. Everywhere the endless northern plain at the beginning of night, at the beginning of winter. No sense of locality; no ingrained quaintness of ancient local histories and customs. It might be Alberta or the Dakotas or Tasmania or Patagonia, any untrampled unfenced section of the earth's surface where men, tortured by the teasing stings of hope, can strain every apprehension of the mind, every muscle of the body to lay the foundations of a new order. It's a tremendous thing to walk alone, even a short distance, at night at the beginning of winter over the Russian plains. (*IAC*, p. 72)

This sense of the isolation and powerlessness of the individual amidst great historical forces—even those forces which men and women themselves set in motion—would inform the novel he was working on while in Russia, *U.S.A.*

The Role of the Middle-Class Writer

After Dos Passos's return from the Soviet Union and after the collapse of the New Playwrights Theatre, he headed for Key West, in March, 1929, to visit his friend Hemingway, whom he had first met as a fellow ambulance driver in 1918 and whose bravado the shy Dos Passos enjoyed, so long as it was tempered with humor. Dos Passos was also eager to visit Key West in order to spend time with Katharine Smith, whom he had probably met there the previous year. Far from the political tangles of Moscow and of New York, he relaxed in the sun for several weeks, before heading north again to continue working on *The*

42nd Parallel. By fall, the novel was finished and he and Katy were married. As a friend remembers it, the young couple "understood each other uncommonly well." They traveled frequently in their first two years together: to France, Switzerland, Mexico, Havana, and Key West. At the same time, since Katy owned a house in Provincetown, Dos Passos seemed to become, as Edmund Wilson wrote to Fitzgerald, "more and more of a respectable householder every day."[26]

In fact, during these years, as Dos Passos was finishing *The 42nd Parallel* and then writing *1919*, his radicalism intensified. He came increasingly to understand—and reject—American capitalism as a system, although he never formulated any coherent strategies for change, or even came to believe very deeply in the possibility of change. "I guess the trouble with me," he wrote Wilson early in 1931, "is I cant make up my mind to swallow political methods. Most of the time I think the IWW theory was right—Build a new society in the shell of the old—but practically all they did was go to jail." Still, he gave his name, time, and sometimes his money to a variety of causes—from signing a protest against the Kuomintang's oppression of revolutionary writers to serving as chair of the National Committee to Aid Striking Miners Fighting Starvation.[27]

Communist and anti-Communist alike tend to gauge Dos Passos's radicalism by his relationship to the Communist party and to Communist causes. Dos Passos never seriously considered joining any party; nonetheless, his frequent associations with Communists were inevitable, given the party's status as the major left-wing organization in the 1930s. Just as his endorsement of and his participation in organizations created by the party do not mean he embraced the entire Communist analysis and program, his frequent criticism of the party in no way suggests an acceptance of capitalist institutions and liberal methods. He was an independent radical.

Dos Passos bore far more hostility to American capitalism than he did to the Communist party. He never hesitated to defend Communists, or any other victims of persecution. Although the depression did not hurt him personally—he continued to live quite comfortably and stay in good hotels when he traveled—he clearly perceived its effect on others. In a *New Republic* article the year after the Crash, he compared the growing repression to the postwar "red scare," and found it "curious" and "sinister" that newspaper headlines referred to the swelling numbers of unemployed workers as "the idle"—"as if there were something innately vicious about not having a job." He reported four thousand arrests of real and alleged Communists in four months, listed some of the more significant court cases, and attacked the manipulation of racism to thwart organizers who tried to unite black and white workers. In the introduction to a 1930 pamphlet, *Story of the Imperial Valley*, he defended framed and arrested Communist organizers of "brutally exploited" Filipino and Mexican farm workers in California and pleaded for contributions to the International Labor Defense, a Communist group.[28]

The intensification in the early 1930s of what the Communists called class struggle prompted Dos Passos to think more about the class structure of American society and about his own place in that structure. Although he could still envy the proletarian background of Michael Gold—"lucky to have worked on a real garbage dump, instead of on the garbage dumps of dead ideas the colleges are"—it was time for him to go beyond the rather crude notion of "declassing" himself. He praised Robert and Helen Lynd's sociological study, *Middletown*; and of the three classes it defined—"the Middle Class or Business Class, the Owning Class, and the Working Class"—he thought the middle class the most important in determining the nature of future social change in America. Most members of the middle class, he wrote, are simply "mercenaries and dependents of the owners" and thus tied to the system. But a layer of this class—engineers, scientists, writers, technicians—would be essential to any society and therefore has no real stake in the perpetuation of capitalism. For this reason, such people could afford to have humane feelings and could be persuaded to help stop the violence against workers and the arrests. To get their support, to avert the "serious repressive measures" still ahead, Dos Passos even suggested hiring a public relations adviser, such as Ivy Lee or Edward Bernays.[29] Unlike the Communists themselves, Dos Passos had no real hope for total victory in the class war and might have feared the consequences of such a victory. Therefore, at this point, he simply sought ways to make the struggle less violent.

Dos Passos seemed to feel that his position as a writer defined his political role. "I speak as a writer and therefore," he wrote, confusingly, "as a middle-class liberal whether I like it or not." Surely Michael Gold, for example, was no "liberal," although also a writer. Critics cite this self-designation as a "middle-class liberal" as evidence that

Dos Passos was never very radical politically.[30] But he must have been using *liberal* in an idiosyncratic way here, since he repeatedly attacked "liberals"—as being, for example, too "neurotic" about Communists. "By middle-class liberals," he wrote, "I mean everybody who isn't forced by his position in the economic structure of society to be pro-worker or anti-worker."[31] Dos Passos was talking here not about his political opinions but about a writer's limited potential participation in class struggle. Eight years earlier, paraphrasing Pío Baroja, he had written that the "discipline" necessary for a builder of a new society "can only come from common slavery in the industrial machine" (*RRA*, p. 93). As a middle-class writer, Dos Passos was still searching for his role in the transformation of society.

Bloody Harlan

The role of reporter, almost irresistible to Dos Passos, continued to prove difficult. In November, 1931, Dos Passos joined Sherwood Anderson and others in an expedition—organized by Dreiser and by the Communists' International Labor Defense—to investigate the conditions of striking miners in Harlan and nearby eastern Kentucky counties. This was brave, since two reporters sympathetic to the miners had already been shot by local authorities. Dos Passos and the rest of the writers' committee spent four days gathering testimony, visiting miners' meager homes, and holding mass meetings. Back in New York, they publicized the deplorable conditions they found, in letters, articles, and a book, *Harlan Miners Speak*. For their trouble, the committee members were later indicted (though never tried) for criminal syndicalism. The following February, two members of a second committee (which did not include Dos Passos) were "severely beaten about the head with revolver butts" by local police.[32]

There was a great deal to report on in Harlan County. The depression had struck the coal industry hard, and mine owners were laying off workers and cutting wages. In one Kentucky village that winter, "not a single child had shoes, and very few possessed underwear." United Mine Workers of America organizing drives met violent resistance: coal company guards, quicky sworn-in sheriffs' deputies, and hired gun thugs terrorized the miners, who soon began shooting back. Miners were frequently arrested and evicted from their homes. The UMWA gave up, the Communist National Miners Union took their place, and the violence continued.[33]

That November, as he later recalled, Dos Passos first "understood the meaning of the word 'depression.' " He saw miners and their families living in flimsy shacks, scarcely protected from "the lashing mountain winds, rain and snow." They subsisted on a "few crumbs of cornbread usually—a piece of salt pork occasionally—a few pinto beans for the more fortunate." The coal company's mules lived better.[34]

Though Dos Passos sympathized deeply with the miners' plight and admired their simple eloquence at meetings and their bravery, he felt powerless to help them. While "bright young men from the *Daily Worker* [make] stirring speeches" about the international proletariat and the Soviet Union, the writers' committee can at best promise "shakily" that public opinion is being awakened (*IAC*, p. 193). A middle-class writer from New York, Dos Passos "shamefacedly" (*IAC*, p. 194) enters the dilapidated cabin of a miner dying from an injury he suffered at work. When another miner, enthusiastic about the NMU, eagerly asks Dos Passos if he too is working for the revolution, Dos Passos answers, uncomfortably, that writers are "people who stayed on the sidelines as long as they could" (*IAC*, p. 197). The end of his *New Republic* article expresses Dos Passos's painful awareness of his distance from these people: he and Dreiser ride off in a taxi, into "the quiet breathless night" (*IAC*, p. 197), much as he had left the Passaic strike five years earlier.

Dos Passos seemed to envy the Communists' optimism and clear sense of purpose: writers, organizers, workers, they understood their role in history. Though he confessed, even thirty-five years later, that the Communists had performed "a useful function" in Harlan, he very much disliked their tactics. The party, then in its "Third Period," was pursuing a policy of dual unionism. Since their union, the NMU, was competing with the UMWA, the Communist International Labor Defense refused to help get miners from the non-Communist union out of jail. This outraged Dos Passos, and when the central committee head Earl Browder, who repeatedly scorned Dos Passos's "liberalism," later tried to persuade him to return to Kentucky to stand trial—presumably for further publicity—Dos Passos refused.[35] Unable to find a democratic and libertarian, yet genuinely radical alternative to the rigid Communist party, Dos Passos would find himself increasingly alienated by left politics later in the 1930s.

Depression Politics

Events were confirming Dos Passos's anti-capitalist sentiments. By 1933, unemployment had reached 25 percent, and millions more were suffering wage cuts and underemployment. While many were hungry —some even dying of malnutrition—crops were burned and milk was dumped into rivers. Idle factories, jobless workers, and families desperately in need of what those factories and workers might produce existed side by side. The irrationality of capitalist production was once again apparent; the depression, as Dos Passos later wrote, *"provided the Marxists with their great I told you so."*[36]

Dos Passos agreed that the "collapse" of American capitalism was "inevitable," but unlike most leftists in the early 1930s, he hardly thought it imminent. To him, the depression revealed the "failure" of American economic institutions. In a *New Republic* article, "Detroit, City of Leisure," he reports on that failure: unemployed men, with nowhere else to go, fill a city park, lying on the grass "in a hundred helpless attitudes of sleep"(*IAC*, p. 199). But Dos Passos's title is not really sarcastic: unlike those who work in the nearby automobile plant and hurry silently through a fifteen-minute lunch, these park dwellers have time to talk, to dream, even to debate "whether the workers could run the banks"(*IAC*, p. 206). Some inspired by ideological conviction, and many more by necessity, have overcome passivity and despair and sought direct solutions to the problems of hunger— from a communal boarding house to mass nonviolent raids on chain grocery stores. As Dos Passos wrote Katy, Detroit gave him the impression "that main street was reddening up."[37]

From Washington, D.C., Dos Passos reported sympathetically on the Communist-led National Hunger March in December, 1931.[38] The not so numerous marchers seemed rather pathetic to him, but they promised more hope than nearby congressmen, with their "close-set eyes full of lawyer's chicanery," their "pursed, selfrighteous" mouths, and their "flabby selfsatisfied" jowls (*IAC*, p. 219). These faces, together with the tired, hungry faces of the marchers, expressed the truth of depression America for Dos Passos; this was reality, and not the "antiquated mirage of a Greco-Roman republic set among the fine lawns and the magnolia trees of the Washington parks" (*IAC*, p. 221).

The turnout was larger six months later, when the "Bonus Army," twenty-two thousand veterans strong, camped out on Anacostia Flats, in Washington, D.C., determined to stay until Congress agreed to grant them their war bonuses early. The spontaneity and especially the democratic organization of this protest inspired Dos Passos and reminded him of the Wobblies' direct action methods.[39] Dos Passos makes their point of view his own in his reporting as he describes their war experiences, their manipulated patriotism during the "red scare," and finally their realization that their country owed them something now that they were jobless. He seems to endorse the veterans' argument that granting them bonuses would stimulate the economy and help everyone. A month after Dos Passos's article appeared in the *New Republic*, government troops under General Douglas MacArthur were driving out the veterans with tear gas and burning down their shacks.

Many looked to the presidential elections of 1932 for a way out of the depression, but Dos Passos—as his reporting on the Republican and Democratic nominating conventions reveals[40]—had little faith in politicians. He contrasts the Republicans' "myth of the keeneyed pilot [Hoover] at the helm of the ship of state" with the Democrats' myth of a new leader who would take the government away from "Republicans, Wall Street, Privilege, Graft and Corruption," give it back to the people, and "in some mystic way" restore prosperity for all (*IAC*, p. 235). The unreality of both visions is reflected in the phony conventions themselves: the Republican "Wild West show" (*IAC*, p. 229) and the Democratic "vaudeville show" (*IAC*, p. 233). Dos Passos mocks the Republicans with great élan, piling one comically grotesque metaphor on top of another. He describes the Democrats more soberly, juxtaposing their great popular appeal with the despair of jobless men, the "discards" outside, who understand that "Hoover or Roosevelt, it'll be the same cops" (*IAC*, p. 237).

Even the Socialists and Communists gave Dos Passos little hope in 1932. At a Socialist party rally he attends—a "Pink Tea," he calls it —everyone is pleasant and agreeable. Their program seems calculated to offend no one and accomplish little. A Communist party rally he finds livelier: stalwart singing of the "Internationale," a triumphant pageant about the Five-Year Plan, and a sense of "the tremendous intoxication with history that is the great achievement of communist solidarity" (*IAC*, p. 245). But even this organization strikes Dos Passos as far removed from the everyday problems of "the forgotten man" (*IAC*, p. 246).

Nonetheless, Dos Passos publicly supported William Z. Foster and James W. Ford, the Communist party candidates, in the 1932 presidential elections. Along with over fifty other "professional workers," including Wilson, Malcolm Cowley, Sidney Hook, Waldo Frank, and Sherwood Anderson, he signed a press release proclaiming that "the only effective way to protest against the chaos, the appalling wastefulness, and the indescribable misery inherent in the present economic system" was to vote Communist. The Republicans and Democrats alike, the statement argued, were agents of the rich, hopelessly corrupt, and incapable of leading the nation out of the crisis. The Socialists, though theoretically anticapitalist, were doing nothing to build a movement for change. The Communists alone were educating the dispossessed class and organizing them into "an efficient instrument for establishing a new society."[41]

Still, Dos Passos had conflicting feelings about the Communist party. He continued to praise its practical work, and through his writing he supported a wide variety of causes the Communists took up, from the Scottsboro defense to the National Student League. But he remained critical of their ideology, and some of their tactics—as in Harlan County—continued to disturb him. But whatever Dos Passos's doubts about capitalism's most vocal enemies, he was becoming every day more convinced of the necessity of replacing it.[42]

Dos Passos's travels and reporting were abruptly interrupted by an attack of rheumatic fever, in April, 1933. He was taken to the hospital, Katy wrote Edmund Wilson, "helpless and unable to walk"; the pain in his joints was so severe he could not move. Friends were sympathetic and generous. Hemingway, after reading a description of this agonizing illness in a medical dictionary, sent him a thousand dollars. Dos Passos seemed a bit embarrassed by such responses. "This sickness," he wrote Hemingway, "has turned out to be a gigantic panhandling enterprise. The wily portugesee shakes down his friends."[43] But by late May, he was off to Spain, for more reporting and for the hot weather his doctor recommended.

JOHN DOS PASSOS

Depression Drama: *Fortune Heights*

Dos Passos's interest in the theater had not died with the New Playwrights, and in 1933, he finished a third and final play, *Fortune Heights*. The Chicago Workers' Theatre produced it in 1934, and that same year two separate productions of *Fortune Heights* played simultaneously in Moscow. Dreiser and Dos Passos apparently considered basing a movie on the play, but none was ever made.[44]

Fortune Heights grew out of Dos Passos's witnessing the effects of the depression and reflects his pessimism about the chances for social change. All the action of this formally realistic drama takes place at Owen Hunter's small filling station, luncheonette, and motel business on the edge of a major highway. In three acts—"The Bull Market," "The Great Depression," and "The New Deal"—we meet a wide variety of characters: a comically unprincipled blowhard of a young mystery writer, Ike Auerbach; Owen's frustrated assistant, Morry; a slick real estate promoter, Ellery Jones; and a whole soupline of hitchhikers, hoboes, and other down and out people who pass through Owen's establishment. The vulgar and destructive cupidity of Ike, Ellery, and others, along with the great inequalities of wealth we see, condemn capitalist values and capitalist economics alike.

The main plot thread concerns the fortunes and the consciousness of Owen himself. Generous and weak, Owen has failed financially in the past, but he is "out to win this time."[45] Determined never again to work for a boss as a "wageslave" (*TP*, p. 188), he wants the life of *"ownership and independence"* (*TP*, p. 163) that the nearby realtor's sign promises. Although he barely meets his mortgage payments, he identifies with the successful speculator Ellery and half echoes his blustery optimism. Against his real nature, he cheats a customer or two. Eventually the depression and a robbery undermine his already precarious financial situation; he, his wife Florence, and their child face eviction. When local farmers and farmhands show up en masse to block the sheriff and deputies, Owen is inspired by this act of solidarity and friendship, abandons his entrepreneurial aspirations, and rejects the world of business. "That's no life for a man any more," he proclaims. "We gotto have a new idea. Somethin' better than dawg eat dawg" (*TP*, p. 292).

The central drama of *Fortune Heights* is the transformation of Owen's *petit bourgeois* individualism into a humanitarian and collectiv-

72

ist spirit. Much like *Airways, Inc.*, the play reflects Dos Passos's continuing concern with the potential of middle-class individuals to align themselves with either the owning class or the working class. Owen feels uncomfortable all along in the role of business competitor —"it's a pretty lousy business that the only way you can make a living is by steppin' in some other guy's face," he tells his wife (*TP*, p. 219)— but it takes an economic setback and then the actual experience of collective action to bring about so complete a break with his past. This, of course, was the path to radicalism of many in the 1930s.

Dos Passos's political statement in *Fortune Heights* is as open-ended as it is militant. The farmers who fill the stage express a very nonideological radicalism in their speeches against the eviction. They invoke the Constitution and the Declaration of Independence, not the Bolshevik revolution. Their loosely populist threat is somehow to "relieve the men higher up, them Wall Street wizards, of the care and responsibility of ownin' this country" (*TP*, p. 285). The play makes very clear that politicians' promises are no substitute for direct action. Ellery Jones, the realtor, now bankrupt, is running for the legislature as an independent New Deal candidate. He pledges that, if elected, he will work to stop all evictions. But Ellery is no more to be trusted now than ever. His recent marriage to Mrs. Stead, the diamond-laden banker's widow, is symbolic: even New Deal politicians are wed to capital.

Fortune Heights is hardly triumphal, however. Although Owen's transcendence of "dawg eat dawg" values and his decision to abandon business upstage the antieviction battle, making its outcome dramatically less important, it does in fact fail. Deputies drive the farmers off with tear gas and Morry is fatally shot. Rather suddenly, Dos Passos has displaced the central dramatic struggle from an economic plane to an almost spiritual one. Perhaps this is the only way he felt he could resolve it positively. Yet he undercuts even this weak optimism. In the final scene—which Lawson objected to as an "ironical defeatist twist" and which both Soviet directors eliminated [46]—a real estate agent is selling Owen's and Florence's place to a new couple, by promising them independence and wealth: the American dream, no matter how flawed, does not die easily. As *U.S.A.* would, *Fortune Heights* combines sharp criticism of capitalism with deep sympathy for its victims and opponents, yet it offers little hope for an easy road to a new society.

JOHN DOS PASSOS

Fascism, Communism, and Americanism

The years between Dos Passos's 1933 trip to Spain and his final, traumatic return there in 1937, were active and productive. He traveled
to Washington, Boston, Hollywood, and to Key West for his health
and for the exuberant, though occasionally crusty, company of Hemingway. He continued to write articles for a wide variety of publica-
tions—the large fees *Esquire* paid for his "used paper" pleased him
greatly[47]—and early in 1936 he completed *The Big Money*, the third
volume of his trilogy, *U.S.A.*

Dos Passos was happily married and had many friends. Katy was
witty and herself an occasional writer, though she lived in Dos Passos's shadow. Despite the frequent miscarriages that left them child-
less, they seemed to share a very pleasant existence. Wilson and others
visited them frequently in Provincetown, where Dos Passos's regular
routine—when he was not off traveling—included early morning
swims, big breakfasts, full workdays, and early nights seven days a
week. Although he had to work hard and sometimes scramble for
money to do so, he maintained what Ludington calls a "comfortable,
if not luxurious" standard of living.[48]

Dos Passos was widely admired and respected for his honesty and
generosity. Katy's sister-in-law recalls his great patience with young
writers who would drop in without an appointment to show him their
work. Militant in print, he was shy and humble in person and seemed,
as Robert Cantwell remembered, "to attach slight importance to his
own opinions." "Tall, baldish, bobbing and very nearsighted," he
struck one interviewer as "a clever, kind, slightly startled Bill the Liz-
ard in *Alice in Wonderland.* "[49]

So Dos Passos felt out of place when, in July, 1934, he found himself in Hollywood—"the world's great bullshit center," he called it—
at work on the screenplay for *The Devil Is a Woman*, a Josef von Sternberg film, starring Marlene Dietrich. Curiosity and hospital debts had
brought him out to "the red-light district," a town where people
seemed to have "that frank innocent viciousness of little children left
alone in study hall on a rainy afternoon." Soon after he arrived, rheumatic fever struck again, confining him to bed, but he continued writing. He soon discovered, though, that the real screenplay was being
written by a young unknown; Dos Passos was being paid for the use of
his name, like "Queen Marie endorsing a vanishing cream." He was

74

not unaware of the irony of working in Hollywood while writing *The Big Money.*[50]

Shortly after his return from Hollywood, Dos Passos published a review article that suggests that his political outlook was growing angrier and gloomier. It was a monstrous war that had originally inflamed his youthful rebelliousness and led to his hatred of capitalism; now he was convinced that capitalist institutions themselves caused war. To satisfy their hunger for profits, he argued, war-related monopolistic corporations whipped up nationalist and militarist sentiment. The "logic of the profit system's need for war" had brought carnage to Europe in 1914 and threatened to bring the world to war again. Of course, business could often achieve its aims short of armed conflict, as in Cuba, a nation Dos Passos describes elsewhere as virtually owned by American finance capital. To protect investments after the fall of Machado, in 1933, the State Department backed "one of the most atrocious reigns of terror in all history."[51]

Such bloody thoughts were fed by the accelerating events in Europe. In a 1933 article entitled "Thank You, Mr. Hitler," Dos Passos drew a lesson from Germany: American capitalists might very well back fascist elements, as their German counterparts had, if necessary to keep the exploited powerless. He did not expect that a centralized fascist state—what he later called "the Hitler-Mussolini style of capitalist consolidation"—would come to America, since democratic traditions remained alive. But he feared an intensification of "Hearstian demagoguery" and "repressive violence." As the decade grew darker, Dos Passos wrote with a greater sense of urgency, compelled "to hurry to get stuff out before the big boys close down on us." Impatient with the very personal, introspective *Esquire* articles his friend Fitzgerald was then writing, he asked: "Christ man how do you find time in the middle of the general conflagration to worry about all that stuff?"[52]

A symbolically important incident helped destroy what little hope Dos Passos had that a united American left might prevent violent repression. In February, 1934, a Socialist-led rally in Madison Square Garden, staged to protest the brutality of the Austrian fascist Engelbert Dollfuss, was broken up by a group of Communists. Socialists, the Communists later insisted, had insulted them at the door, while inviting people like Mayor Fiorello LaGuardia to speak, though the day before "his police had clubbed and ridden down Socialist and

75

Communist workers on the steps of the New York Public Library."
Heckling at the rally led to fights and finally to total chaos; Communists were hurling chairs from the balcony. Dos Passos and twenty-
four others signed "An Open Letter to the Communist Party," criticizing the disruptive actions. The *New Masses*, by now a party organ,
published the letter and, in a reply, lamented this betrayal by "Dos
Passos the revolutionary writer, the comrade." Dos Passos replied in
turn that such "unintelligent fanaticism" could only destroy any
chance there was for creating "a workers' and producers' commonwealth."[53]

Stalinist terror in Russia added to Dos Passos's dismay with American Communists. In an exchange of letters with his old friend Edmund Wilson, Dos Passos debated events in the Soviet Union and
their significance for America. Wilson insisted that Stalin, despite his
"limitations," was still moving Russia towards socialism; for Dos Passos, events there had "no more interest—except as a terrible example
—for world socialism." By early 1935 he could tell Wilson that he
would prefer the despotism of Henry Ford, United Fruit, and Standard Oil to that of Earl Browder, Mike Gold, and others.[54]

Dos Passos had already written off the Communists—though not
Marxism or socialism[55]—by the time their line softened in 1935. As
Hitler's strength grew, Stalin and hence the CPUSA decided that
Communists desperately needed allies against fascism. Suddenly, liberals and Socialists ceased to be "social fascists," and communism was
"Twentieth Century Americanism." World revolution was no longer
on the agenda; the Comintern, as Malcolm Cowley put it, had
decided "to let sleeping dialectics lie."[56] In the 1936 elections, though
the party formally nominated Browder for president, it worked to
elect Roosevelt. Dos Passos supported Roosevelt as well, but by then
his thinking and the Communists' were worlds apart.

Dos Passos had been very suspicious of the Roosevelt administration and the "Raw Deal" at the start, in part because he distrusted all
government. His reporting on New Deal Washington contrasted
pompous, irrelevant politicians (as well as insensitive AFL bureaucrats) with the successful mass action of the Unemployed Councils.
Roosevelt himself he described as "Delano the Magician," dazzler
and manipulator of the press and the public; in a letter to Hemingway, Dos Passos predicted "the slow extinction of the working stiffs
and white collar grinds to a sound of lovely oratory."[57] But his dissat-

76

isfaction with the organized left, his gradual appreciation of the New Deal's achievements, and perhaps also his increasing fear of the kind of instability that characterized European politics led him to vote for Roosevelt's reelection in 1936.

Thus Dos Passos began to wax patriotic. His was not the "Americanism" of the Communist party, but a genuine search for American traditions that might explain the present and help build a future. Earlier he had challenged Marxists to "Americanize Marx," not "to junk the American tradition." Now he was beginning a reading course in American history to learn about "the old days I tend to begin to find attractive." He remained aware of the potential abuses of patriotism, though, and could still remember the great postwar effort "to bulldoze the average man into believing that the general interests of the nation coincide with those of the boards of directors of big business, by festooning the profit system with red white and blue bunting." But he was clearly beginning to move in a new direction. He finally abandoned the *New Masses* and began publishing frequently in *Common Sense*, a journal whose philosophy was firmly rooted in the American populist tradition.[58]

Another source of Dos Passos's alienation from the Communists and of his search for alternatives was the party's attitude toward language and literature. He had mocked the writing in the *Daily Worker* as "clippings from Bukharin's scrapbasket" and had felt that a major role of the radical writer was to introduce "a more native lingo" into political discourse. While he recognized the element of propaganda or "preaching" in all writing—"not to admit that is to play with a gun and then blubber that you didn't know it was loaded"—the independent and individualistic Dos Passos could never have accepted the prescriptive doctrines of Granville Hicks and others. To say, as many did, that literature is a weapon in the class struggle is merely to recognize its inevitable ideological component, to recognize that all literature, to some extent, is shaped by and shapes political consciousness. But to insist, as Hicks does, that "all literature" should embody the viewpoint of "the vanguard of the proletariat" and should be judged by its ability to "lead the proletarian reader to recognize his role in the class struggle," is to develop narrowly political and instrumentalist literary values which would have pleased Marx as little as they pleased Dos Passos.[59]

In any case, Dos Passos found this literary communism increas-

77

ingly irrelevant not only to the needs of "the real guys . . . being framed and jailed in all parts of the country," but also to his own concerns as a writer. And in a paper he sent in 1935 to the first American Writers' Congress, organized by Communists, he rejected any interference in the work of writers, whether by capitalist managers or bureaucratic leftists. Total freedom of speech and thought, he insisted, were essential to any struggle for liberty.[60]

Dos Passos was no longer the aesthete he had been in his youth: he now saw the novelist as a "second-class historian of the age he lives in." His own theorizing about what constitutes good writing was realistic, if inconclusive. He tells a friend that good writing is "reality," but hastens to add that he would hate to have to define the term. While conceding that all writing is subjective and didactic, he insists that beyond this exists something objective and impersonal, something he honors with the label "straight writing." He explains: "The mind of a generation is its speech. A writer makes aspects of that speech enduring by putting them in print. He whittles at the words and phrases of today and makes of them forms to set the mind of tomorrow's generation. That's history. A writer who writes straight is the architect of history."[61] This formulation raises more questions than it answers, for the choice of which "aspects of speech" to put into print is a subjective one. Novels built of "speech" are not necessarily any "straighter" than others. More consonant with the very political nature of Dos Passos's own writing is the suggestion—when he writes of "set[ting] the mind of tomorrow's generation"—that the writer's role is to intervene in history. This is ultimately the struggle of the autobiographical "Camera Eye" character in U.S.A., a novel powerfully shaped by its author's quite personal criticism of American society.

The Individual in History: U.S.A.

U.S.A. proved to be a more ambitious undertaking than Dos Passos realized when he first began writing it in the months after the execution of Sacco and Vanzetti. Originally conceived as a single book, a "series of reportages in which characters appeared and re-appeared," it grew over a decade into a 1,450-page trilogy whose subject was nothing less than the history of American life in the first thirty years of the twentieth century. Though the consummation of Dos Passos's experiments with literary form, *U.S.A.* represents neither a conclusion to the evolution of his political thought, nor a totally coherent analysis of American society. Its contradictions and tensions contribute to the trilogy's great energy and continuing appeal.[62]

In order to make American society as a whole his subject, Dos Passos creates an elaborate structure out of four distinct modes of expression in *U.S.A.* The bulk of the trilogy consists of twelve conventional narratives, the lives of twelve people, each told from the viewpoint of its central character. Their stories interrupt each other, so that each life is broken into as many as eight blocks, and their stories often intersect, so that, for example, Janey Williams is a character in the narrative line devoted to Joe Williams, and vice versa.

Dos Passos further fragments his novel by placing three innovative devices at various junctures between narrative blocks. The first, the "Newsreel," consists primarily of newspaper headlines, and fragments of news stories, political speeches, advertisements, and popular song lyrics. Sixty-eight Newsreel sections chart the course of popular consciousness over the thirty-year period *U.S.A.* covers. They help re-create the world the major characters move in and they reproduce the chaos and superficiality of public opinion. But the choice of Newsreel items is not random: telling juxtapositions—of a headline announcing American entrance into the European war, for example, and a story describing soaring corporate profits—condemn capitalist society as well as its shallow mass culture.

The second innovation is the introduction into the novel of brilliantly condensed biographies of well-known individuals. These twenty-seven brief "lives" of powerful or influential people—Woodrow Wilson, Thomas Edison, Eugene V. Debs, Isadora Duncan, and William Randolph Hearst among them—further detail the historical setting of the fictional narratives. These sections directly express Dos Passos's own opinions. Though factual, they are frequently ironic, even sarcastic, and Dos Passos achieves a compact eloquence in these portraits of heroes like Debs and villains like Wilson. In contrast to the Newsreels, in which history appears as a headlong rush of virtually unrelated incidents, the biographies suggest some of the underlying forces that condition historical events: the needs of finance capital, as represented by the house of Morgan; the rationalization of the labor process and the disciplining of the work force, symbolized by F.

79

W. Taylor; or the revolt of workers against such conditions, led by figures like Big Bill Haywood.[63]

Through the fifty-one "Camera Eye" sections, we trace the life of the artist, the growth of political and aesthetic awareness that has culminated, presumably, in the writing of *U.S.A.* These autobiographical Joycean fragments express the pain experienced by an intensely sensitive child and then young man growing up in the troubling world depicted by Newsreels, biographies, and narratives. We have here again "the poet against the world." But *U.S.A.* is not really an "Art Novel," to use Cowley's term, for the Camera Eye sections, we learn by the end of the trilogy, have traced the development of a radical.[64]

The paths of these structural elements often converge. Woodrow Wilson's biography, for example, comes roughly at the point where a major character attends the Versailles Peace Conference and the Newsreel entries are alluding to that same conference. More important is the continuous implicit interaction of these elements. Montage creates meaning.[65] The fictional lives, the historical currents we see in the Newsreels and biographies, and the inner world of the Camera Eye character illuminate one another in complex ways. As in *Manhattan Transfer*, the fragmentary form prevents our easy identification with individual characters; the focus is shifted instead to the larger social patterns, and the reader is driven to an active participation in the political analysis. *Manhattan Transfer* dramatizes the essential aloneness of its characters at the expense of any real sense of the social nexus that relates their individual alienation to the nature of the city's institutions. *U.S.A.* re-creates that social nexus. Alienated and isolated as its major characters may be, they exist in history; the historical developments of the Newsreels and biographies impinge on their everyday lives.

Most of those lives end in defeat, corruption, or premature death. A gulf between virtue and success informs *U.S.A.* as it does *Manhattan Transfer*. In this fast-paced novel of rootlessness and social mobility, those who rise are often corrupted in the process. Those few who try to act morally—namely, the radicals: Mary French, Ben Compton, and sometimes Mac—meet repeated defeat. All seem to move through their lives too rapidly to comprehend what is happening to them; their experience and their understanding of their own lives are almost as chaotic and confused as the Newsreels' version of public events.

Only the reader is allowed to see the larger patterns, the causes as well as the effects.

Existence itself is often degraded in *U.S.A.*, characters alienated from themselves and others. Flat characterization depicts lives flattened by society.[66] Joe Williams, for example, is an itinerant seaman, a perpetual outsider, a failure. Dos Passos describes Joe's marriage proposal to Del: "When he kissed her goodnight in the hall, Joe felt awful hot and pressed her up in the corner by the hatrack and tried to get his hand under her skirt but she said not till they were married and he said with his mouth against hers, when would they get married and she said they'd get married as soon as he got his new job" (*NN*, p. 65). Though narrated in the third person, this is Joe's own language, the "speech" Dos Passos refers to in his description of "straight writing." The very externality of the description—"awful hot" is a diminished token for passion—suggests an impoverished inner life, as does the absence of imagery. As in *Manhattan Transfer*, parataxis helps create this externality and dramatizes the hurried, uncontemplative, almost driven lives these characters lead. This "behavioristic" style,[67] as he called it, is not relentless in *U.S.A.*—some characters are more introspective than others and some passages are almost lyrical—but Dos Passos makes clear from the start that his is a debased world.

Obviously, and sometimes superficially, Dos Passos uses alcohol and sex to dramatize this debasement, to highlight the driven nature of his characters' lives. The frequency with which drunkenness is a symptom as well as the cause of a character's decline prompted Upton Sinclair, in a letter to Dos Passos, to call *The Big Money* a "temperance sermon." Sexual encounters—themselves often drunken—are often depicted as sordid and degraded, almost to the point of making *U.S.A.* seem puritanical. University of Texas students defending the inclusion of *The Big Money* on a reading list against the charge by conservative regents that it was "indecent, vulgar and filthy" could, with some justice, argue that the novel was in fact "deeply moral," for the characters' "sin" almost inevitably resulted in unhappiness.[68]

U.S.A. goes deeper than this and illustrates the kind of systemic evils of American society that Dos Passos wrote about in his nonfiction: poverty, unemployment, political repression, imperialism,[69] and the degrading mechanization of work. We see the destructive effects of

81

"dawg eat dawg" values and the psychological damage done to both rich and poor by great disparities of wealth. Beneath the images of *U.S.A.* is what Dos Passos calls "the sabotage of life" (*BM*, p. 101) by capitalist institutions.

Dos Passos devotes an entire volume of his trilogy, *1919*, to the war. He suggests that the United States entered the war solely to fatten the armament industry's profits and to "mak[e] the world safe" (*NN*, p. 16) for powerful American bankers with loans in Europe. As significant as the causes of the war are its consequences, which Dos Passos knew quite well: a general coarsening of American sensibilities, the stifling of dissent, and an explosion of propaganda and lies. "The war was a blast that blew out all the Diogenes lanterns" (*NN*, p. 15). The bitterly ironic biography of the Unknown Soldier powerfully evokes the war's cost in lives. Dos Passos presents American involvement in the war as the grotesque expression of twentieth-century American values, a logical and organic unfolding of the destructiveness inherent in the present organization of society. "*War*," writes Randolph Bourne, "*is the health of the state*" (*NN*, p. 104).

The life of Charley Anderson dramatizes what Dos Passos calls "the sabotage of production by business" (*BM*, p. 101). A talented mechanic with vaguely radical sentiments, Charley joins a friend after the war in starting a successful business manufacturing airplane starter motors. As he moves up into the world of high finance and begins speculating in the stock market, Charley's technical skill degenerates. In a quarrel with his loyal friend and mechanic, Bill Cermak, he defends speed-ups in his factory—it is the pressure of competition, he explains. When the two of them go up for a test flight, the plane fails mechanically, and Cermak is killed. Charley has lost his last contact with his former way of life. The big money has lured him away from his true calling, and his personal life deteriorates. In the figure of Charley Anderson the connection between historical forces and individual lives is actual as well as symbolic.[70]

Several biographies in *U.S.A.* expand the historical dimension of Charley's experience and indicate a significant development of Dos Passos's views here beyond the simple anxiety about technology per se expressed in "A Humble Protest" and *Rosinante to the Road Again*. Dos Passos often judges scientists by their social consciences in *U.S.A.*: he admires but pities the mathematician Steinmetz who, though a principled socialist, was absorbed and used by General Electric; he disparages Edison, who "cashed in" on his inventions and "never worried about . . . the social system" (*FSP*, pp. 297, 301); and he praises the Wright brothers as simple, hard-working mechanics, though he alludes darkly to the military use of their inventions. But the real direction of contemporary technological development is determined by the work of Frederick Winslow Taylor and Henry Ford. As Dos Passos wrote in a manuscript version of *The Big Money*, "the same ingenuity that went into improving the performance of a machine [the automobile] could go into improving the performance of the workmen producing the machine."[71] It is the exigencies of profit that guide the use of scientific management—"the substitution for skilled mechanics of the plain handyman . . . who'd move as he was told / and work by the piece" (*BM*, p. 24)—and that increase the pace of the assembly line until "every ounce of life was sucked off into production and at night the workmen went home grey shaking husks" (*BM*, p. 55). The need for and the creation of a worker "who didn't drink or smoke cigarettes or read or think" (*BM*, p. 51) debases not only work itself but all social life. The 1920s wave of capitalist expansion that carries Charley Anderson to the top drags down others as it corrupts him.

Dos Passos particularly fears the great concentration of power that capitalism creates. A large number of his biographical subjects aid or manage that concentration (Carnegie, Keith, Morgan, Wilson, Hearst, Taylor, Ford, and the scientists, for example) or else, however ineffectively, oppose it (Haywood, Debs, La Follette, Reed, Hibben, Everest, Joe Hill, Veblen). In the world of *U.S.A.*, the majority of individuals are powerless; the real centers of power are beyond their reach. This helps explain the shallow lives and moral passivity of most of the novel's major characters. Much as he had once insisted that "organization is death," Dos Passos in his later years would vehemently attack any concentration of power—the Kremlin, labor unions, the New Deal—whatever its origin or consequences. But in *U.S.A.* his subject is "a society dominated by monopoly capital" (*BM*, p. 101).

This domination is not static: it intensifies as history moves forward. Nor is domination total, for characters often possess a great deal of individual freedom and social mobility. Joe Williams may be doomed to a life of transient and unremunerative labor; and Mary French, Ben Compton, and even Mac for a while, may forsake middle-class comforts on principle; but many do climb or connive toward success. Throughout, *U.S.A.* bitterly condemns the American Dream: success not only corrupts, but fails to bring satisfaction. Moneyed lives are easier, to be sure, but no more fulfilling than other lives. The exploitation of the many by the few brings genuine happiness to none.

That the rich are not much happier than the poor might seem to undercut Dos Passos's attack on economic injustice. But inequality itself is destructive. It creates dehumanizing ambition, an isolating individualism, and feelings of inferiority among the losers. Janey Williams, for example, cruelly shuns her brother Joe once she moves into middle-class circles; Joe knows his place, and sadly keeps his distance.[72]

The destructive nature of racial injustice gets far less attention than that of class injustice in *U.S.A.* There are hints, though. With obvious sarcasm, Dos Passos places the headline "PLAN LEGISLATION TO KEEP COLORED PEOPLE FROM WHITE AREAS" (*FSP*, p. 362) right in the middle of a Newsreel announcing American entry into the war to make the world safe for democracy. He touches on the harm racism can do to whites by suggesting, as one critic points out, [73] a connection between the traumatic racist taunts—"Niggerlover"—that greet young Janey Williams as she plays with a black friend and her later development into a cold and stiff adult. The racism of Dos Passos's white characters —when we do see it—is depicted as part of their very degraded consciousness.

Blacks themselves are almost invisible in *U.S.A.*, however. Of the twelve major characters in the trilogy, meant in some sense to be representative of the nation, none are black. Nor are any of the subjects of the twenty-seven biographies black, though A. Philip Randolph— to give but one example—a man whom President Wilson once called "the most dangerous Negro in America,"[74] might have fit quite well beside Debs, Bourne, and the other radicals and pacifists. The few black figures that do appear in the novel appear as minor characters, their experiences seen only from another's point of view. Perhaps worst is Richard Savage's night in Harlem bars—itself meant to dramatize his decadence—where the black people he runs into are no more than stereotypes.

At least two critics have read *U.S.A.* as a sexist novel: Bianca T. Lalli has written of the "misogyny" of the trilogy, and Eleanor Widmer has suggested that Dos Passos's major women characters are merely stock female stereotypes.[75] Dos Passos's flat characterization and his effort to focus on social more than individual history inevitably involve some stereotyping of all characters; and unless informed by a feminist impulse, conscious or unconscious, such writing is bound to reflect not only its author's unexamined assumptions but the sexism of the society it depicts. There is no analysis in the novel of the oppression of women as there is of the oppression of the working class. And many important women—birth control advocate Margaret Sanger, for example, whose work certainly had bearing on the lives of the novel's many characters troubled by unwanted pregnancies—are noticeably absent from the gallery of biographies. Only Isadora Duncan appears. But fully half of Dos Passos's twelve main characters—whose perspectives he fully develops—are female, and Mary French earns our sympathy and respect (for her political commitment) above any other character in the trilogy—hardly a misogynist's vision of the world. Nonetheless, the radical social criticism of *U.S.A.*, however thoroughgoing, is male as well as white.

Those at the top in *U.S.A.* have the power to influence, even manipulate the consciousness of the vast majority. There are reasons why characters like Joe or Janey see themselves and the world the way they do. When, for example, Charley Anderson sees *The Birth of a Nation*, the "battles and the music and the bugles [make him] all jelly inside" (*FSP*, p. 385). He thrills as the Ku Klux Klan charges and feels, for a moment, a great urge to enlist and fight in the war, which he eventually does. William Randolph Hearst, a deliberate manipulator of public opinion, succeeds in "putting his own thoughts / into the skull of the straphanger" (*BM*, p. 474). In Dos Passos's biography of Rudolph Valentino, whose funeral ignites mass hysteria, we learn of Hollywood's great image-making power; through the rise to stardom of one character, Margo Dowling, we learn of its vulgarity. The public mind that the Newsreels exhibit—much like the mind of Fuselli in *Three Soldiers*—is largely the product of mass culture, not the creator of a genuinely popular culture.

The career of J. Ward Moorehouse epitomizes the growth of the public relations industry and its political use. Key to this major character's rise from humble roots to international prestige as a publicity man is his discovery of "this new unexploited angle of the relations between capital and labor" (*FSP*, p. 258). His client, of course, is capital. In the free marketplace of ideas, bargaining is unequal. Public relations, a part of mass culture, helps legitimate a social order.

The effectiveness of such propaganda is not total, however. Various characters in *U.S.A.* read Marx, Veblen, Edward Bellamy, and Upton Sinclair as well as the Hearst papers. Mary French learns firsthand not to trust the press when, as a reporter in Pittsburgh, she is fired for writing an honest story about striking steelworkers; the editor of this company town newspaper wants an article about extravagant wages, lazy immigrants, and red agitators paid by Russia with stolen jewels. Even casual political conversations can loosen the hold of the prevailing ideology. Dissenters as well as rulers are subjects for biographies; occasional signs of protest, like the Wobbly song "Pie in the Sky," appear in the Newsreels; and the Camera Eye records one individual's long struggle toward genuine understanding of his society.

Still, defeat pervades the trilogy. The truth does not liberate characters like Mary French and Ben Compton; as radical activists they can be as "deadalive" and as unhappy as anyone else. Their triumph is at best a moral one. Some critics have seen an ironclad determinism in this: characters are "billiard balls" in this "closed system of despair." Others describe *U.S.A.* as a self-defeating novel of protest: characters are so degraded they seem incapable of full human development in any social order; there is nothing to be saved. As in *Manhattan Transfer*, there are naturalistic elements in *U.S.A.* Dos Passos strives to show environment shaping character, because he wishes to attack society as a whole. But the twelve major characters possess varying degrees of will. Joe Williams is passive, almost deterministically conceived, but Richard Savage is capable of choice and is the target of Dos Passos's severe moral criticism when he callously abandons pregnant Anne Trent. The tension between naturalism and the intense moral indignation that pervades *U.S.A.* gives the novel much of its energy. Its bleak vision of nearly universal defeat demands radical social change.[76]

Dos Passos portrays himself, through the Camera Eye, least deterministically of all. His various experiences—his privileged but lonely childhood and his participation in the war, for example—certainly condition his development. But the almost totally subjective point of view, the internal characterization, focuses our attention on the exercise of his will. His halting development into a radical appears as a series of choices, though in the context of the novel as a whole, his own choice ironically seems to be the only possible, the only moral path for a sensitive individual. None of these choices is easy, however; his eyes "sting from peeling the speculative onion of doubt" (*BM*, p. 151). In a world as complex as the Newsreels make it seem, and as hopeless as the fictional characters make it seem, action is indeed difficult. When he speaks, "urging action in a crowded hall," he wants to give his audience "the straight dope," but it is triumphal slogans that bring him applause. He is ashamed for not having told the truth: "that we stand on quicksand," that "doubt is the whetstone of understanding" (*BM*, pp. 149–50). *U.S.A.* itself is that more complex truth. Like the hero of *One Man's Initiation—1917*, he moves gradually from observer —a mere camera eye—to committed radical. He eventually writes and marches to save Sacco and Vanzetti, although, like those symbols of martyred virtue, he too ends in defeat.

Despite his eventual political commitment, the Camera Eye character (like Dos Passos himself) experiences much uncertainty about his role as a middle-class writer. Everyone is isolated in the atomized world of *U.S.A.*, and as an artist he is doubly isolated: the formal separation of the Camera Eye sections from the world of the fictional characters helps dramatize this.[77] From his earliest fearful attraction to "laborers travailleurs greasers" (*FSP*, p. 25) to his impotent despair at the plight of Harlan County miners—"what can we say to the jailed?" (*BM*, p. 524)—he feels isolated from the working class whose cause he wants to champion.

The Camera Eye character often sees his struggle to become an actor in history as a struggle with language. For Dos Passos, people like Woodrow Wilson, William Jennings Bryan—"a silver tongue in a big mouth" (*FSP*, p. 172)—and above all Moorehouse are particularly villainous for their abuse of language, for using it to distort rather than discover and express the truth. The Newsreels overflow with the patriotic cant phrases of politicians and others. The Camera Eye character strives to expose the hypocritical use of the vocabulary of liberty and democracy. He hopes to "rebuild the ruined words worn slimy in the mouths of lawyers districtattorneys collegepresidents judges" (*BM*, p. 437). But these are "only words" against the concentrated power of monopoly capital, against men like electric utilities king Samuel Insull, the legendary "POWER SUPERPOWER" (*BM*, p. 525).[78]

Dos Passos also dramatizes his own conflicts and choices through the contrasting lives of Richard Savage and Mary French. Savage's experiences at Harvard and in the war, as well as the radicalism and aesthetic interests of his youth, are very similar to Dos Passos's own. But Savage sells out. He hasn't even the strength of his own weak political convictions and ends up as the right-hand man and probable successor to J. Ward Moorehouse. Mary French, however, grows politically more committed every day. Like Dos Passos, she works madly to save Sacco and Vanzetti and raises money to aid striking miners. Her total devotion to causes and her too close association with the Communist party impoverish her personal life. While Savage cares only about himself, she seems to care only about others. Thus, as Savage's life demonstrates the moral decline inherent in abandoning political ideals, and French's suggests the perils of political commitment, the Camera Eye shows us the path Dos Passos himself struggled to find.

The contrast between the IWW and the Communist party is also central to *U.S.A.* Liberals—such as Woodrow Wilson and George Barrow, the "laborfaker" (*BM*, p. 146)—discredit themselves throughout the trilogy; only explicitly radical groups promise any real hope for change. Through Mac, in *The 42nd Parallel*, Dos Passos portrays the IWW—which he long admired—as a loose, exciting, energetic organization. We share their easy, glad comradeship when fellow Wobblies run into each other on the road. "The boys" drink, talk socialism, and fight hard for the rights of "the working stiff." The "cooperative commonwealth" they envision seems appealing and necessary.

The Communists, on the other hand, insist upon hard work, discipline, and ideological conformity in order to bring about the revolution. While the local party member Eddy Spellman may be as happy and friendly as a Wobbly, it is the suspicious, extremely unpleasant Don Stevens who rises in the organization. If Dos Passos romanticizes the Wobblies, he seems to caricature the Communists.

The war divides these two worlds, and the experiences of Ben Compton in *1919* help explain the differences. At first, Ben works with the Wobblies and is brutally beaten by sheriff's deputies in Seattle. When the war comes, his unrelenting opposition to it lands him in jail. At every turn he refuses to compromise his principles; as those around him give in to prowar pressures, his almost fanatical behavior comes to seem admirable. He eventually becomes the "wellsharpened instrument" (*NN*, p. 431) he wanted to be, and joins the party. Only after he is expelled for deviationism does he realize that he and Mary French should have had that child he insisted on postponing until after the revolution. The contrast between the IWW and the Communist party is an integral part of Dos Passos's vision of a gulf between virtue and success. The appealing Wobblies dissipate their energies in disorganized behavior, as when Mac impulsively goes off to Mexico to "see the revolution" (*FSP*, p. 123) and ends up a bourgeois store-owner. And they are repeatedly crushed by force—the castration of Wesley Everest epitomizes this. The Communists, on the other hand, seem to be building a strong organization, despite the setbacks they suffer. But they are almost dehumanized in the process. The violent course of Revolutionary Russia—suggested by a long, detailed Newsreel account of the execution of the czar and his family, striking as the only single-item Newsreel in the trilogy—casts a shadow over the revolutionary hopes of Ben Compton and others. So the future holds little real promise. We are left at the end with the image of the vagrant, "Vag"—"wants crawl[ing] over his skin like ants" (*BM*, p. 561)—who hitchhikes hungrily down the road, as a plane filled with self-satisfied, well-fed passengers flies overhead.

Vague nostalgia creeps into the later parts of *U.S.A.* The prewar heyday of socialism is over. Radical heroes, except for the embittered Veblen, have disappeared from the biographies. The night Sacco and Vanzetti are executed, the Camera Eye character reaches far back into the American past to invoke the Founding Fathers: "America our nation has been beaten by strangers who have turned our language inside out who have taken the clean words our fathers spoke and made them slimy and foul" (*BM*, p. 462).

A formerly great land corrupted by nebulous "strangers" somehow alien to the American way of life is not what Dos Passos saw his country as in 1927. *Facing the Chair* and his many essays and articles make this clear. The biographies in *U.S.A.* of people like Morgan, Wilson, Hearst, and Ford show how quintessentially American are those who helped mold the world in which Sacco and Vanzetti had to die.[79]

U.S.A. chronicles not only the changes America underwent over three decades, but also the evolution of its author's own social thinking. The muted optimism of *The 42nd Parallel*, the anger and militance of *1919*, and the despair of *The Big Money*—these contrasts cannot be completely explained by the varying epochs Dos Passos re-creates, nor by any plan such as the transition, as he suggested in a 1932 letter to Cowley, from "competitive capitalism" to "monopoly capitalism."[80] Between 1927 and 1936, Dos Passos experienced an intensification of his radicalism with the onset of the depression, and, later, a growing pessimism and disillusionment with the Communist party that led him to search America's past for a viable radical tradition. The trilogy thus is strained with tensions that even its elaborate formal structure cannot entirely hold.

Such tensions, along with the complexity of its form, may help account for the wide spectrum of critical opinion about *U.S.A.* American Communist critics in the 1930s looked eagerly to this talented and prestigious writer as a potential supporter, hoping he might give literary expression to their view of the world. Consequently, they often saw too much or too little in *U.S.A.* Granville Hicks heaped praise on *The 42nd Parallel*, but saw "the characteristic futilitarianism of the age creep[ing] slimily" across its pages. The more militant *1919* brought Dos Passos greater tribute: V. F. Calverton placed him in "the mainstream of the proletarian tradition," and Michael Gold saw him growing politically "like corn in the Iowa sun," although Hicks, again, pointed out that Dos Passos had "yet to master the whole body of revolutionary theory." The pessimistic ending of the trilogy no doubt surprised many overly optimistic Communist readers of *1919*, for *The Big Money*, along with Dos Passos's increasing public criticism of the party itself, brought harsh attack. Gold thundered that *U.S.A.* was nothing but a world of "merde," that its author was trapped in "the muck of bourgeois nihilism" and must "hate the human race."[81] Dos Passos, it seems, had been read out of the Communist literary pantheon.

Soviet critics fiercely debated the political implications of *The 42nd Parallel* and *1919* in a three-day symposium on Dos Passos in the spring of 1933. Much of the disagreement was over the acceptability of the "unconquered Joyceanism" of the Camera Eye, with its emphasis on the subjective and even unconscious aspects of life, rather than on the structure of society. Some critics were troubled also by the technical complexity of the novels: they suggested, provocatively, that "the diversity of literary devices used by Dos Passos sprang from his own ideological uncertainty." As Deming Brown points out, the debate— the largest ever over an American writer—really concerned the course Soviet literature should be allowed to take. The champions of Socialist Realism eventually prevailed over the defenders of Dos Passos and of literary freedom, and by 1937 Soviet publication of Dos Passos had stopped. *The Big Money* never appeared in the USSR, and Dos Passos "nearly vanished from the pages of Soviet criticism."[82]

In general, critical discussion of *U.S.A.* has focused on its technical devices and on its seeming determinism. Most French critics have delighted in its complex structure; Sartre in 1938 called Dos Passos "the greatest writer of our time." But Marshall McLuhan thought *U.S.A.* an "extreme simplification" of what Joyce had achieved and complained that Dos Passos saw "nothing inevitable or meaningful in human suffering." Alfred Kazin praised the narrative style of *U.S.A.* highly, but thought the trilogy too tightly sealed in despair, too "symmetrical a series of hell pits," and concluded that Dos Passos's "opposition to capitalism [was] no greater than his suspicion of all societies." Diverse political perspectives lurk somewhere behind all these critical evaluations of *U.S.A.*, but few would disagree with Kazin's praise that Dos Passos "brings energy to despair."[83]

The Anatomy of Socialism

In 1939, Max Eastman published "Motive-Patterns of Socialism," an article that sheds light on the difficulties Dos Passos had as a socialist in the 1930s. Eastman divides those for whom socialism has great appeal into three main groups:

> first, the rebels against tyranny and oppression, in whose motivation the concept of human freedom formed the axis; second, those yearning with a mixture of religious mysticism and animal gregariousness for human solidarity—the united-brotherhood pattern; third, those anxious about efficiency and intelligent organization—a cerebral anxiety capable of rising in times of crisis to a veritable passion for a plan.[84]

Most individuals, he adds, combine traits from all three types, but usually one of the three passions—for freedom, for solidarity, or for efficient planning—predominates. All three types, though for differing reasons, are opposed to war.

Dos Passos is an almost pure example of the first type: the rebel against tyranny and oppression, the lover of freedom. Though the intense loneliness of the Camera Eye character may suggest a yearning for "human solidarity," Dos Passos, always the individualist, never discusses this as an aim of social change. While his anger in *U.S.A.* at "the sabotage of production by business" may seem like an interest in efficiency, his major concern is with its effect on the worker, as the Taylor and Ford biographies indicate, and with the moral decay of people like Charley Anderson.

The Wobblies, too, particularly the Wobblies in *U.S.A.* were very much this first type, which Eastman calls "libertarian socialists." Even their goal of a "cooperative commonwealth"—which was really a vision of brotherhood, not a plan for an efficient society—must have appealed somehow to a young Dos Passos eager to share the vitality he saw in the lives of the working class, the "muckers" of the early Camera Eye sections of *U.S.A.* and the poor of *Streets of Night*. Basically a prewar movement, the IWW was tied to the era of Dos Passos's youth, ensconced in the past, and spared the difficult choices of the 1930s. Thus they continued to inspire him for years.[85] The Wobbly reminiscences of Blackie Bowman form the emotional core of *Midcentury*, published in 1961.

The Communist party, however, came to stand for planning and efficiency in the 1930s. Elements from all three of Eastman's patterns motivated individual Communists, and many fought hard and selflessly against oppression of all kinds. But the party's support for Stalinist Russia and its criticisms of depression America almost inevitably stressed the importance of efficient economic planning, not individual liberties. While the party spoke often of class solidarity and international solidarity, its divisively sectarian practice at times negated both. By 1935, the beginning of the more conciliatory Popular Front period when intellectuals began joining the party in greater numbers, Dos Passos had virtually given up on "the comrats."[86]

Dos Passos saw no radical alternative to the Communists. Socialists, like liberals, were mere reformists, he felt; Trotskyists were marginal and ineffective. Neither Leninist nor reformist strategies could have entirely appealed to Dos Passos, for both looked to a strong state —not to local autonomy and self-government—as a means to transform society. Dos Passos had based his early hopes for the Russian Revolution, he later recalled, on the "democratic possibilities of the original town meeting type of soviet," not on a strong, efficient Bolshevik state. Anarchists could offer an idealistic vision of liberty—as well as the martyrs Sacco and Vanzetti—but they lacked a significant movement. As the Communist party grew in the 1930s, it monopolized the definition of "socialism." Dos Passos began studying the Founding Fathers, and using words like "libertarian" to describe his political views.[87]

The Civil War in Spain

Liberty was doubly imperiled in the Spanish civil war, which Dos Passos reported on in 1937. While fascism—which he still saw as "a disease of sick capitalism, not a disease of democracy"—was threatening to destroy the shaky Republic, the republican government itself was busy crushing a genuine social revolution underway in Catalonia and other areas. George Orwell had found Barcelona the previous December, "liker to a worker's city than anything I had conceived possible." Self-governing, cooperative communities were being organized, albeit violently, that embodied many of Dos Passos's own political ideas. But whether driven by the exigencies of war, fear of popular revolution, or the requirements of Soviet foreign policy, the central government—an alliance of liberals and Communists—repressed this surge of local insurrection. Dos Passos found the complicated and ultimately tragic events in Spain "much too instructive."[88] The civil war left him demoralized.

Dos Passos had been to Spain in 1933, at the peak of his radical anger, to report on the young Republic. He found the often "wellintentioned" liberals and Socialists in the central government unwilling "to change the basic setup of power" (*IAC*, p. 143). Attached to their comfortable jobs in the bureaucracy, their café life, American cars, and investments, they feared "el reparto," the "division of lands and wealth" (*IAC*, p. 152) the anarchists demanded. Although critical of the violence of some anarchists, Dos Passos recognized their desperate poverty. The repressive violence of the government—the mass shootings, arrests, deportations of rebels—he found inexcusable. "The Republic of Manual and Intellectual Workers," he wrote, "turn[s] out to be the Republic of those who work others so that they shan't have to work themselves" (*IAC*, p. 139).

The civil war broke out in July, 1936, and by the following March,

Dos Passos had begun raising money for a film to support the lesser evil in this struggle between Republicans and Fascists. With Hemingway, Lillian Hellman, and Archibald MacLeish, he formed a corporation called Contemporary Historians, and they chose Joris Ivens to direct the film. Once in Spain, old friends quarreled over the filming: Dos Passos wanted to stress the people's suffering, Hemingway the military battles. The film, which Hemingway narrated, ultimately did both, and in July, Hemingway and Ivens showed it to President and Mrs. Roosevelt in the White House. Other showings brought thousands of dollars in contributions to save the beleaguered Republic.[89]

The fate of José Robles, an old friend, intensified Dos Passos's doubts about the cause he was supporting. Robles taught Spanish literature at Johns Hopkins, was visiting his native Spain when the war broke out, and remained there to help in the fight against Franco. Late in 1936, he was arrested, accused of treason, and secretly executed by a republican "special section," probably Communist-led. At the request of Robles's wife, Dos Passos began inquiring noisily into the charges against her husband, who had disappeared. Spanish officials, fearing Dos Passos would desert the cause if he knew Robles had been killed, lied to him; Hemingway, refusing to question the official explanation, was more than insensitive to his friend's distress. Dos Passos did uncover the truth, much to his horror, before he left Spain, and what Ludington calls "the first cracks" in his friendship with Hemingway, already apparent for several years, suddenly became a decisive split.[90]

The motivation for the execution remains unclear: some Spaniards told Dos Passos that Robles had indiscreetly discussed military plans in a café; Malcolm Cowley insisted from New York that Robles was a fascist spy; and Dos Passos himself came to believe that his friend, not a Communist, simply knew too much about "the relations between the Spanish war ministry and the Kremlin." Dos Passos made the story public only after the war was over—perhaps to avoid harming the Loyalists. But he returned from the war bitter and despairing.[91]

During the winter of 1937–38, in a series of *Esquire* articles and a fifteen-page book—*The Villages Are the Heart of Spain*—Dos Passos cautiously described his experiences. As in his reporting ten years earlier on his trip to the Soviet Union, he is reluctant to criticize those under attack from the right. He, therefore, expresses more uncertainty than he feels. Superficial descriptions which carefully avoid political judgments tease the reader. What does he really think of that extremely dedicated but rigid and condescending Communist doctor who insists on the need for better organized food production and transport? Dos Passos refuses to say.[92]

Dos Passos shows no reluctance to praise the socialist enterprises in Spain's small villages. Without killing anyone, the people of San Pol organized public recreation centers and an agricultural cooperative that brought the village self-sufficiency and plenty. Almost alone among American observers, he admires the revolutionary idealism of POUM—the left wing anti-Stalinist socialist organization—whose headquarters he visits. But war, factionalism, and the repressive central government are threatening to destroy all hope. Already "the popular movement in Catalonia [seems] doomed, hemmed in by ruthless forces of world politics too big for it" (*VHS*, p. 14). Dos Passos is left with the question he is each day more afraid to ask: "How can the new world win?" (*VHS*, p. 15).

Dos Passos gave up on Spain, and on all Europe, where "infectious formulas for slavery" were "preparing . . . on every side" and where politics was degenerating into "the business of plain and fancy massacre." In an article entitled "Farewell to Europe," he finally announced that only in the American tradition could ways be found to resolve the conflict between individual liberty and "bureaucratic industrial organization." This represented a retreat for Dos Passos, no longer a total opposition to all such bureaucratic organization, but a search instead for methods to preserve some liberty *within* it. Given the intensity of his recent criticisms of the ways in which capitalist institutions mold all life around them to serve their ends, he may be whistling in the dark when he writes the following:

> Not all the fascist-hearted newspaper owners in the country, nor the Chambers of Commerce, nor the armies of hired gunthugs of the great industries can change the fact that we have the Roundhead Revolution in our heritage and the Bill of Rights and the fact that the democracy in the past has been able, under Jefferson, Jackson, and Lincoln, and perhaps a fourth time (it's too soon to know yet) under Franklin Roosevelt, to curb powerful ruling groups.[93]

Fifteen years earlier, in *Rosinante to the Road Again*, Dos Passos had expressed his fears for the future through his Spanish sketches, but he had also expressed his hopes. Although he never confused industrialized America with agrarian Spain, his idealized, almost pastoral vi-

sion of Spanish anarchism and community life infused his criticisms of
his own country with energy and hope. The Spanish civil war
changed that, and his later embracing of Jeffersonian thought proved
a weak substitute for the utopian dreams Spain once inspired. Dos
Passos's farewell to Europe turned out to be a farewell to any real
hope for radical change in America, and the blow to his idealism
proved to be a setback for his art.

Despair and Defeat: *Adventures of a Young Man*

Adventures of a Young Man, Dos Passos's first novel after the civil war,
has none of the power of *U.S.A.*: it is despair without energy.[94] The
fate of Glenn Spotswood, the book's hero, is the fate of American radical idealism in the 1930s. The son of a Christian pacifist whose principles cost him his teaching job, Glenn grows up with a sharp moral
sense and a passion for truth and justice. He reads Henry George
while a Columbia student, spends a summer traveling with a Wobbly
as a migratory worker, and hangs around with New York liberals and
Communists. In Texas, he discovers the harsh realities of class struggle when the Ku Klux Klan and the American Legion run him out of
town for getting involved with striking Mexican pecan shellers. As a
Communist, he is beaten and jailed for helping to organize desperately poor miners in Slade County. When he protests the party's
abandonment of jailed miners—the party's main concern was "to
educate the American workingclass in revolutionary Marxism"
(*AYM*, p. 241)—he is expelled. He publishes an opposition newspaper, *Workers' Unity*, but remains isolated and lonely. He goes to Spain
to fight for the Loyalists, but his deviationist reputation has followed
him, and he is jailed by the Communists, sent on a suicidal mission,
and killed by enemy gunfire. The betrayal of his idealism could not be
more complete.

The significance of Glenn's adventures is made clearer through his
relationships with three women. Glenn's first sexual experiences are
with Gladys Funaroff, a beautiful, bohemian Communist. Naïvely,
Glenn immediately asks her to live with him. But Gladys is committed to no one individual, not even her husband Boris. When she turns
him down, Glenn feels depressed and betrayed, as he later would
when the party he loved further corrodes his romantic innocence.

The wealthy, liberal Marice Gulick will do anything for Glenn. Though a bit overbearing, and rather ludicrous with her dilettantish interests in psychoanalysis and suffering workers, her heart is in the right place. But when, during the Popular Front era, she becomes infatuated with "the most wonderful Russian" (*AYM*, p. 270), the Communist Stanov, and ends up in bed with a party leader, Irving Silverstone, Glenn moves out of her apartment. Through Marice, a still radical Dos Passos is attacking liberals for the superficiality of their social criticism; even more strongly he is attacking their vulnerability to manipulation by Communists.

Wheatly, sister of one of the imprisoned miners, loves Glenn, but skeptically. Her major concern is to free her brother, and she acts as Glenn's conscience, reminding him of his duty to the men in jail. By supporting the party's position on the jailed miners, Glenn unwittingly betrays her and carries the burden of guilt all the way to Spain. The Communist party itself has come between Glenn and the working class he wants to help.

This moral fable in the form of a conventionally realistic novel never really comes to life. As an idealistic youth, Glenn is briefly interesting and convincing. Once Glenn becomes involved with Communists, Dos Passos's hatred for the party overwhelms all else. Glenn is reduced to a foil, a virtuous innocent who exists primarily to highlight Communist duplicity and, near the end, to pronounce the already obvious lessons he has learned. His boyhood friend, Paul Graves, makes periodic appearances to enunciate eminently sensible criticisms of the Soviet Union and of American Communists. And lest the reader miss the point, Dos Passos repeats his scenario of Communist manipulation of popular movements three times: in Texas, in Slade County, and in Spain. The Communist characters themselves are caricatures: the endlessly sinister Irving Silverstone seems to "hiss" (*AYM*, p. 260) on the telephone, and the flighty Gladys Funaroff says to Glenn, before he joins the party: "You represent the confused ignorant masses of America....Here is my hand" (*AYM*, p. 106). This all might have been good satire if presented less earnestly.[95]

Glenn never succeeds in filling the role of moral hero, martyr for social justice and democratic socialism that Dos Passos intended for him. The portrayal of Glenn is external, flat. He lacks what Georg Lukács calls a carefully delineated "intellectual physiognomy." We see his idealism in action, but rarely in thought, and since the Communists' struggle to possess his mind and soul is the central drama of the novel, this externality is a significant weakness.[96]

Glenn, in fact, is portrayed like a character in *U.S.A.* Without the counterpoint of eleven other narratives and without the expanded historical, moral, and subjective dimensions that the Camera Eye, biographies, and Newsreels create, such characterization is empty. *U.S.A.* was moral as well as complex. It achieved an exciting multiplicity of perspectives without a relativity of values. In *Adventures of a Young Man*, Dos Passos hammers his point. Once Glenn is defeated by Communism, nothing remains. The novel ends abruptly: "He was dead" (*AYM*, p. 322).

The character of Glenn Spotswood is vaguely autobiographical. His experiences are in part an exaggerated version of the author's own: he joins the party where Dos Passos only sympathized, organizes miners rather than writes about them, and loses his life in Spain, where Dos Passos lost only his radical faith. But nothing of Dos Passos's complex and contradictory sensibility—what we see so clearly, for example, in the Camera Eye of *U.S.A.*—enlivens *Adventures of a Young Man*. Instead, we have a tedious polemic, an outpouring of disgust for the Communist party, that is interesting primarily as a symptom of the defeat of its author's own hopes.[97]

Dos Passos's hatred of the Communist party—"stalinoids," he now called its members[98]—was growing ever more intense. In the absence of the more democratic, more libertarian radical movement he hoped for, Dos Passos would eventually come to see democracy and socialism as incompatible, even as opposites. The work for left-wing causes that once helped accelerate his radicalization had begun by the late 1930s to erode his radicalism; his despairing rejection of all leftist aspirations—expressed most dramatically in *Adventures of a Young Man*— marked the start of a long drift to the right. By the end of his life, Dos Passos would be championing American militarism, defending Joseph McCarthy, and making businessmen heroes of his novels.

CHAPTER THREE
WORKING DOWN AT THE
BOTTOM OF A WELL: 1939–70

> One of the bitterest things about growing older is the sense of solitude that hedges you about. Old friends harden into fanatics and stop liking you because they don't like the things you say. Sometimes I feel as if I were working down at the bottom of a well.
>
> Dos Passos to Max Eastman, Christmas, 1953[1]

Escape into the Past

As the turbulence of European politics turned with seeming inevitability into a second bloody world war, Dos Passos was burying himself in America's history, reading seventeenth- and eighteenth-century print until his eyes were "like a pair of badly poached eggs."[2] To escape from a troubling present, he turned to a glorious past. Recent events, particularly in Spain, seemed to have foreclosed the possibility of meaningful radical political action, but he was rediscovering hope through his study of earlier generations of radicals, individuals who appeared able to exercise human will for noble ends. Dos Passos's search for lessons in America's colonial and revolutionary eras would continue for the rest of his life.

The first early American hero Dos Passos wrote about was Tom Paine. Probably the most radical and thoroughly democratic American revolutionary figure, Paine was the logical choice. In a two-part essay in *Common Sense* late in 1939, Dos Passos praised Paine for the simple honesty of his words and deeds. Dos Passos was eager to identify with this relentless enemy of privilege for whom writing was "the direct putting down of plain speech." In Paine's revulsion with the violent turn the French Revolution had taken, Dos Passos must have seen his own distress over events in the Soviet Union; Paine, he wrote,

99

"recognized . . . that no useful social order can be founded on massacre."³

In *The Ground We Stand On*, published in 1941, Dos Passos undertakes a broader study of America's early history. Through the lives of Roger Williams, Samuel Adams, Benjamin Franklin, Thomas Jefferson, Joel Barlow, and Hugh Henry Brackenridge, we find him tracing with pride the growth of what he sees as the particularly American concepts of self-government and individual freedom. His aim is to "give that cantilever bridge into the future that we call hope a firm foundation in what has been."⁴

Dos Passos attempts to strengthen this bridge by carefully differentiating American democracy from American capitalism. He argues that young radicals of his generation, disgusted by politicians and businessmen who used the language of the American tradition to mask self-interest, erred in rejecting their own political heritage entirely, failing to realize that perhaps "the republic was something more than a painted dropcurtain hiding the babyeating Moloch of monopoly capital" (*GWSO*, p. 6). Needing an escape from his pessimism and despair, Dos Passos seized upon this democratic political heritage as a source of hope, a ground to stand on. This represented a shift of emphasis for him, away from economic toward purely political questions. As he became more interested in political processes, Dos Passos began to wonder if America could transcend capitalism without destroying it; this was an important aspect of his transformation from democratic radical to radical democrat.

Dos Passos also attempts in *The Ground We Stand On* to draw clear distinctions between Anglo-American and continental European traditions. Their divergence is a major focus of his study of the seventeenth and eighteenth centuries. "The Englishspeaking peoples," he finds, "are heirs to the largest heritage . . . of self-government there has ever been in the world" (*GWSO*, p. 8). Lacking such a heritage, Europe today has succumbed to "deathdealing illusions" (*GWSO*, p. 12), both Fascist and Communist. But the American political process is elastic enough and our democratic habits strong enough, Dos Passos believes, to allow for necessary change without discontinuity, social progress without the risk of instability or chaos. As in "Farewell to Europe," Dos Passos here is hoping to prove America exceptional. Years of doing so would eventually help transform him from something of an internationalist to the most chauvinistic of American patriots.

The introductory chapter of *The Ground We Stand On* is entitled "The Use of the Past." But Dos Passos never makes clear precisely what that use is, how his historical studies can guide our actions in the present. His discovery of the virtues of self-government through the lives of early Americans seems a priori: he comes to conclusions his own thinking and experience had already led him to. He finds hope, but few insights, and his ransacking of the American past at times verges on antiquarianism, as in his detailed descriptions of Jefferson's gardens. He never fully explains just how we learn from history. This was an important question, for he was beginning a decade-long study of the life and thought of Thomas Jefferson.

The Anxious Democrat: *Number One*

The democratic processes Dos Passos celebrates in *The Ground We Stand On* fall prey to the deft and sinister manipulation of Chuck Crawford in *Number One*.[5] The novel, published in 1943, describes the rise to power of this pseudopopulist demagogue, roughly modeled on Huey Long, and the growing disillusionment of Crawford's secretary and campaign manager, Tyler Spotswood. Crawford's political enemies eventually expose his crooked financial dealings, but Tyler takes the blame, and his boss's political climb goes on.

"Number One," as his servile subordinates call Crawford, can charm almost anyone. The role he plays best is the humble, folksy man of the people: not a revered and distant United States congressman, but—as he tells two dirt farmers—just "ole Chuck Crawford . . . doin' chores for the American people" (*NO*, p. 15). In his speeches, and occasionally even in action, he defends the common people, the real producers, against "the bankers an' usurers an' predatory interests that never did a lick of real work in their lives" (*NO*, p. 53). Hunger for power and wealth is what really drives him, and he soon collaborates with those very "predatory interests" in order to build his political machine and fill his own pockets. In public he trumpets his love for the Bible, the family, and American political ideals; behind the scenes we see his vanity, his debauchery, and his petulant despotism over his subordinates. One of Dos Passos's most vivid characters, Chuck Crawford embodies many of the evils that most concerned his creator: the abuse of the language of radicalism and democracy, the placing of ends above means, and the concentration of great power in the hands of an individual.

Five italicized prose poems, depicting five representative Americans, highlight the hollowness of Crawford's claims to represent "the real people" (*NO*, p. 89). Dos Passos shows us the genuine needs of these people—for love, community, dignity, adequate income, and meaningful work—which Crawford manipulates so successfully. The formal separation of these passages from the main narrative emphasizes the distance of the average American from the real centers of political power; it underscores the great gap between what Crawford calls democracy—the empty forms of electoral politics—and the actual needs of people for some control over their own lives. The picture is not so bleak as all that, since these portraits also reveal a people of great decency and strength of character. However, as if to compensate for his fears, Dos Passos romanticizes these Americans. He slips at times into banality as he strains too hard to assert his democratic faith in the face of the threat to democracy represented by "Number One."[6]

The real drama of the fall and redemption of the democratic spirit is acted out by Tyler Spotswood, from whose point of view the novel is narrated. Tyler begins as an idealistic, devoted, and almost unbelievably naïve supporter of Crawford. He feels a "warm musclerelaxing rush of belief" (*NO*, p. 13) whenever he hears "Number One" speak. His muscles, however, are often relaxed to start with, since Tyler has a serious drinking problem. To be sure, Dos Passos uses this alcoholism to dramatize Tyler's moral confusion—but also, it seems, to cover up a haziness in characterization. Despite rapidly accumulating evidence of Chuck's crookedness, Tyler somehow maintains enough faith in his leader's worth to continue working for him. When it becomes apparent that Crawford has framed Tyler in order to escape conviction for his illegal dealings in oil leases and in a radio station, Tyler refuses to turn state's evidence. He decides instead to accept the punishment. His first responsibility, he insists, is not to stop Chuck, but to get his own life in order, to straighten out "number one" (*NO*, p. 297).

While this ending may make certain psychological sense—a guilt-ridden man embracing punishment—Dos Passos is trying for more.

He wants us to accept Tyler as a moral hero and to see his act as the result of a great political awakening. Just before Tyler decides not to testify against Crawford, he receives a letter from his brother Glenn, written shortly before he was killed in Spain. Glenn, the hero of *Adventures of a Young Man*, speaks with the moral authority of a martyred idealist. He explains to his brother the importance of "*seeing the other fellow's point of view,*" the value of "*every man woman and child,*" and the need not to let "*them sell out too much of the for the people and by the people part of the oldtime United States way . . .* [which] *has given us freedom to grow,*" (*NO*, pp. 281-82). Reading this letter suddenly fills Tyler's mind with "a bright clear sorrowful light" (*NO*, p. 283) and inspires his liberating decision.

That Dos Passos brings his novel to a positive resolution with so blatant and banal an authorial intrusion suggests something of the conflict he was experiencing at the time. Tyler might have stopped a powerful demagogue, even sent him to jail; but he decides instead to stand up for democracy by taking all the blame himself and letting Crawford continue his political career. Dos Passos's attempt to make this the basis of an optimistic ending is forced, distinctly willed. As in *U.S.A.*, we have the moral individual alone against an immoral world, but instead of defeat we have an artificial triumph. The ugly political realities Dos Passos depicts in *Number One*—and Chuck is shown as only symptomatic of a corrupt system—clash with the proud faith in American democracy Dos Passos expresses in *The Ground We Stand On*. Impatient to resolve this conflict, he covers it with moralizing. A final prose poem, sentimental in its celebration, ends with the broad exhortation: "*weak as the weakest, strong as the strongest, / the people are the republic, / the people are you*" (*NO*, p. 304).[7]

Number One warns against the potentially fascistic enemy within, but it was written while the United States was at war with the Axis powers. This may help explain its forced optimism, as well as its insistence, as Glenn writes, that "*everything every one of us does counts*" (*NO*, p. 282). It may also help explain Dos Passos's sole focus on the importance of democracy, not on the problems of capitalism, as well as his insistence that "*the people is everybody,*" even "*the boss glaring you in the eye*" (*NO*, p. 303). Class and other divisions are to be forgotten as we unite against a common enemy.[8] *Number One* reflects a shift in Dos Passos's views: away from his earlier angry concerns with class and

103

with economic justice toward a more optimistic, but narrower, emphasis on the virtues of a political democracy he wanted to see as peculiarly American.

America at War

Dos Passos's defense of democratic values was not always so awkward and so abstract as in *Number One*. Amidst work on his novels, historical research in Virginia archives, and a trip to England to see the war and address a PEN congress, he found time for new political causes. In 1941, as national secretary of the New World Resettlement Fund, he helped create an agricultural colony in Ecuador for refugees from fascist Spain. An eager defender of civil liberties, he signed the founding statement of the Committee for Cultural Freedom, and in 1942 became a "sponsor" of the American Civil Liberties Union's National Committee.[9] He counted himself among the "men of our time for whom Freedom of Thought is a matter of life and death." When the federal government used the newly enacted Smith Act to indict twenty-nine Minnesota truck drivers, including members of the Socialist Workers party, he helped in their defense, as vice-chairman of the Civil Rights Defense Committee. He also protested the indictment in an open letter to Roosevelt, reminding the president of the destructive hysteria that had been unleashed by the previous war, and insisting that the best defense of "the American cause" was "a democracy that is wholeheartedly, even recklessly, for freedom."[10]

In spring of 1942, he set out on a year-long tour of wartime America. "Continually tortured by curiosity" about the "big untidy soul-stirring country we live in," he visited, among other things, New England shipyards, farms in the South and Midwest, Congress, the Pentagon, and public power projects in Oregon. To pay his way, he wrote more articles than he would have liked to, for *Fortune*, for *Liberty*, and, in a series called "People at War," for *Harpers*. He gathered these and other writings into a 1944 volume entitled *State of the Nation*.[11]

Dos Passos's reporting is filled with the often contradictory voices of the people he talks with, and he is reluctant to take sides openly in a dispute. But the reader soon realizes that an old farmer "with a blue flash in his eye" or a Dane with "a thoughtful look" is more likely to speak the truth than a lawyer with a "richly modulated courtroom voice" or a man on the radio who wins the applause of men "with fat wallets on their hips" (*SN*, pp. 263, 265, 154, 39). The war had stimulated prodigious economic growth and infused great energy into the American people, and the author of "A Humble Protest," the critic of Taylor and Ford, is now obsessed with productivity. Dos Passos asks everyone he meets how to increase it even more, and the "immense gentle insistent explosion of new growth" (*SN*, p. 134) that he can feel in the air seems to intoxicate him and fill him with hope for the future.

Dos Passos feels less sanguine about America's political future than about its technological development. He sees some potential for "industrial democracy" (*SN*, p. 43) in the new labor-management committees established by the War Production Board and is encouraged by the growth of farmers' cooperatives. But he fears that federal regulation is increasing the power and wealth of the largest corporations and destroying the independent family farm, which he, like Jefferson, sees as a cornerstone of "popular selfgovernment" (*SN*, p. 81).

In the 1930s Dos Passos had denounced war as the epitome of capitalist evil and as "the health of the state" (*NN*, p. 104); now he found himself praising a war effort that was enriching capitalists and strengthening the federal government. The introductory chapter to *State of the Nation* expresses the hope that in our still flexible society, "our liberties" (*SN*, p. 2) would endure. Its homiletic tone suggests—much as the prose poems in *Number One* do—that Dos Passos has doubts. The survival so far of freedom and equality, he writes, "has been a sort of miracle," and "miracles only happen when enough people want them to happen" (*SN*, p. 2). Unable to reconcile his idealized vision of America, drawn largely from his studies of its past, with the actuality of its present insititutions, Dos Passos would increasingly tend to substitute moral exhortation of individuals for a thorough, critical analysis of their society.

Whatever fears and doubts Dos Passos had as he surveyed the home front disappeared when he began observing the war itself. The Londoners he visited in 1941 had emerged from the bombings "twice the people they had been before," and American successes in the Pacific theater made him "puff [his] chest out and say . . . 'By gum, I'm on the winning side.' "[12] As a correspondent for *Life*, he found himself reporting with enthusiasm the progress of this second war to make the world safe for democracy.

Dos Passos began his island-hopping tour of the Pacific late in

1944. He traveled by jeep, bomber, and battleship; talked to enthusiastic fighting men; and enjoyed "raging" good health. Eager for optimism, he was quickly caught up in the excitement of this very successful campaign. He was fascinated by the logistics of supply and astounded by the ability of his country's technology and organization to transform each island practially overnight into "a farflung scrap of America" (*TD*, p. 19). The loyalty and, as he describes it, servile gratitude of "little Filipinos" (*TD*, p. 142), "little . . . smiling chirping" Chamorros, and other native populations seemed to swell his pride in the American way of life.[13] "The word liberation," he wrote Katy from Guam, "gives you a lot to think about." It all must have struck him as the dawning of what his editor Henry Luce called an "American Century."[14]

Dos Passos saw little of the gore that had so shocked him as an ambulance driver in France twenty-five years before, and he returned from the Pacific "cheered and stimulated," confident in American ability to handle "the terrific problems that face us everywhere." When he traveled to Europe late in 1945 to cover the American occupation, he was plunged into gloom and despair, and was soon wondering "how to make the horror not conquer us."[15] The cities he loved were rubble, their inhabitants hungry and desperate. In a Berlin train station he saw men, women, and children whose "skin hung on their bones like candledrippings" (*TD*, p. 325). He was particularly shaken by the callous, often barbarous treatment of the German people by the occupying forces, American as well as Russian. He was equally horrified by the results of American behavior at Big Three conferences, where, he felt, "all the trumps" (*TD*, p. 286) had been dealt out to the Russians. It seemed as if the war had been fought for nothing.

Dos Passos experienced extremes of pride and shame as an American. He describes how the prosecutor at the Nuremberg trials, his compatriot Robert Jackson, fills the courtroom with what all agree are "great and courageous words" (*TD*, p. 306). But afterwards, a stranger persuades Dos Passos of the utter hypocristy of the proceedings; the massive Allied bombings of Dresden and other heavily populated areas, the stranger points out, are also "crimes against humanity" (*TD*, p. 308). Dos Passos finds solace in defending his country and its traditions in a debate with a young *Stars and Stripes* reporter enamored of the Soviet system, but leaves Europe with very little faith in the future.

The Socialist Menace

Despite what Dos Passos saw as America's abandonment of eastern Europe and shameful behavior in occupied western Europe, he continued to urge greater American leadership in international politics. There was still hope, he wrote, that we might "recover our manhood as a nation." While he stood nearly alone in his early criticisms of American tactics in the last years of the war, he was very much in the mainstream of burgeoning cold war opinion when in 1947, the year of the Truman Doctrine, he wrote that the world "could not endure half slave and half free."[16]

Communists played an ever greater role in Dos Passos's postwar nightmares. In the 1930s, his sympathy for the party had given way to disillusionment and then, with the Spanish civil war and the death of his friend José Robles, to hatred, and this hatred grew in the 1940s. In 1943, he assumed rather hastily that Communists were responsible for the assassination of his friend Carlo Tresca, the anarchist leader; this assumption, in turn, gave fuel to his anti-Communist angers. Like many, Dos Passos suspended overt criticism of America's wartime ally, the Soviet Union. But in the later 1940s he repeatedly warned his fellow Americans of a malevolent and nearly omnipotent Kremlin.[17] Eventual war between the United States and the Soviet Union was thus almost inevitable. "The time will come," he wrote, "when we shall have to bow down or fight."[18]

Dos Passos found even the moderate socialistic measures of the Labour government in Great Britain a threat to freedom. He traveled there with Katy in the summer of 1947 and wrote two articles for *Life*. The first, "Britain's Dim Dictatorship,"[19] despite its forthright title, criticizes the Labour government largely by insinuation. Like *State of the Nation*, it pretends to neutrality and objectivity by describing scenes and quoting various presumably representative Britons. But the descriptions are often loaded: the air, for example, the landscape — "everything"—seems "stagnant" (pp. 120, 121), like the socialized economy apparently, and Dos Passos provides obvious clues to help the reader decide which of the various speakers to believe. The anti-socialists "patiently" explain their ideas to "a hostile crowd" (p. 122) or speak in a voice "clear with conviction" (p. 130), while the defense of the government is left to "a plump little politico smooth as a plum " (p. 133) or a "young idealist" with adopted Oxford mannerisms, "the overenunciated speech, the smirks and smiles, the little mouths" (p. 139). Dos Passos's earlier writing, both fiction and journalism, often used caricatures and stereotypes, but never so heavy-handedly and disingenuously before his disillusionment with left politics in the late 1930s.

The second and more important article, "The Failure of Marxism,"[20] is straightforward. It draws broad conclusions from Dos Passos's observations. Britain is a stagnant, unproductive, highly bureaucratic society. Labour's policies have improved the economic position of the working class at the expense of the middle class and have destroyed individual initiative by reducing economic incentives. Dos Passos repeats Bernard Baruch's claim that socialism distributes not wealth but poverty.

The Labour government, he writes, has not created a new society, but "a new ruling class" (FM, p. 106), namely those trade union leaders and Labour intellectuals who have moved up in the hierarchy since the change of government. The hierarchy itself remains, and "The Established Order"[21]—title of an early version of "The Failure of Marxism"—has in fact tightened its control over the people. Regulation of the economy and a "direction of labor" order, which limits the freedom to choose employment, have brought a frightening decline in "personal liberty" (FM, p. 105). In its "ultimate implications," Dos Passos insists, "British socialism is turning out to be not so very different from the Russian brand" (FM, p. 105).

The British Labour government represents, for Dos Passos, only one small corner of a world that "is becoming a museum of socialist failures" (FM, p. 98). "The revolutions have happened" (FM, p. 98), he writes (a bit prematurely), and have only proved the bankruptcy of socialist idealism and Marxist theory. Individual liberty "inevitably" (FM, p. 108) suffers greatly when enterprises are socialized; our only hope is to turn away from "the dazzle of socialist illusions" and fight to "keep the avenues open for the freedom and growth of the individual man" (FM, p. 108).

Reviewers and critics saw "The Failure of Marxism" as a wholesale rejection of Dos Passos's former radical beliefs, and many attacked it resoundingly. Norman Thomas pointed out that Great Britain was in fact making a remarkable recovery, political and economic, from a devastating war. Granville Hicks reminded Dos Passos of the evils of an unregulated capitalism, which he surely could not have forgotten in only fifteen years. And Philip Rahv attacked Dos Passos's "purely speculative analogies" between Great Britain and the Soviet Union.[22]

In his eagerness to prove the failure and the danger of socialized institutions, Dos Passos does indeed dismiss too quickly the considerable problems the Labour government faced, which included an economy shattered by war and the severest winter of the century. In his fears for the fate of the individual in a mass society, Dos Passos saw temporary and rather limited controls as permanent and extensive. Most of the economy remained in private hands, and the "direction of labor" measure affected very few people and lasted only two and a half years.[23] While the use of German prisoners to do agricultural work without pay was indeed a "sinister" (*FM*, p. 106) sign, this broad condemnation of a government in power only two difficult years was premature.

Dos Passos's fears that British socialism would prove no different from Soviet tyranny seem particularly exaggerated, especially in light of his own long discourse in "The Failure of Marxism" itself on the history of Russian communism. The "hopes of free development for the new social system" (*FM*, p. 102), he writes, were thwarted by outside intervention in the civil war and by inherited traditions of autocracy. Yet he claims the same fate awaits Britain, seeming to forget its democratic traditions, relative independence, higher level of technological development, and the great difference between Labour and Bolshevik political methods.[24]

Unlike the Communists, Dos Passos refused in the 1930s to identify the Soviet Union with the socialist ideal. Nor did the state-managed capitalism of the Labour government have much in common with the "cooperative commonwealth" he dreamed of. But having lost hope in the possibility of a libertarian, truly democratic socialism—and having found himself at odds with those, whether Communists or social democrats, who called themselves socialists—he renounced socialism after the war as the greatest, most dangerous illusion of his time.[25]

Dos Passos could not endorse governments that called themselves socialist because even when they did succeed in distributing wealth they failed to distribute power. This fear of concentrated power, central to his political thinking by the 1940s, represents a continuity with his earlier views, with his cry in 1918 that "organization is death," and with his attacks on capitalism and on the Communist party in

109

U.S.A. and in his journalism. For Dos Passos the radical democrat, bureaucracies, hierarchies, and manipulative politicians are still favorite targets. The real contradiction, he writes in "The Failure of Marxism," is "not between 'capitalism' and 'socialism' but between the sort of organization that stimulates growth and the sort that fastens on society the dead hand of bureaucratic routine or the suckers of sterile vested interests" (*FM*, p. 98).

"The Failure of Marxism" marks one turning point in the evolution of Dos Passos's political thought. His complaint that Labour policies stifle "individual initiative" and interfere with "the normal operations of buying and selling necessary to carrying on a business" (*FM*, p. 106) suggests that free enterprise has crept into his conception of freedom. Such a definition of freedom is central to capitalist ideology, and for Dos Passos represents a significant retreat from his earlier radicalism. Whether free enterprise itself might inevitably lead to monopolies and to great inequalities of wealth and power, whether the freedom to carry on a business might undermine the very democracy and individual freedom Dos Passos values so highly, whether, in other words, there was, as he wrote in the 1930s, a conflict "between property rights and human rights"[26]—such questions, basic to his earlier thinking, would concern him less and less in later years.

World War II contributed a great deal to these changes. The war ended the depression and brought America unprecedented prosperity. Impressed by wartime productivity, Dos Passos thought little about the sort of economic injustices that had angered him in the 1930s. Change itself became frightening; European ideologies of change had led to war, he felt, and the Soviet domination of eastern Europe exacerbated his fears of communism. As a reporter in Europe in 1945, he saw the world growing grimmer daily. Pessimism bred conservatism. It was time to reconsider his earlier sweeping criticisms of American capitalism: "The untrammeled power of the ruling class in the Soviet Union," he told a reporter in Paris, "makes you wonder whether the profit motive is as bad as it has been painted" (*TD*, p. 327).

The Liberal Menace:
The Grand Design

In "The Failure of Marxism," Dos Passos implicitly contrasted the

American "self-governing community" (*FM*, p. 98) with an allegedly undemocratic Great Britain; in a moment of patriotic fervor, he had forgotten his own analysis of the New Deal administration, which after all must have suggested some disturbing parallels to Britain's Labour government. He had voted for Roosevelt in 1936 and over-came his anger over the "filthy hypocracy" of the administration's "hasty" recognition of Franco to do so again in 1940. But he raised troubling questions about the wartime New Deal in *State of the Nation*, and by November, 1944, he was ready to vote Republican. He later characterized his support for Roosevelt's third term as the "*political act I have most regretted in my life.*" He atoned for that act by writing *The Grand Design*, published in 1949.[27]

This long novel is set primarily in the political tangle of Washington, D.C., during the administration of a certain unnamed New Deal president. The central drama of *The Grand Design* involves the ideal-ism, the frustration, and the eventual resignation of two men—Paul Graves, a scientist, and Millard Carroll, a successful entrepreneur—who come to Washington to serve their country by taking unremuner-ative positions in the Department of Agriculture. Subplots centering around love, ambition, conspiracy, and greed in the nation's capital introduce numerous less important characters in something of a *roman à clef*.[28] Twenty prose poems, like those of *Number One*, outline the broader historical context of the main action and, like a too insistent chorus of earnest American opinion, bemoan the betrayal of our deepest hopes and aspirations by "the President."

Dos Passos depicts New Deal programs as a mixed blessing. They strengthen the position of the working class, but they also create a stratum of prosperous, careerist union officials like Joe Yerkes. Agri-cultural programs help some small farmers and impoverished share-croppers, but are easily manipulated by the "Farm Bureau lobby" to serve the narrow interests of the "big boys" (*GD*, p. 75). Everything deteriorates as the novel progresses. The early New Deal holds great promise, but amidst the mobilization for wartime production and po-litical maneuvering around the 1940 election, the interests of the powerless are easily forgotten. The ultimate betrayal of New Deal ideals and of the Founding Fathers' grand design comes when the president appoints Jerry Evans, the smooth financier and power bro-ker, to head the new War Procurement Board.

While exposing the failings of the New Deal, Dos Passos is also

111

making a more general point: that strong central government can create more problems than it solves. The sincere efforts of Paul and Millard to implement real reform are perpetually thwarted by red tape, obscure political machinations, and the inability of even the most selfless bureaucrats to stay in touch with the needs of ordinary people. Big government, Dos Passos suggests, interferes with the salutary functioning of science, as represented by Paul, and of entrepreneurial capital, as represented by Millard. Like the argument in "The Failure of Marxism," the implication here that science and capital, if left alone, would together serve the people well marks a significant departure from the Veblenian critique in *U.S.A.* of "the sabotage of production by business" (*BM*, p. 101).

The New Deal threatens not only efficiency, but, more important, democracy in *The Grand Design*. It centralizes decision-making in Washington and, beyond that, concentrates great power in the hands of one man. The president never appears in the narrative sections of the novel—dramatizing, perhaps, his aloofness and his isolation from his subordinates and his constituents—but the prose poems portray him as a skillful and sinister manipulator of the public, like "Delano the Magician," as Dos Passos called Roosevelt in 1934. His "*insinuating*" voice, "*carefully tuned to the microphones*," deceives us again and again: "*We danced to his tune. Third Term. Fourth Term. Indispensable*" (*GD*, pp. 60, 4, 417). Power corrupts him and he corrupts us, as we passively accept "broad executive power," "concentration camps" for Japanese-Americans, and Big Three negotiations which "*divided up the bloody globe and left the freedoms out*" (*GD*, pp. 6, 416, 419).

Of course, the popular election of so evil a president—like the election of Crawford in *Number One*—ought to disturb the deep faith in the common people and in democratic processes that Dos Passos expresses throughout *The Grand Design*. But it does not. By portraying Roosevelt as an extraordinarily skillful political operator, the consummate schemer, Dos Passos avoids such a challenge to his growing faith in American traditions, and makes Roosevelt not a product of our society, but someone alien to it, like the "strangers" (*BM*, p. 462) in *U.S.A.* who have corrupted our nation.

The Communists in *The Grand Design* are also "strangers"—in fact, hardly recognizable as human beings. Like the cardboard comrades in *Adventures of a Young Man*, they forever sneer, smile cruelly, and make preposterous statements, like Joe Yerkes's claim that love is "a disease of the personality" (*GD*, p. 53). Dos Passos makes many of his Communist characters antipathetic by portraying them, very ham-handedly, as stereotypical homosexuals and lesbians: mannish and manipulative Greta Greenberg; hard, cold, sneakily lecherous Jane Sparling; and passive, whimpering Winthrop Strang, with a falsetto voice and an overbearing mother. Even the heterosexual Communists are deviant: Joe Yerkes lacks all human feeling, and Jed Farrington is cruelly exploitative, taking command of a woman "as if she were a squad of wretched farmboys he was lashing into shape for partisans" (*GD*, p. 391). All this contrasts sharply with Millard's earnest love for his wife and Paul's manly (though illicit) passion for Georgia Washburn.

This ludicrous portrayal of Communists undermines the novel's insistence that they represent a genuine threat to American freedoms. More important, it suggests a failure, or else a refusal, by Dos Passos to think very deeply about communism. In *U.S.A.*, the public relations executive J. W. Moorehouse was an imaginative creation, understandable as well as despicable. But the distorting hatred behind the portrayals of the Communists in *The Grand Design* prevents understanding and marks another step by Dos Passos away from the serious exploration of American communism and toward simple, and simplistic, denunciation.

However, the real emotional and political center of *The Grand Design* is neither the insidious president nor the grotesque Communists, but rather the conflict between rural and urban values, between local self-reliance and the administration of life from afar, which Paul observes and experiences in his excursions into "the field" to study the farm problem firsthand. Paul is struck, for example, by the insensitivity of one middle-class New Deal supporter who brings him to the cabin of a destitute, toothless woman and pokes a big finger at her mouth sores and bleeding gums as evidence of the need for more relief money. Paternalistic aid from Washington only humiliates such people, Paul realizes; reform must "start at the bottom instead of the top" (*GD*, p. 163). The poor need neither a handout nor a lecture, but "daily control over their destinies" (*GD*, p. 143). The answer to poverty and to powerlessness, Paul decides, is independence "at the source of [one's] livelihood" (*GD*, p. 143), and he crusades to save the family-sized farm.

Given Dos Passos's long-time concern for the problems of a highly

113

industrialized society, it is significant that *The Grand Design* focuses on agriculture instead of industry and finds the greatest threat to individual freedom, as well as the best real hope for its rejuvenation, on the farm. A sharp contrast between the country and the city dominates the novel. The Carrolls' idyllic drive across the Ozarks on their way to the capital, and Paul and Georgia's refreshing journey through farming country, which culminates in their love affair, oppose the destructiveness of the frenetic politicking in the capital. Just as he caricatures urban Communists, Dos Passos idealizes successful small farmers; their thriving crops, bounteous hospitality, and "gleaming clean aluminum milking machinery" (*GD*, p. 251) are out of a Norman Rockwell painting. There has always been a touch of almost pastoral romanticism in Dos Passos's writing—most obviously in *Rosinante to the Road Again*—and his own life was becoming ever more countrified in the 1940s, as he developed a close friendship with an Iowa farmer, Bob Garst, and acquired part of his father's Virginia farm.[29] More than this, *The Grand Design* reflects Dos Passos's increasingly Jeffersonian vision, hinted at in *The Ground We Stand On*, and later to be fully articulated in his biography of Jefferson—a vision in which the foundation of freedom lay not in the inevitable collectivism of the industrial working class, but in the independence and individualism of the property-owning farmer.

Dos Passos's attack on modern liberalism in *The Grand Design* is an attack on its methods. Although his is not the criticism leveled by New Left historians—that New Deal reforms served primarily to save a capitalist system in crisis[30]—he does share their view that reform from the top, highly centralized power, and secret maneuvering at "the level of the leaders"(*GD*, p. 435) contradict basic democratic principles. Dos Passos has abandoned the class analysis that informed *U.S.A.* and grudgingly made his peace with capitalism, though not with monopolies. By focusing on questions of power and organization, he saw what liberals and Communists failed to see: that government bureaucrats can be as oppressive as capitalists. Nonetheless, in describing virtually all change as the product of one evil president's manipulations, he tends to ignore the deeper historical currents that helped to bring such change about: with depression and the war, greater government regulation was an idea whose time had come.

His blaming all on Roosevelt, however, seems an effort to allow more hope to emerge from *The Grand Design* than from the less superficial and more deterministic *U.S.A.* If Roosevelt, not history, is the villain, then the damage can be undone. Undoing, in fact, seems to be how Dos Passos now envisions positive social change. The family farm that his hero Paul fights for derives from an earlier era; Paul wishes to recapture for the present the independence of the "oldtime American farmer" (*GD*, p. 143). It is an old woman in "Daniel Boone Country" who first hints at the novel's central theme, when she tells Millard and his wife,"Us folks don't have no truck with no government" (*GD*, p. 20). In rejecting liberalism in *The Grand Design*, Dos Passos looks backwards and begins to develop his particular brand of conservatism.

Although it is a novel about bureaucracy, *The Grand Design* has some life, and its attempt to capture New Deal Washington in fiction is a bold and ambitious undertaking. Unfortunately, Dos Passos usually fails to dramatize effectively the important political conflicts that make up its theme. As a scientist and former farmboy trying to use the government to save the family farm, Paul successfully embodies the struggle between centralized administration and local autonomy. A scene in which he rolls up the sleeves of his bureaucratic white shirt and eagerly helps a farmer pull a calf is one of the most vivid and expressive in the novel.

All too often, though, Dos Passos gives us debate, not drama. Paul and Millard become rather wooden characters who merely expound their creator's opinions. Even without the loud editorializing of its prose poems, *The Grand Design* is too didactic; Dos Passos knows the answers to his questions before he even raises them. Chapters rotate among the viewpoints of five different characters, but the viewpoint is always Dos Passos's. Most reviewers faulted the novel, no doubt in part because it attacked the liberal hero Roosevelt. But the real problem was that ever since *U.S.A.*, Dos Passos had become less the angry artist than the weary lecturer, and as one critic wrote, quoting Blake, "the tygers of wrath are wiser than the horses of instruction."[31]

Dos Passos yoked *The Grand Design* to *Adventures of a Young Man* and *Number One* to form the trilogy *District of Columbia*, published in 1952. As a trilogy, it lacks the unity of *U.S.A.*, though some characters reappear, and the theme of misdirected idealism—Glenn's, Tyler's, and Paul and Millard's—loosely binds the three novels together. In addition, certain minor parallels and ironies emerge from the juxtaposition: Georgia Washburn, like Marice Gulick of *Adventures of a Young*

JOHN DOS PASSOS

Man, exemplifies the vulnerability of liberalism to Communist pressures; Georgia's death, by finally impelling Paul to leave Washington, helps redeem him, much as Glenn's death redeems Tyler; and the pathos in *The Grand Design* of Herbert Spotswood's manipulation by Communists at a rally to commemorate the civil war in Spain is deepened when we remember that his son Glenn was killed there as a "Trotzkyist-Bukharinist wrecker" (*AYM*, p. 317). However, the moods of the three novels mix poorly: the overwhelming despair of *Adventures of a Young Man*, the forced optimism at the end of *Number One*, and the antiliberal scolding of *The Grand Design* neutralize each other.

Changing Prospects

The last months Dos Passos worked on *The Grand Design* were a time of frightening loneliness and disorientation. In September, 1947, he and Katy were driving from Provincetown to see friends in Connecticut. Momentarily blinded by the sun, Dos Passos hit a truck. Katy was killed instantly and Dos Passos, as Ludington recounts it, was left "cupping his gouged-out right eye in one hand." Once out of the hospital he distracted himself with work and visits to friends, but a year later, as he wrote, "the void [was] as deep as ever." In 1949, he married Elizabeth Holdridge, and the next year announced with pleasure "the arrival of a tiny squalling leaky little character named Lucy Hamlin Dos Passos."[32]

By then, Dos Passos had settled in as a gentleman farmer on his eighteen hundred acres in Virginia's Westmoreland County—away, as Ludington suggests, from the most "overpowering" memories of Katy.[33] His letters of the early 1950s abound with cheerful references to working their garden, selling timber, building a new wing on the house, and raising cattle. On frequent trips to Baltimore, he continued his research on Jefferson and revolutionary America.

He missed old friends and the intellectual excitement of New York. "Conversation," he wrote Edmund Wilson, "has entirely disappeared from my life." His isolation was in part political as well as geographical. His views were rapidly diverging from those of Wilson and others, and he was finding himself and his ideas at the fringes of intellectual debate, not at the center, as they had been in the 1930s. This made his protracted project on Jefferson particularly frustrating, "a hell of a lot of work, with only the prospect of another goddam book to shove down the goddam rathole."[34]

Dos Passos did, however, publish another volume on contemporary social problems, *The Prospect Before Us*, in 1950. Tired of what must have seemed to him a losing battle, he called it "the last work I shall ever do pertaining to the public welfare."[35] Of course, it was not, but some of it suggests that Dos Passos felt his influence as a political writer was coming to an end.

The Prospect Before Us brings together fragments of earlier writings, such as "The Failure of Marxism" and wartime reporting, with much unpublished material, in an effort to provide a broad examination of the fate of individual freedom in three areas of the world: Great Britain, South America, and the United States. Dos Passos awkwardly structures the book as a series of public lectures; a representative American audience asks the questions necessary to bring out the speaker's exceedingly digressive argument. Dos Passos casts himself as a kind-hearted, occasionally bumbling "MR. LECTURER," and gently mocks his own fears of irrelevance by allowing the audience to dwindle steadily. At the end, a janitor begins switching off the lights while MR. LECTURER is still talking, and as the last light goes out, MR. LECTURER must assure a "VERY YOUNG MAN" that his ideas are indeed "on the level" (*PBU*, p. 375).

Dos Passos aims in *The Prospect Before Us* to generalize and to extend to new areas the sort of criticism of centralization and bureaucracy he makes in "The Failure of Marxism" and in *The Grand Design*. An "eighteenth century libertarian like Tom Paine," he writes, "would find more similarities than differences" among American "Capitalism," British "Socialism," and the Russian "Dictatorship of the Proletariat" (*PBU*, pp. 5-6). Under all three systems, "stratified corporations" (*PBU*, p. 8)—whether business, governmental agencies, or unions—exercise too much power over individuals. The problem transcends ideologies because it lies "in the structure of industrial society itself" (*PBU*, p. 6); the solution is "decentralization" and greater citizen "participation in local selfgovernment" (*PBU*, pp. 373, 363).

Dos Passos's reproaches are against what James Burnham calls "managerial society,"[36] and he seeks a radically democratic alternative. However, still enthusiastic about the sort of technological miracles he witnessed during the war, Dos Passos greatly admires efficiency and productivity, values potentially in conflict with democratic ones. This conflict leads him to judge "stratified corporations" very unevenly. He deals evasively with the issue of industrial democracy in his celebratory descriptions of the vast, complex, and productive operations of General Mills. But he is critical of large unions—the enemy of productivity from the viewpoint of managers—even though such unions offset the concentrated power of large corporations. Further, he argues that "wage workers and managers alike must forget the class war and think only about saving the Republic" (*PBU*, pp. 366–67). Dos Passos's earlier urge to "declass" himself, stimulated perhaps by his recent fear of the instability caused by class struggle, has given way to an effort to deny the significance of classes in American society. He could not have had much hope that workers and managers would "forget the class war"; he concludes, unsurprisingly, that "the prospect before us is one of mighty effort against great odds" (*PBU*, p. 372).

Protesting Too Much:
Chosen Country

Jay Pignatelli, hero of *Chosen Country* (1951),[37] takes one small step toward "saving the Republic" by saving himself. The illegitimate son of a prominent American lawyer, he spends much of his childhood in Europe, moving from place to place, never really feeling at home in America. He rejects his country, first by fleeing it for the ambulance service in France and the Middle East Relief, then by defending its alleged enemies as a lawyer for the Sabatinis, whose case resembles Sacco and Vanzetti's. After falling in love with the wholesome, endlessly charming, very American Lulie Harrington, he is able fully to embrace his native land and put an end to the confusion and loneliness of his existence as an outsider. The novel ends with their idyllic honeymoon, "alone in the green world" (*CC*, p. 484). Their vows to build a life together represent salvation for Jay and hope for the rebirth of the nation he is part of.

The structure of *Chosen Country* reinforces the romantic nature of its plot. Jay and Lulie meet early in the novel and lead their separate lives; the narrative point of view alternates chapter by chapter between his and hers. The point of view alternates *within* the last chap-

118

ter, the chapter in which they meet again, court, and marry. In addition, three short sections labeled *"Prolegomena"* reach back into the past to detail the life stories of Jay's and Lulie's parents. Dos Passos relies on marriage, the oldest convention in comedy, to resolve history happily. In a novel so structured, the risk of sentimentality is great, and *Chosen Country* does not escape it, as can be seen in the final lines. Their first morning alone together, Jay and Lulie stand side by side looking out at the ocean: " 'Husband,' she said. 'Wife,' he said. The words made them bashful. They clung together against their bashfulness. 'Together we begin,['] he said, 'to make...' 'This wilderness our home,' she said. The risen sun over the ocean shone in their faces" (*CC*, p. 485).

Dos Passos, like many novelists, writes better about despair and defeat than about joy and affirmation, and the most successful passages of *Chosen Country* are those that depict Jay's early troubles: his "horrible . . . hotel childhood" (*CC*, p. 26), his sexual shame and frustration, the repeated failures in what one critic calls his "search for belonging."[38] The interpretive crux of the novel lies in how completely Jay's problems are solved by the end. His new-found love, his all-embracing patriotism, and his future career with a prosperous law firm merge in Jay's mind and form what seems to be the foundation of enduring happiness. Such a resolution is inconceivable in the world of *U.S.A.*, where love is almost impossible, patriotism a racket, and a lawyer somebody who makes "slimy" (*BM*, p. 437) the language of democracy. (Now, of course, it is not lawyers but Communists and other "dogooders" who "mouthed the words but at the same time . . . let the substance dribble down their chins" [*CC*, p. 466].) That *Chosen Country* is autobiographical explains in part its exceptional nature. As a tribute to the memory of Katy, whom Lulie resembles in many ways, it had to conclude in celebration. With Katy dead, Dos Passos needed desperately to look to a brighter future. The novel reflects too Dos Passos's happiness about remarrying and about the birth of his first child.

Dos Passos's personal needs for affirmation also helped shape *Chosen Country* as a political statement. In novels such as *The Grand Design*, Dos Passos simultaneously praises and censures his country. Here, through Jay, without a trace of irony, he unabashedly declares his love for America, for "the country of his choice that made him feel so proud and humble when he saw the striped flag fly" (*CC*, p. 466).

119

Jay's is a very apolitical sort of patriotism. Working on the Sabatini defense, Jay learns to distrust the hissing Communists and misguided "dogooders"; more important, he learns to avoid causes entirely. Politics repeatedly proves confusing and treacherous, and just as he flees the stifling city for the "raw magnificent country" (CC, p. 465), he flees political involvement for the soothing simplicity of Lulie's affections. In the same way that Dos Passos's own sorrows and pleasures in this period were not political, but deeply personal, he roots his protagonist's troubles in a lonely childhood and resolves them in a happy marriage.

With three short sections—"Footnotes"—that depart from the main narrative and momentarily rise above it stylistically, Dos Passos highlights the rightness of Jay's embracing of family, country, and financial success, and at the same time tries to give the novel greater historical specificity and depth. The "Footnotes" develop three characters who eventually play minor roles in Jay's life and suggest various paths idealism such as his might take: Eliot Story Bradford, 1872–1918, abandons some of his youthful aestheticism for a sort of aristocratic, nonpolitical social conscience and admirably creates a volunteer ambulance corps during the war; Anne Comfort Welsh, 1892–1929, like Mary French in U.S.A., sadly gives too much of herself to various causes, including the Communist party; and Elisha Croft, 1865–1930, overworks himself in the legal defense of miners who in the end prove unworthy of his faith in them. Jay's own political choices, then, come to seem as right as his choice of a wife.

Chosen Country fails as a novel in part because it awkwardly imposes present feelings on past experiences. It is Dos Passos's most autobiographical novel: Jay's childhood isolation, his powerful but distant father, the various college and war experiences, the defense of two Italian immigrants, the Hemingway figure—all the elements are there.[39] But Dos Passos is too busy disowning his early political radicalism to make very comprehensible his own rebellious past. He pushes Jay too rapidly through involvement in and then disillusionment with the Sabatini case and with all such causes, as if he, Dos Passos, could not wait to bring him to his final patriotic awakening.[40] Jay learns in a few short years what Dos Passos came to believe only after twenty; this, perhaps, is what Dos Passos at fifty-five wished his own youth had been. The point, however, is not that Dos Passos revises his own past, but rather that he never fully reimagines it. Jay comes alive as a character in the elaborate memories of his childhood, but as an adult, he is reduced to a lifeless vehicle for his creator's editorializing on his own past mistakes.

Permanent Red Scare

In the late 1940s and in the 1950s, Dos Passos had little hope that the idealized America of his imagination would become a reality. The retreat from politics that helps save Jay Pignatelli was not the path Dos Passos himself would take. In subsequent novels and in his journalism, he escalated his verbal attacks on those he saw as his nation's most dangerous enemies: the Communists. Ironically, in an era of declining Communist influence at home and unprecedented American military power abroad, Dos Passos's fears grew: he wrote of breaking out "in a cold sweat," afraid for his country. He saw Communists everywhere, insidious and extraordinarily successful. The Kremlin, he wrote, controlled "two-thirds of the world," and American Communists were involved in a "conspiracy of assassins." In 1959, after numerous leftists had been driven out of the universities, he complained that a faculty member who defended "the profit system often finds it hard to hold his job." He feared we might be "doomed," but he hoped that at least we would "go down fighting."[41]

Just as Dos Passos's radicalization in the 1920s preceded the leftward journey of many intellectuals in the 1930s, he also turned angrily against communism earlier than most. Much as the depression, when it came, deepened his hatred of capitalism, the hysterical atmosphere of the late 1940s and early 1950s deepened his hatred of communism. Once again he was in tune with the times. The congressional investigations, the loyalty campaigns, and the ranting headlines and politicians that built an anti-Communist consensus must have confirmed for Dos Passos what he had believed for years—that Communists were ruthless and pervasive and had to be stopped at any cost. The cold war, as Randolph Bourne might have said, was the health of the state—and the American crusade against communism became the very sort of threat to individual freedom Dos Passos feared from communism itself.

His virulent anticommunism distorted Dos Passos's political values. In some of his statements of the 1950s, it is very hard to recog-

121

nize Dos Passos so recently the radical democrat and civil libertarian. He defends J. Parnell Thomas's work as head of the House Committee on Un-American Activities as "clumsy" but "necessary" and insists, in 1959, that "the hysteria of McCarthyism was generated chiefly by those who opposed him." He admits that a few people had been "inconvenienced" by the crusade, but can call McCarthy nothing worse than "a clumsy man who tripped over a good cause."[42] Dos Passos had already dissected the political racketeer in *Number One*; that he could now apologize for McCarthy suggests the extent to which his anticommunism overwhelmed his critical judgment.

The phenomenon of the ex-Communist as the angriest and eagerest sort of crusader against communism was a recurrent one in the 1950s. Though Dos Passos was not an ex-Communist, and never really became what Issac Deutscher calls "an inverted Stalinist"[43]—a sectarian in a new sect—his former radicalism helped shape his later conservatism. Communist sins there certainly were, and, as in the case of the death of José Robles, they sometimes touched Dos Passos personally. But while American Communists never presented a threat to the United States, their continued existence must have threatened Dos Passos psychologically. Like an ex-Communist, he felt perhaps the need to atone for his past errors, to exorcise the devil, and to see Communists as unusually powerful and seductive, because once they had nearly seduced *him*.

Dos Passos's anti-Communist anger also helped still his doubts about America, doubts which themselves may have stimulated his anti-communism. As *Chosen Country* suggests, he very much needed to be patriotic. Yet, as *The Grand Design* and other writings of this period show, he was alarmed by the path he saw America following. At times he would tautologically identify the United States with democracy and pose the Soviet Union as its opposite; at other times, he would write that "*the same sort of new ruling class that reached power by violent means in the Soviet Union has reached power by peaceful means in this country.*"[44] He could praise "our failure to create an empire when empire building was easy" yet on occasion write that internationally the United States is "really an expanding power unit and that all our idealism is eyewash." With so unstable a foundation for his patriotism, he needed to affirm that patriotism ever more emphatically. Deeply critical of the country he loved, he tended to displace his criticism onto an "unAmerican" group, the Communists. His striving to integrate himself into American society left him only more alienated. As Norman Mailer wrote, of writers who had returned to the patriotic fold, "the artist feels most alienated when he loses the sharp sense of what he is alienated from."[45]

Spiteful Novel:
Most Likely to Succeed

Dos Passos poured all his anti-Communist vitriol into his next novel, *Most Likely To Succeed*,[46] published in 1954. In a straightforward manner, without *Prolegomena* or prose poems, the novel describes the aggressive climb to success of Jed Morris, whom we first meet as an energetic, rebellious, self-dramatizing, young playwright straining to seduce a wealthy woman on a transatlantic voyage to New York. He joins the left-wing Craftsman's Theatre, in which the Communists exploit his talents and tamper with his plays. Soon he finds himself in Hollywood, where his career skyrockets, thanks to connections in the party. Jed eventually signs up, but the pressures of his political work add to those of his professional work to strain his physical and emotional resources. When the party, suspecting the woman he needs and thinks he loves of being a federal agent, forces him to abandon her, Jed—in a final scene—collapses with a heart attack.

Most Likely to Succeed is a moralistic novel with no moral drama. Jed is punished in the end for having let his vanity, his need to feel important, lead him into Communist hands. But from the start, he is such a despicable character that his victimization by the party leaves us nearly unmoved. His affectations, his self-importance, his opportunism, and his unfeeling use of other people as means to his own ends make him one of Dos Passos's most repulsive characters. He is proud of his great capacity for love, yet, as one woman rightly tells him, he "think[s] women are dirt" (*ML*, p. 32). In rare moments when he realizes his own failings, he crumples in self-pity and blames it all on capitalism.

So grotesque an individual is perfectly suited for the Communist party as Dos Passos depicts it. Yet, because the novel is narrated from Jed's point of view, we find ourselves reluctantly granting him some small measure of sympathy owing to his treatment by the party. Those who exploit Jed are even worse than he is. These Communists leer and sneer and "dribble . . . words" (*ML*, p. 100) out of the corners of their mouths from the start, while Jed only hisses for the first time (*ML*, p. 234) when he is just about to sign his membership card. His old friend Sam Faust, one of the "men that count for something" (*ML*, p. 186), has sold his soul to the party for power and money, and his ever more corpulent body testifies to his accumulating sins. By the end, as America is entering the war, manipulating Communists not only control Jed, but—it seems—are on their way to controlling Hollywood, radio, and the press.

Were it not written so solemnly and imbued with so much hatred, all of this might be read as satiric comedy. Occasional comic scenes do provide much needed relief from Dos Passos's grim anti-Communist mission. The family of Jed's second wife, Felicia, whom he eventually drives to drink, are humorous, not deadly serious, caricatures: her lazy, ineffectual, philosophizing father Schol; her flinty, spirited mother Agatha; and her dreamy, Oxonian brother Yeats Hardestie, who swoons over the delights of English prosody. Jed's brief fling with "Dr. Olga Swenson, Chiropractic" (*ML*, p. 121) is also mildly amusing. But such moments remain incidental to the main thrust of the novel, to its unrelenting assault on the Communist party and those whom it attracts. *Most Likely to Succeed* is not satire but invective.[47]

The novel's major dramatic weakness—its effort to make Jed both villain and victim—derives in part from Dos Passos's great clumsiness, worse here than in *Chosen Country*, in imposing his current views on his own past and that of others. Though Jed resembles John Howard Lawson more than Dos Passos, there are many autobiographical elements in the early part of the novel—particularly in Jed's stories about the Near East and in his experiences with the Craftsman's Theatre, obviously a fictionalized version of the New Playwrights Theatre. While recreating the past in *Chosen Country*, Dos Passos led a wiser former self through a more corrupt world of leftist politics than he had actually known; in *Most Likely to Succeed*, he degrades almost beyond recognition both that world and what there is of himself in his protagonist. So impatient is he to disown his own past radicalism that he makes Jed unbearably unpleasant from the very start. There is not a hint in the novel of the social ills that might have driven people— Dos Passos included—to seek change through leftist organizations. Jed's motivation, like that of Sam and the other Communists, is reduced to vanity, hatred, and a hunger for money and power. The novel is lifeless, the few points it makes belabored. In the political climate of the early 1950s Dos Passos let his obsessions destroy his art.

Self-Evident Truths:
The Head and Heart of Thomas Jefferson

Not all was bitterness and fear during these years, however. Dos Passos continued to find inspiration in his historical studies, which had begun with *The Ground We Stand On* and his essay on Tom Paine and would absorb him the rest of his life. Despite the "unending drudgery" of research and writing, he persisted; each book took far longer than he anticipated. Once it was done, he quickly began another. At the expense of his fiction, he threw his best energies into historical work for which he seems to have had little talent.[48] Dos Passos must have felt such work exceedingly important, since he sacrificed so much for it.

Dos Passos's most significant historical volume—the first after *The Ground We Stand On* and the culmination of more than a decade's work —is *The Head and Heart of Thomas Jefferson*, published in 1954. It describes the world Jefferson lived in and follows his life until 1793, eight years before he became president. We learn more about his heart and less about his head than we might expect in a biography of so important a political thinker, for the portrait is warmly personal and only vaguely intellectual. Jefferson emerges as a more rounded and more appealing character than most characters in Dos Passos's novels, but the book is flawed by a profusion of irrelevant detail, an accumulation for its own sake of what one reviewer called "the jangling bric-a-brac of Americana."[49]

There was much about Jefferson and his era to appeal to Dos Passos. The study of the past—any past—might have satisfied his need to escape from a politically troubling present. Revolutionary America— an almost preindustrial age, and an age often viewed as one of individuals, not corporate institutions—might have easily taken the place in Dos Passos's imagination of the Spain of *Rosinante to the Road Again*. As a patriotic American unhappy with his country, Dos Passos turned eagerly to the moral and political triumphs of Jefferson and others, proof of the American superiority for which he found only mixed evidence in the present. The gap betwen virtue and success that struc-

125

tured the worlds of *Manhattan Transfer, U.S.A.*, and even *The Grand Design* had been the product of Dos Passos's own political frustrations; in Jefferson's world virtuous individuals succeeded in doing good. The values of the Enlightenment were Dos Passos's own values: reason, liberty, and the improvement of human kind. His father, after all, had given him "an eighteenth-century education," and he himself had once, as a young man, called for "a new Enlightenment."[50] Whereas once the more radical Tom Paine embodied these values for Dos Passos, now it was Thomas Jefferson who did, a man so much at one with his own country he could eventually become its president.

The Head and Heart of Thomas Jefferson presents an idealized version of Jefferson and his times. Dos Passos, the iconoclast, here becomes an idolater, a maker of new myths. Not content with a great but flawed Jefferson, Dos Passos constructs a hero flawless beyond belief. Much as he attributed all evil to Roosevelt in *The Grand Design* and to Communists in several novels, he now attributes all virtue to Jefferson. The republic that Dos Passos shows Jefferson laboring to build in fact has all the beauty and simplicity of a "storybook democracy" (*BM*, p. 150). As John P. Diggins writes, Dos Passos is a "romantic historian," and the orderly, democratic world he depicts is "more willed than true, a triumph of imagination over inquiry."[51]

The most undemocratic aspect of revolutionary America was, of course, slavery, and Dos Passos treats the institution casually and Jefferson's views on it gingerly. Jefferson himself made somewhat contradictory statements about blacks and slavery, and Dos Passos emphasizes the more liberal ones, smoothing over Jefferson's belief in the innate mental inferiority of the Negro race.[52] Dos Passos was no defender of slavery, but its existence in no way dampened his enthusiasm for the "libertarian" (*TJ*, p. 207) Jefferson and the great experiment in "selfgovernment" (*TJ*, p. 160) he took part in. Dos Passos could thus suggest, without irony, that Jefferson was well qualified to plan for democratic government because of his experience running his plantation (thirty-four whites, eighty-three black slaves), "a laboratory for the practical management of men" (*TJ*, p. 179). Jefferson, of course, is the product of his age, but Dos Passos, in his efforts to establish that age as a moral exemplar, obscures some of its most significant characteristics.

Slavery remains in the background because *The Head and Heart of Thomas Jefferson*, like virtually all of Dos Passos's later historical writing, is the history of political elites. Most of the books and documents he could draw upon were written by and about the upper classes, so the choice of this era may have shaped his approach in part. But by failing to investigate or even speculate upon the experiences and the points of view of the lower classes, Dos Passos contributed to the tendency of historical research to ignore those voiceless individuals whom Jesse Lemisch—in an essay entitled "The American Revolution Seen from the Bottom Up"—calls the "inarticulate." At its most idealized, *The Head and Heart of Thomas Jefferson* suggests that powerful men, impelled neither by historical forces nor by class interests, acted upon moral and philosophical principles to build a republic that embodied the best interests of all. Throughout, Dos Passos seems to assume that such men represent all people and that their freedom defines a free society. Once, long before, Dos Passos had traveled to Passaic and to Harlan County to learn about his country from the bottom up. In *U.S.A.* he had proudly described America as "a publiclibrary full of . . . dogeared historybooks with protests scrawled on the margins." Since that time his perspective had changed considerably, despite his assertion, so late as 1949, that he tended "to see things from the point of view of the man on the bottom, instead of the man on top."[53] Had he really done this in his study of Jefferson's times, he might have seen things differently and come to very different conclusions. The conflict a very young Dos Passos once felt between elitist and democratic impulses is dissolved too easily in his admiration for political elites who acted in the name of democracy.

His focus on those at the top in part explains the great harmony Dos Passos finds in revolutionary America. By limiting his inquiry to the activities of the upper classes, Dos Passos presents what seems to be an almost classless society. Jefferson's supporters and those of Hamilton debate how strong the central government should be, for example, but both sides agree—though Dos Passos never dwells on this—that popular sovereignty should be held in check, that elite gentlemen should rule. Of course the consensus, as Dos Passos describes it, is a very pragmatic and prodemocratic one; he sees it as the product of a particularly American outlook, which he takes great pains to contrast with the rigid class distinctions of the English and the "lack of realism" (*TJ*, p. 342) of the French. As recent commentators have pointed out, such insistence on consensus and on the existence of a peculiarly American character is, like the focus on elites, a common

127

characteristic of postwar American historiography.[54] Dos Passos's views of the past, though colored by his own particular concerns, have much in common with those of his contemporaries.

Like many other historians, Dos Passos has the present fully in mind as he examines the past. "Today," he writes, "when the need to take sides in the struggle for the freedom to seek individual happiness again confronts every man alive, we can understand, as the Americans of 1776 understood, what a bold enterprise it was" (*TJ*, p. 175). Walker Watson, the naïvely idealistic pawn in Roosevelt's machinations in *The Grand Design*, has a living room filled with history books he "never get[s] a chance to read" (*GD*, p. 226). Dos Passos very much wants his readers to do better than Watson, to enter into the present struggle for freedom well armed with historical knowledge. *The Head and Heart of Thomas Jefferson*, like his novels of this period, is thus baldly didactic. The study of Jefferson, he hopes, will help us "find a formula for individual liberty."[55]

But how? At the center of the Jeffersonian democratic ideal is a community of independent small farmers. The gap between the idealized past Dos Passos describes and his own society, strangled by corporate institutions, is so great that all we can learn from such history is how much we have lost. It is not even clear what Dos Passos himself feels he has learned, for he saw the need for "selfgovernment" in the present long before he discovered it in the past. Dos Passos's historical studies suggest no real analysis of historical change, but rather a moralistic and simplistic criticism of the present by comparison with a nobler, purer, freer age now gone.

Dos Passos's historical search for "a formula for individual liberty" lasted thirty years. In later volumes—*The Men Who Made The Nation* (1957), *Prospects of a Golden Age* (1959), and *The Shackles of Power* (1966)— he continued his examination of the early years of the republic.[56] None was the product of so much effort and love as his work on the early Jefferson. Dos Passos's identification with his subject in *The Head and Heart of Thomas Jefferson* must have been, at least for a while, emotional as well as political, for he writes that: "As Jefferson grew older and found no one to replace his dead wife in his inner affections he was becoming hedged in with a peculiar private solitude . . . In the bitterness of that solitude the driving passion that kept him trudging ahead through the routine and drudgery of public life was love of country" (*TJ*, p. 292).

Sad Decline: *The Great Days*

Much as *The Head and Heart of Thomas Jefferson* seems to lament the passing of a more glorious era in his country's history, Dos Passos's first novel to follow it is steeped in an aging man's nostalgia for the bright joys of his own earlier days. Ro Lancaster, hero of *The Great Days*,[57] wants to begin his life anew at fifty-nine and sets out for Havana with a beautiful woman, Elsa, thirty years younger than he. By the end of their vacation, he has lost much of his pride, all of his money, and Elsa. Ro's real life is in the past, in endless reveries of the "great days" (*TGD*, p. 9) when, as a famous journalist and happy family man, he felt important and he felt loved.

The contrast between past and present is dramatic in *The Great Days*. In Cuba, Ro despairs of ever communicating his deepest feelings to the bored and restless young woman he has brought along. He feels humiliated by his sexual failure with her and by the frequent sniggering the disparity in their ages evokes. His very act of reminiscing underscores his distance from her, his loneliness and isolation in the present. While much of his past is shrouded in a romantic mist, the people and landscape of Cuba are constantly unpleasant and ugly. In addition, though the narrative point of view is always Ro's, the third-person present seems far less immediate, less intensely felt, than the first-person flashbacks. In past as well as in present narratives, life loses its joy as the novel progresses: Ro's friend Roger Thurloe kills himself, his own journalism career declines, and his wife Grace dies of cancer in the course of his reminiscences. If the structure of *Chosen Country* is romantic, with all action leading up to Jay's and Lulie's marriage, the structure of *The Great Days* is nostalgic, with successive events ever sadder compared to those early days when Ro and Grace, newly married, were "so happy [they] could hardly bear it" (*TGD*, p. 11).

Ro's frustration in Cuba, when not pathetic, is almost farcical. But his past suffering achieves a certain grandeur, in large part because it is tied to world events; his tragedy parallels the nation's. As Ro's reporting in the Pacific and in Europe documents, America is winning the war but losing the peace. His close friend Roger Thurloe, a cabinet member, knows this too, but Roger's warnings about the Soviet Union, "the great ally who wants to cut our throats" (*TGD*, p. 200), go continually unheeded. Roger and Ro alone, it seems, truly under-

129

stand how imperiled our freedoms are, and when Roger (modeled on James Forrestal) is driven from the cabinet and when Ro's views make it difficult for him to publish, the future begins to look dark. Roger, Grace announces ominously, "is the only great man we have left" (*TGD*, p. 270), and his suicide at the end marks the death of all hope for American leadership in the world.

The political views Ro and Roger express are, of course, Dos Passos's own. In fact, Ro's endless reminiscences of his travels in the Pacific and in Europe for "Picture Magazine" are taken, often verbatim, from *Tour of Duty*.[58] Among the many other autobiographical elements are Ro's trip to England during the bombing, his strained friendship with a belligerent fellow writer resembling Hemingway, his strenuous efforts to develop "an American democratic theory" (*TGD*, p. 280) in a book not unlike *The Prospect Before Us*, and—in the novel's most effective passage—the sudden death of his wife. Dos Passos, like Ro, did in fact take a trip to Cuba with a younger woman. More important, though, Ro's feelings in Cuba of weariness, frustration, and isolation reflect Dos Passos's own despair in his later years; like Ro, he felt past the peak of his career, rejected by the public, "a back number" (*TGD*, p. 236). Perhaps, like Ro, he also hoped that some day, again, he "might be needed" (*TGD*, p. 312).

The Great Days, as Robert G. Davis points out, is too "uncomfortably personal." Unloved, unread, unappreciated, Ro Lancaster is crying out for sympathy and understanding. He has sacrificed a great deal for his country—spending much of the precious little time left with his wife away reporting on the war—only to be cast aside later for disagreeing with "the right thinkers" (*TGD*, p. 295). Whenever he publishes, he reminds himself, "the critics tear down his poor old name" (*TGD*, p. 2). There is no narrative distance from all this, unfortunately, and Ro's self-pity very quickly becomes Dos Passos's own. *The Great Days* is truly one of his saddest novels.[59]

Reinterpretations in the Fifties

His fiction alone could not contain Dos Passos's growing concern with his own past. In articles and interviews he had often touched upon the changes in his political views; in 1956, he published a short history of his ideas and activities from impetuous youth to sober old age. *The*

Theme Is Freedom combines excerpts from his journalism over the years with narrative passages that fill in the gaps and try to make sense of what he wrote long ago. There is some projection of current views on a former self[60] and some politically charged editing of past writing,[61] but in general *The Theme Is Freedom* is rather evenhanded as such difficult political autobiography goes.

Dos Passos proceeds in two contradictory ways in explaining his past radicalism. At times he seems to argue that not he but the world has changed, that all his life he has simply defended individual freedom against whatever *"vested interest"* (*TF*, p. 246) threatened it. Once, that vested interest was business; now the vested interests are government, trade unions, and communism.[62] He exaggerates the change in the nation and does not recognize enough in himself. Business, after all, has hardly vanished from the scene. In addition, individual freedom is an elusive concept, and valuing it does not define a political position very precisely, certainly not Dos Passos's; great political controversy swirls around just what "freedom" is and how best to establish it.

At the same time that he insists on the continuity of his thought, Dos Passos often disowns his earlier opinions, much as he does in *Chosen Country* and *Most Likely to Succeed*. In Spain in 1937, he now realizes, he was a *"blundering"* liberal, in Greenwich Village a narrowminded radical, and during the depression, *"too busy booing the capitalist bogyman to look into the facts very carefully"* (*TF*, pp. 115, 164, 101). No longer misled by manipulative Communists or by his own naïve enthusiasms, he sees clearly now, and objectively. This interpretation mixes uneasily with his claim of constancy, and the real dynamics of his political history—combining elements of both continuity and change—are more complex than anything Dos Passos himself offers. The hindsight in *The Theme Is Freedom* provides little real insight.

In the decades after World War II, Dos Passos's thinking about his own role as a writer changed as well. Once unsure of his place in the class struggle as a middle-class radical "wordslinger," he now settled comfortably into his duties as staunch defender of the republic. Once frustrated, perhaps, as a novelist, as merely a "second-class historian" of his age, he now, quite proudly, saw himself as a writer of history, "the greatest of the literary arts." But his journalism must have frequently disappointed him; written too often in a race with the bill collector, it rarely achieved the level Ro Lancaster aspired to, that of a "kind of journalism . . . that's between history and prophecy" (*TGD*, p. 68).[63]

Dos Passos also reinterpreted his own novels, or "contemporary chronicles," as he began to call them. He now regularly referred to his fiction, past and present, as satire and to himself as a "satirist." He suggested that a novel like *U.S.A.* is not realistic social criticism, but rather "a dark and garish picture" of human failings, and that his novels represent only the vaguest sort of political expression. They abound with ideological statements and implications, but only because such things are "part of the scene." Stung many times by narrow and vindictive political judgments of his fiction, alienated from the politics of his best novels, eager perhaps to avoid further partisan judgments of his writing, Dos Passos was understandably interested in characterizing his work as almost apolitically satirical. But the minor satiric elements in his novels do not change their essential character: sober, analytical, and above all deeply political.[64]

Some things from his past Dos Passos never questioned, however. His love of travel remained as strong as ever, and in the 1950s he visited Japan, Mexico, Brazil, and the western United States. Dos Passos also retained his old distrust of professional politicians, at least living ones. Though he voted—consistently Republican—and served in 1952 as honorary head of the Artists and Writers for Taft Committee, he thought election campaigns superficial and degrading. "If any American politician ever stopped grinning," he wrote in 1956, "all the TV sets would short-circuit, the blended tones on all the two-tone cars would begin to clash, everybody's shaving cream would turn to sand."[65] The old irreverent Dos Passos was still alive.

Strange Bedfellows: Dos Passos and the New Conservatives

Despite his irreverence, Dos Passos threw his name in with the circle of new conservative intellectuals that centered around William F. Buckley, Jr., and the *National Review*. The founding of the magazine struck him as a "bloodheating project," and, between 1956 and his death in 1970, Dos Passos contributed at least a dozen articles to it, as well as writing the introduction to Buckley's book, *Up from Liberalism*, and a "foreword" to *The American Cause*, by Russell Kirk. At a 1962

Young Americans for Freedom rally in Madison Square Garden, Dos Passos—along with Strom Thurmond, John Wayne, and others— proudly accepted a "Freedom Award." Two years later he enthusiastically supported Barry Goldwater for president. Dos Passos was a valuable feather in the conservatives' cap; eager to end his own political isolation, he gladly joined their cause. He took a liking to Buckley's "high spirits and sheer animal warmth."[66]

The conservatism of Buckley and the others is complicated and indeed contradictory. Allen Guttmann, in *The Conservative Tradition in America*, makes a useful distinction: he calls "Conservative" and "Liberal" the traditions of Burke and Locke respectively, and "conservative" and "liberal" the opposition to and the advocacy of change. Whereas Conservatives value tradition (especially religious tradition), community, and authority, Liberals value reason, individualism, and freedom. The *National Review*'s politics are a confusing mixture of Conservatism and Liberalism, but consistently conservative—that is, resistant to change, particularly change toward a more powerful central government. For example, while the magazine defends, as its "Credenda" state, "Truth" and "the organic moral order," it also champions free enterprise, in which individuals amorally pursue their self-interest and social decisions are made by the market place. The "victory" it demands against communism—for it finds coexistence "neither desirable nor possible, nor honorable"—can never be had by the weak central government it deems essential to freedom. Such contradictory views, whether between or within individuals associated with the *National Review*, are bound tightly together by an undying hatred of monolithic world communism and its paler cousin, modern liberalism. To quote Guttmann again: "the followers of Burke have joined the followers of Paine in order to combat programs they imagine to originate from Marx."[67]

Much in this awkward synthesis was contrary to Dos Passos's own political thinking. Although he had waxed soft on capitalism in his later years and had begun on occasion to invoke ethical and even "Christian" ideals, he scarcely shared Buckley's double faith in God and in "the omnicompetence of the free marketplace."[68] While Dos Passos often turned to the British and American tradition for inspiration, he never echoed Buckley's appeal to received or revealed sources of political principles; instead he put his faith in reason and hoped "first rate rigorous thinking" would bring solutions to social problems.

133

Dos Passos's political values were more individualistic, even anarchistic, and more deeply democratic than Buckley's; he disliked hierarchies, and praised, even idealized the "common man." As Diggins writes, a great gap lay between "Dos Passos's libertarian and Buckley's authoritarian conservatism."[69]

In fact, Dos Passos may have had as much in common with the libertarian socialist editors of *Liberation* as with Buckley and his colleagues. Four months after the *National Review* first appeared, Dave Dellinger, A. J. Muste, Bayard Rustin, and others announced, in the opening editorial of *Liberation*, their desire to bring socialism back into the "American tradition"—the tradition of Jefferson, Paine, Thoreau, Emerson, Debs, Bourne, and other American rebels. They rejected both liberal and Communist orthodoxy, insisted "means" were as important as "ends," and called for "decentralization" and the "direct participation of all workers or citizens in determining the conditions of life and work." This echoed Dos Passos's vision of the 1930s—*Liberation* was, in some ways, a descendent of the journal *Common Sense* he wrote for then—and even twenty years later his fundamental values were not so different from theirs. All the same, his blinding hatred of any individuals in any way resembling the *"Abominable Snowmen,"* as he now called Communists, put the socialist editors of *Liberation* on the opposite side of the barricades.[70]

Dos Passos's most important reason for allying himself with the *National Review* circle was no doubt their shared aversion toward modern liberalism. Both saw liberalism as the ruling ideology of the age, long unopposed at the presidential level until Goldwater ran in 1964—Eisenhower and Stevenson, for example, shared, if unequally, the urge to strengthen the federal government. Never finding Arthur Schlesinger, Jr.'s "vital center" very vital, Buckley denounced the federal government as a "gigantic, parasitic bureaucracy," and Dos Passos argued, with some justice, that "today's tired liberal idealism reflects the apathy and self-interest of the bureaucrat." Both perceived concentrated, centralized power as the main enemy, though neither Buckley nor Dos Passos, as simmering cold warriors, directed much criticism against what Eisenhower labeled "the military–industrial complex."[71] For Dos Passos at least, the answer was, all too simply, greater individual freedom.

But expanding freedom is anything but a simple process; and Dos Passos's search for freedom's foundations in the age of Jefferson did not prove very fruitful. In a nation of numerous independent small farmers, a weak central government may have meant more freedom than a strong one, and for white property owners, property itself made such freedom more secure. Dos Passos's too direct application of what he learned from Jefferson to an era of agribusiness and gargantuan corporations and banks made little sense. In a world of such powers, minimizing government would hardly leave the vast majority free. Few citizens have sufficient property to be independent, and real democracy and self-government are impossible where wealth and thus power are held so unequally. Moreover, to the extent that the New Deal and similar liberal programs mitigate social ills like poverty and unemployment, an attack on big government—particularly if combined with criticism of unions and a call to "forget the class war" (*PBU*, p. 367)—can become, however unwittingly, an insensitivity to such problems. Buckley, who cherished above all "the freedom of the individual to acquire property and dispose of that property in ways that he decides on,"[72] felt comfortable defending privilege; Dos Passos, still concerned with the dispossessed, with those forced to work for others' profit, was more troubled.

Dos Passos's plunge into historical studies led him away from a critical examination of contemporary historical reality. He saw limited government as the basis of freedom in part because he never examined very deeply the reasons why government grew. By blaming the expanding power of "the superstate we live in" on liberal ideology, on a satanic Roosevelt, as in *The Grand Design*, and on Communist propaganda, he ignored the dynamics of capitalist growth itself. War, depression, threats to overseas investments—all call for intervention by the state, which is itself influenced by increasingly powerful capitalist interests. An ahistorical application of Jeffersonian principles to postwar America can only mislead. As one writer puts it, "the classical liberal ideals . . . were wrecked on the realities of capitalist economic forms"; not the new conservatism, but "libertarian socialism" —or what Dos Passos himself called "humanitarian socialism"—is truly "the inheritor of the liberal ideals of the Enlightenment."[73]

Form and Content: *Midcentury*

As he grew older and as political disappointments accumulated, Dos Passos exhibited less and less of one essential ingredient of Enlighten-

135

ment thinking, its optimism. His conservatism resulted in part from his belief that American civilization was deteriorating, and thus change, which liberals advocated, would almost inevitably be for the worse. Such pessimism rumbles through *Midcentury* (1961),[74] the last novel Dos Passos published during his lifetime, and in many ways his best since *U.S.A.*. This long novel opens and closes with references to *"the century's decline"* (*MC*, pp. 4, 495), and its judgment of the postwar era is gloomy, almost lugubrious: *"Man drowns in his own scum. / These nights are dark"* (*MC*, p. 496).

Midcentury, as Dos Passos wrote a friend, is "a long documentary narrative in the (modified) manner of U.S.A."[75] Six fictional narratives, which share several characters and many themes, make up most of the novel. In addition, through biographies of public figures— Douglas MacArthur, Sam Goldwyn, Eleanor Roosevelt, and J. Robert Oppenheimer, among them—Dos Passos re-creates some of the historical context in which the narratives unfold and expresses directly, often with penetrating sarcasm, his own crusty opinions of the times. Numerous short "Documentary" sections assemble headlines and fragments from newspapers, magazines, and other sources. Whereas the more strictly chronological Newsreels of *U.S.A.* trace historical events, the Documentaries as a group simply develop certain themes: the absurdities of advertising, the corruption of unions, the trivial and amoral uses of advanced technological skills. In place of the lyrical, questioning, personal Camera Eye of *U.S.A.*, four short italicized prose poems present the rather impersonal musings of *"a man"* (*MC*, p. 3) walking his dog, his gloomy pronouncements on the human condition. In seven sets of "Investigator's Notes"—to which nothing in *U.S.A.* corresponds—victims of labor racketeering tell "the investigator" their painful stories. As in *U.S.A.*, juxtaposition creates meaning and the aim is to portray a society, not individuals.

Three of the six narratives bear directly on the novel's central theme: the degeneration of unions into oppressive organizations. In 1958, Dos Passos was permitted to see the files of John L. McClellan's Senate Select Committee on Improper Activities in the Labor and Management Fields. These "hair-raising" files, along with subsequent correspondence and discussions with union members, provided Dos Passos with endless stories of labor racketeering and other abuses, upon which much of *Midcentury* is based.[76] Idealistic Frank Worthington, for example, rises quickly in the novel to a position of union leadership, only to find himself isolated by bureaucratic tangles and corrupt fellow officials from the workers he represents. Terry Bryant helps establish a badly needed union in the rubber factory where he works, but gangsters quickly take it over and drive him out. Later, he is murdered while trying to fight a monopolistic taxi company controlled by businessmen and union bosses with close ties to organized crime. Metaphorically for Frank, literally for Terry, organization is death.

The emotional center of *Midcentury* is the deathbed reminiscing of Blackie Bowman, an old Wobbly who, like Dos Passos, once dreamed of "the cooperative commonwealth" (*MC*, p. 64). The only full-length first person narrative in the novel, intersecting none of the others, Blackie's story occupies a special place in *Midcentury*. His memories of IWW struggles, Greenwich Village, and the 1913 Paterson strikers' pageant in Madison Square Garden are more alive than anything else in the book. Through Blackie (who, like his creator, has a glass right eye), Dos Passos is expressing his own sense of betrayal; he criticizes contemporary unions most harshly by opposing to them the ideals and the sacrifices of those who fought for earlier unions. Along with the Investigator's Notes, occasional Documentaries, and caustic biographies of union leaders—Harry Bridges, John L. Lewis, Walter Reuther, and Teamsters Tobin, Beck, and Hoffa—the narratives of Blackie, Terry, and Frank strongly indict present-day large unions as at best undemocratic, at worst criminal.

Union members are not the only ones caught in the strangle hold of corrupt and tyrannical organization in *Midcentury*. Will Jenks, a bold young entrepreneur, buys the ailing Swiftservice Company for $100,000 and, believing that "everybody would benefit by competition" (*MC*, p. 445), he launches an aggressive campaign to challenge the near monopoly of his rival, Redtop. The gangsters who control Redtop, backed by union muscle, retaliate: they picket his business, burn his cabs, and kill one of his employees, Terry Bryant. In a parallel plot, Jasper Milliron, an executive in a nationwide milling corporation, falls victim to the machinations of more sophisticated gangsters. Through financial manipulation, Judge Lewin and others, greedy for power and profits, squelch his efforts to modernize, decentralize, and streamline the administration of company operations. Lewin, it turns out, has interests in Redtop as well. To him, all is "a problem in pure finance," his only concern, the bottom line. He explains at a dinner party: "I can't be distracted by worrying about administration, who gets fired from what job, all the grubby little lives involved" (*MC*, p. 475).

Such a mentality, Dos Passos suggests, rules America at midcentury. Not just individuals, but individual autonomy itself is imperiled. Organization threatens to destroy the rights of union members and the entrepreneurial energies and creative ideas of men like Will Jenks and Jasper Milliron. Institutions, as Dos Passos told a reporter the year he finished *Midcentury*, are turning people into ants.[77] All this contrasts sharply with the world of Blackie Bowman's reminiscences, a world much like that of *The 42nd Parallel*. Wobblies "were all leaders" (*MC*, p. 157), not pawns of union bosses; people were freer then and valued freedom more. Now, as Blackie reminds himself in his hospital bed, "there's no place left in this world for a philosophical anarchist" (*MC*, p. 60). The contrast is pessimistic as well as nostalgic; Dos Passos embraces individual self-government as a lost cause.

According to Dos Passos, America's culture is both responsible for and a reflection of the sorry state of its individuals and institutions. The proliferating consumer culture that the Documentaries endlessly illustrate is a culture of conformism, amorality, and shallow materialism. As technology promises to fulfill all desires, those desires—shaped by advertising campaigns—themselves become increasingly trivial and alienated. Freudian psychology further reduces the stature of human beings; by "dispos[ing] of thou shalt not" (*MC*, p. 30), it denies the individual responsibility for his or her own behavior. Though there is little evidence that Dos Passos studied Freud seriously, he knows what he dislikes.

The younger generation is the deplorable product of this culture. To show how far we have fallen, Dos Passos juxtaposes biographies of Major General William Frishe Dean, whose stiff moral fiber enabled him to resist three years of torture by his Communist captors in Korea, and of James Dean, the "sinister adolescent" (*MC*, p. 484) whose narcissism and resentment captured the imagination of millions of teenagers. Stan Goodspeed is one such teenager; in a brief monologue, the last of the six narratives, he describes the spree he went on with credit cards and cash he stole from Jasper Milliron, his uncle. Dos Passos becomes the stern puritan here—the sort of parental figure he once criticized in *Streets of Night*—as he attacks this decadent generation, spoiled by "wartime prosperity" (*MC*, p. 420). He seems to reach up toward religion as a solution when he writes of "God's spirit in man" (*MC*, p. 422), and he descends to platitudes as he reminds us that "right and wrong [is] the inner compass that points true north" (*MC*, p. 422). The dissection of a social system in *U.S.A.* had an intense moral force to it, but at its very weakest, *Midcentury*—like much of Dos Passos's later fiction—seems less a novel of social analysis than a tiresome tract.

Dos Passos's attack on American unions is more hortatory than analytical. As many reviewers quickly pointed out,[78] not all unions are run by gangsters, or even run undemocratically. But *Midcentury* presents unions as virtually the only source of working-class oppression, and freedom in the novel comes to mean the freedom not to join a union, that is, the open shop, a favored cause of the *National Review* circle. Blackie Bowman's memories suggest how difficult working can be without a union, but they serve primarily to condemn present practice by comparison with past ideals; imbued as they are with Blackie's (and Dos Passos's) nostalgia, they make the difficulties of the old days seem somehow wonderful. What we do not learn in the novel is how this romantic past became the hellish present; none of the narratives covers the transition, the depression and war years in which the large industrial unions were built. Dos Passos sheds little light on this historical process so essential to understanding the problems he attacks and instead dissolves them in abstractions: "*Man*," he writes, "*is a creature that builds institutions*" (*MC*, p. 119), institutions which inevitably stifle their creators. Elaborate sociobiological comparisons to the insect world (see *MC*, pp. 119–21) suggest even more strongly that biology is destiny, and social progress thus impossible.

Capitalist institutions escape criticism in *Midcentury*. Capitalist evils such as the tyrannical power of concentrated wealth are all embodied in the very minor figure of Judge Lewin, allowing Jasper Milliron, the executive, and Will Jenks, the risk capitalist, to emerge as sterling heroes. Class barriers tumble down as worker and boss face a common enemy, the racketeer. Will Jenks and his employee Terry Bryant, for example, contend only to see who can do more for their common cause: the Swiftservice taxi company. The suggestion that entrepreneurs and modernizing executives like Will and Jasper might limit the wages or speed up the labor of workers like Terry is carefully avoided. As in *The Prospect Before Us*, the struggle for self-government somehow unites all classes.

The denied divergence of class interests becomes clearer if we look at a source of Jasper Milliron's story in Dos Passos's journalism. The modernization Jasper struggles for, an engineer in *Midcentury* explains, would replace the miller's "rule of thumb by the rule of the dial" (*MC*, p. 322). In a 1950 report on General Mills that Dos Passos originally wrote for a company publication and reprinted in *The Prospect Before Us*, a plant manager carries his explanation further, suggesting the implications of such new techniques: "We want to replace the rule of thumb by the rule of the dial. The miller won't need his thumbs any more. We've cut off his thumbs. . . . There'll be no thumbs in the flour milling of the future" (*PBU*, p. 324). Skilled labor, in other words, will be replaced by more profitable but more alienated unskilled labor. In *The Prospect Before Us* Dos Passos raises briefly the question of the consequences for labor, for the miller, and even hints at its connection to the broader issue of democracy in corporate decision-making, but in *Midcentury* this troubling question is avoided, and we have an unqualified celebration of Jasper's efforts—a clear reversal from the scathing portrayal of F. W. Taylor in *U.S.A.*

Midcentury's celebration of the businessman clashes awkwardly with its condemnation of a business culture in the Documentaries and of Stan Goodspeed, the offspring of that culture. This is but one of the contradictions in the novel. While the Documentaries suggest the emptiness of technological progress in the absence of moral and social progress, Jasper Milliron emerges as heroic, though defeated, in his battle for modern milling techniques. At a deeper level, the detailing of social determinants of individual behavior in narratives, Documentaries, biographies, and Investigator's Notes runs counter to the descriptions in the prose poems of an immutable human nature. The heroism of most of the novel's major characters contradicts the near disgust with humanity expressed in the final pages, which end sarcastically with a dog's mistaken respect for "*man*" as the "*paragon of animals*" (*MC*, p. 496).

In *U.S.A.*, we saw a clash between an intense moral outrage at injustice and degraded behavior in capitalist America on one hand, and a deterministic depiction of how capitalism creates that injustice and shapes that behavior on the other. This clash creates a dramatic tension that animates the novel, that makes the struggle for a better world feel imperative to the reader. In *Midcentury* we have disorder, not tension. The interaction of opposing elements creates less counter-point than cacophony.

In its attempt to re-create the energy and excitement of *U.S.A.*, *Midcentury* falls short in other ways. The Documentaries lack the breadth and the punch of the Newsreels. The Investigator's Notes, often melodramatic, begin to repeat the narratives and each other. The prose poems, too Olympian in their generalizing, lack the energy, the sense of growth, and the dynamic interaction with other parts of the novel that make the Camera Eye so effective. Most obviously, *Midcentury* lacks the scope of *U.S.A.*: it documents specific problems, while *U.S.A.* re-creates an era; it rages against teenagers and racke-teers, while *U.S.A.* takes on an entire civilization. In this sense, the panoramic form of *Midcentury* matches its subject only imperfectly; its many-sided attack on corrupt unions, for example, is overkill. Much of the problem is that Dos Passos drew too heavily and somewhat in-discriminately on the McClellan files and on his own material in *The Prospect Before Us*.[79] *U.S.A.*, on the other hand, developed more organ-ically out of single, though certainly complex, vision.

Despite all this, *Midcentury* is Dos Passos's best novel in twenty-five years. The use of the form of *U.S.A.* in some sense liberates his talents. Several of the biographies—a type of narrative Dos Passos found con-genial—are as incisive as those of *U.S.A.*, and the variety of elements enlivens the novel. In addition, in *Midcentury* Dos Passos can allow himself to portray Blackie Bowman's early radicalism without rancor —and thus with considerable imagination and energy—in part be-cause he knows that other sections of *Midcentury* will counteract its po-litical implications. The composite structure enables Dos Passos to express more fully his contradictory feelings and thoughts. This, ironi-cally, makes for better art—however much it lacks overall coherence —than the rather narrow novels that precede *Midcentury*.

The forced optimism of *Number One*, the relentless degradation of *Most Likely to Succeed*, and the dreamy sentimentality of *Chosen Country* were each exaggerations of one aspect of Dos Passos's outlook at the time, each only partially true to his thinking. The deadening didacti-cism of *The Grand Design* and the almost embarrassing self-pity of *The Great Days* likewise resulted in part from a simple form that allowed Dos Passos to be carried away by anger or by despair. The highly structured form of *Midcentury* imposed a discipline on Dos Passos that

141

he needed and benefited from. However much it fell short of *U.S.A.*, *Midcentury* represented a significant improvement over the novels that came between. Harry T. Moore, reviewing *Midcentury* on the front page of the *New York Times Book Review*, ventured that Dos Passos, at sixty-five, had recovered "a long-lost reputation at a single stroke."[80]

The Frightening Sixties

Dos Passos's political views changed little over the last decade of his life. His hatreds grew more intense, as did his passion for an ever more elusive "individual freedom." His fears increasingly overshadowed his hopes, as they had done since the war. Many old friends were dismayed, saddened more than angered, by his public statements; Edmund Wilson wrote him that his writings on current events gave him "the creeps."[81]

Communist demons continued to haunt him through the 1960s, and "Communist" became for him the sort of "mindclosing label" he had criticized the party for using in the 1930s. Their propaganda, he wrote in 1964, had been "the dominant influence" in Washington for twenty years. Even his friend Wilson, when suggesting Alger Hiss and the Rosenbergs might not be guilty, sounded to Dos Passos like "another robot of the ventriloquists of Communist propaganda." Wilson, in turn, criticized Dos Passos for seeing "everything in terms of melodrama." Dos Passos wrote of "spiders anesthetiz[ing] their victims before devouring them," and elsewhere explained the radicalism of South American university students as a desire for big cars and meals in fancy restaurants. He saw Communist subversion everywhere, and, as he wrote a cousin in 1970, could not help "rejoicing" at times that he was "not likely to live much longer."[82]

Dos Passos feared Communists were behind the civil rights movement.[83] He had praised the *New Leader* in 1950 for attacking "racial discrimination," and, much later, he wrote sympathetically of Malcolm X. But he told an audience in 1964 that he did not think the current "agitation" was very useful. Dos Passos in fact found the civil rights movement "very depressing"; it had fallen "into the hands of very sinister people," and he feared racial war. He was in the awkward position of supporting civil rights, but rejecting the methods of the people struggling—whether legally or through civil disobedience

—for those rights. Like Buckley, he argued unrealistically that change should be implemented "at the local level."[84]

Dos Passos had no sympathy at all for New Leftists. He might have found their call for "a participatory democracy" appealing, had he been able to hear it, but to him they sounded like Communist puppets. He saw conspiracy all around, and he explained to *National Review* readers that it is "no accident" that "when part of a graduating class walks out on a speech at some American college the event coincides with the disturbances of certain self-styled Buddhists in Saigon." Dos Passos identified the New Left with the generation of decadent adolescents in *Midcentury*. Unable to accept their protest as legitimate, he saw it as "a tantrum of spoiled children." He was revolted by "the half naked people" at Woodstock who looked as if they had never "done a decent days work, plain physical labor, in their lives."[85]

Dos Passos railed against not only the "rank criminal idiocy of the younger generation," but also against higher taxes, lower moral standards, crime in the streets, and the media, especially television, which he blamed for making poverty a "political bogey" in a land of "almost universal affluence." He continued to denounce liberalism and to trace many problems to Roosevelt and the New Deal.[86] Among the few things that gave him hope were Barry Goldwater's presidential nomination, Ronald Reagan's "breezy common sense," Richard Nixon's invasion of Cambodia, and the Apollo moonshots. But in what he saw as "a nightmare world of violence and delusion,"[87] he had little political hope left.

Yet his own life remained vigorous and productive almost to the end. He wrote books about Brazil, Portugal, and Easter Island, and traveled to a great many other places. In addition to his historical studies and a children's book about Thomas Jefferson, he published two collections of his earlier work in the 1960s, and a memoir, *The Best Times*.[88]

Illness interrupted Dos Passos's last major project. "Congestive heart failure," he wrote friends in 1970, "is an uphill battle which you are sure to lose in the end." In *Century's Ebb*, the novel he never completed, he tries to resurrect Jay Pignatelli, hero of *Chosen Country*, and, in a biography, Walt Whitman as well. Dos Passos spitefully mocks leftists, liberals, believers in progressive education, permissive parents, and other symptoms of what he saw as the amorality of our age. Despite a half-hearted attempt to bring the novel to a joyful climax with

143

the second marriage of the autobiographical Pignatelli, *Century's Ebb* remains, as he wrote in a letter, "a last forlorn Chronicle of Despair." Dos Passos grew weaker over the summer of 1970, and his death in September ended what one critic called his "romantic, constantly disappointed love affair with the United States."[89]

Politics and the Writer

Dos Passos's memoir, *The Best Times*, ends in 1933. The first third of the century was indeed the best time of his life; he was doing his most creative work then, and the political vision that shaped that work was expansive and even hopeful. His youthful radical anger was developing into an informed passion for a "cooperative commonwealth"; and his fiction, particularly *U.S.A.*, depicted forces straining toward a new society within the decaying and deadening shell of the old. The future held promise that individual and collective action could put an end to injustice.

But in the years that followed—as fascism engulfed Europe, civil war crushed all hope in Spain, and communism increasingly betrayed socialist ideals—Dos Passos's expectations dwindled and his vision narrowed. The sweeping social criticism of *U.S.A.* and *Manhattan Transfer* gave way to the often mean-spirited carping of *The Grand Design* and *Most Likely to Succeed*. Nothing would revitalize him after he lost his early radical faith, neither his impractical Jeffersonian dreams nor his somewhat incongruous alliance with the conservative intellectuals of the *National Review*. While *Midcentury* reproduced the form of *U.S.A.*, it failed to recapture its energy and excitement. The best times were indeed over.

Throughout his long journey from left to right, a certain consistency characterizes Dos Passos's thinking. He first came to oppose capitalism through his distaste for industrialism and his hatred of war; later he came to accept American society through his hatred of communism, in which he saw many of the evils he once attributed to industrial capitalism itself: the concentration of power, the crushing of the individual, the aggression of war. The same intense individualism that gave rise to his radical criticism of the Communist party in the 1930s made him an enemy of the increasingly powerful and bureaucratic modern liberal state after the war. Through all his work runs an anger born of misplaced faith. Wilsonian liberalism, American Communists, trade unions, the New Deal, his country's efforts in World War II—all disappointed him. However much he yearned to love his "chosen country," he remained its tireless critic, always the rebel, ready to attack whatever he perceived to be "the interests." He continued to the end, as he wrote of Baroja, "to put the acid test to existing institutions." However "Colonel Blimpish" his later views became, his honesty, independence, and integrity remained.[90]

Most enduring, of course, is Dos Passos's fiction. In it, he grappled with the major political issues of his time and sought to lay bare the operations of an increasingly complex social system. So ambitious an undertaking was bound to succeed only partially, but more than any other American novelist of his generation, he did succeed—brilliantly in *U.S.A.*—in dramatizing the ways, subtle as well as brutal, in which history shapes the lives of individuals. His work as a whole remains an enormously valuable and fascinating chronicle of a turbulent age and of the sensibility of a passionate, decent, immensely curious man trying to understand and to survive it.

NOTES

Preface

1. "Dos Passos: 'No secret Formula For Truth,' " *New Haven Register*, 9 May 1965.

2. Jeffrey Hart, "John Dos Passos," *National Review* 19 (24 January 1967): 96; George Stade, "The Two Faces of Dos Passos," *Partisan Review* 41 (1974): 483; George A. Knox and Herbert M. Stahl, *Dos Passos and "The Revolting Playwrights"* (Uppsala, Sweden: Uppsala University Press, 1964), p. 39; Martin Kallich, "John Dos Passos: Liberty and the Father-Image," *Antioch Review* 10 (March 1950): 106; Robert Gorham Davis, *John Dos Passos*, University of Minnesota Pamphlets on American Literature, no. 20 (Minneapolis: University of Minnesota Press, 1962), p. 44.

3. Melvin Landsberg, *Dos Passos' Path to "U.S.A.": A Political Biography 1912–1936* (Boulder: Colorado Associated University Press, 1972); Townsend Ludington, ed., *The Fourteenth Chronicle: Letters and Diaries of John Dos Passos* (Boston: Gambit, 1973) (hereafter cited as *TFC*); Townsend Ludington, *John Dos Passos: A Twentieth Century Odyssey* (New York: Dutton, 1980) (hereafter cited as *TCO*).

4. The full-length literary studies are: John H. Wrenn, *John Dos Passos*, Twayne's United States Authors Series (New Haven: College and University Press, 1961); John D. Brantley, *The Fiction of John Dos Passos* (The Hague: Mouton, 1968); George J. Becker, *John Dos Passos* (New York: Frederick Ungar, 1974); Iain Colley, *Dos Passos and the Fiction of Despair* (Totowa, N.J.: Rowman and Littlefield, 1978); and Linda W. Wagner, *Dos Passos: Artist as American* (Austin: University of Texas Press, 1979). Dos Passos is one of four radicals-turned-conservative studied by historian John P. Diggins in his *Up From Communism: Conservative Odysseys in American Intellectual History* (New York:

Harper and Row, 1975). Quote in text is from p. 97. Knox and Stahl's book (see note 2 above) is a highly specialized study which discusses Dos Passos's plays and his work with the New Playwrights Theatre group in the late 1920s. In addition, there is, in French, Georges-Albert Astre, *John Dos Passos: de "L'Initiation d'un homme" à "U.S.A."* (Paris: Lettres Modernes, 1974). Two brief studies are Bianca Tedeschini Lalli, *John Dos Passos*, pamphlet series *Il castoro*, no. 21 (Florence: La Nuova Italia, 1974), in Italian; and Davis's *John Dos Passos* (see note 2 above).

Chapter One

1. Quoted in Daniel Aaron, "The Riddle of John Dos Passos," *Harpers* 224 (March 1962): 56.
2. JDP, *The Best Times: An Informal Memoir* (New York: New American Library, 1966), p. 15 (hereafter cited as *Best Times*). The best sources of biographical information on Dos Passos are *Best Times, TFC, TCO,* and Landsberg, *Dos Passos' Path.*
3. See Kallich, "Father-Image," pp. 99–106; Blanche H. Gelfant, "The Search for Identity in the Novels of John Dos Passos," *PMLA* 76 (March 1961): 133–49; and Diggins, *Communism,* pp. 93–97 passim.
4. JDP, "P.S. to Dean Briggs," in *College in a Yard: Minutes by Thirty-Nine Harvard Men,* ed. Brooks Atkinson (Cambridge: Harvard University Press, 1957), p. 64. For a useful overview of Dos Passos's years at Harvard, see Charles W. Bernardin, "Dos Passos' Harvard Years," *New England Quarterly* 27 (March 1954): 3–26.
5. Thomas R. Edwards, "Dos Passos Divided," *New York Review of Books,* 29 November 1973, p. 28; JDP to Rumsey Marvin, 28 August 1915, in *TFC,* p. 24; JDP to Marvin, 29 May 1916, in *TFC,* p. 37.
6. The words are Stewart Mitchell's, recalling his college friend. Quoted in Landsberg, *Dos Passos' Path,* p. 20. On Dos Passos's early *Harvard Monthly* stories, see ibid., pp. 24–31, and Colley, *Fiction of Despair,* pp. 13–17.
7. JDP, "Un Grand Journaliste: John Reed," *Le Monde,* 18 January 1930, p. 3 (my translation). See JDP, review of *Insurgent Mexico* by Jack Reed, *Harvard Monthly* 59 (November 1914): 67–68; JDP, review of *The War in Eastern Europe* by Jack Reed, *Harvard Monthly* 62 (July 1916): 148–49.
8. [John Dos Passos], "Summer Military Camps: Two Views. I," *Harvard Monthly* 60 (July 1915): 156, quoted in Landsberg, *Dos Passos' Path,* p. 41; JDP, "The World Decision," *Harvard Monthly* 62 (March 1916): 23; JDP, "A Conference on Foreign Relations," *Harvard Monthly* 62 (June 1916): 126–27.
9. JDP, "A Humble Protest," *Harvard Monthly* 62 (June 1916): 116 (hereafter cited as HP).
10. JDP to McComb, 26 August 1916, quoted in Landsberg, *Dos Passos' Path,* p. 48.
11. JDP to Rumsey Marvin, 23 April 1916, in *TFC,* p. 35; JDP, "Against American Literature," *New Republic* 8 (14 October 1916): 269 (hereafter cited

as AAL). On the derivative nature of AAL, see *TCO*, p. 93.

12. JDP, "Young Spain," *Seven Arts* 2 (August 1917): 475–76 (hereafter cited as YS).

13. J. Joseph Huthmacher, *Trial by War and Depression: 1917–1941* (Boston: Allyn and Bacon, 1973), p. 26; JDP to Rumsey Marvin, April 1917, quoted in *TCO*, p. 120; JDP to Arthur K. McComb, n.d., quoted in Landsberg, *Dos Passos' Path*, p. 52.

14. JDP to Rumsey Marvin, 30 July 1916, in *TFC*, p. 44; JDP to Arthur K. McComb, n.d., quoted in Landsberg, *Dos Passos' Path*, p. 51; JDP to Rumsey Marvin, 12 December 1916, in *TFC*, pp. 60–61.

15. *TCO*, p. 121; JDP to E. E. Cummings, 14 September [1918], Houghton Library, Harvard University, Cambridge, Mass. For a vivid description of Dos Passos's first days at the front, see *TCO*, pp. 131–38.

16. JDP to Arthur K. McComb, 20 July 1917, quoted in Landsberg, *Dos Passos' Path*, p. 56; JDP to McComb, 10 August 1917, quoted in ibid., p. 56; JDP, "P.S. to Dean Briggs," p. 66; JDP to Rumsey Marvin, 23 August 1917, in *TFC*, p. 92; JDP to McComb, 27 August 1917, quoted in Landsberg, *Dos Passos' Path*, p. 56.

17. Quotes from JDP, diary entry, 15 January 1918, in *TFC*, p. 128; and JDP to José Giner Pantoja, February–March, 1918, in *TFC*, p. 152 (Ludington's translation from French). For interpretations that ground Dos Passos's hatred for authority in his relationship with his father, see Gelfant, "Search for Identity"; and Kallich, "Father-Image."

18. JDP to Arthur K. McComb, 7 May 1918, quoted in Landsberg, *Dos Passos' Path*, p. 58; *Best Times*, p. 70.

19. JDP, *One Man's Initiation—1917* (London: George Allen and Unwin, 1920; reprint ed., Ithaca: Cornell University Press, 1969); hereafter cited as *OMI*. The 1969 edition is, unlike the 1920 edition, unexpurgated. The novel was initially a continuation of *Seven Times Round the Walls of Jericho*, an unpublished novel Dos Passos began in France with Robert Hillyer, and which is discussed in Wagner, *Dos Passos*, pp. 27–29.

20. John Chamberlain, "John Dos Passos," *Saturday Review of Literature* 20 (3 June 1939): 4. On the "unnatural" character of the war in the novel, see Landsberg, *Dos Passos' Path*, p. 59.

21. John W. Aldridge, *After The Lost Generation: A Critical Study of the Writers of Two Wars* (New York: McGraw-Hill, 1951), p. 60. On the literary influences on *OMI*, see Landsberg, *Dos Passos' Path*, pp. 62–63. Quote from JDP, diary entry, 14 January 1918, in *TFC*, p. 127.

22. Richard Stover Donnell argues, interestingly, that a conservative Dos Passos changed the title of *One Man's Initiation—1917* to *First Encounter* when reissuing it in order to emphasize the error of his earlier views: "By 1945, Dos Passos had decided that his hero's initiation into radical politics was not a discovery of reality but only a first step in an educational process." See "John Dos Passos: Satirical Historian of American Morality" (Ph.D. diss., Harvard University, 1960), p. 817 n. 33. Donnell's 977-page dissertation is a valuable source of information about Dos Passos and his work.

23. He called himself "un petit mouton du troupeau de Maman Liberté," a little sheep in Mother Liberty's flock. Maman Liberté, of course, had recently married "M. Militarisme." JDP to E. E. Cummings [September–November, 1918], Humanities Research Center, University of Texas, Austin, Texas. The quote about the "rights of the governed" is from JDP, diary entry, 30 August 1918, in *TFC*, p. 208. According to Landsberg, *Dos Passos' Path*, p. 65, Dos Passos wrote, in a 5 October 1918 letter to Arthur K. McComb, "that he repeated the words 'Organization is death' over and over again—in anagrams and in different languages." Four days earlier, 1 October 1918, he had written in his diary, "Organization kills" *(TFC,* p. 213).

24. JDP to Arthur K. McComb, n.d., quoted in Landsberg, *Dos Passos' Path*, pp. 64–65; JDP, diary entry, 7 October 1918, in *TFC*, p. 219; JDP, diary entry, 15 November 1918, in *TFC*, p. 230; JDP to Thomas P. Cope, 15 May 1920, in *TFC*, p. 293.

25. JDP, "In Portugal," *Liberator* 3 (April 1920): 25; JDP to Marvin, 2 January 1920, in *TFC*, p. 276.

26. JDP to Marvin, June 1919, in *TFC*, pp. 253–54; JDP to Stewart Mitchell, 17 February 1920, in *TFC*, p. 281.

27. JDP, *Three Soldiers* (1921; reprint ed., New York: Modern Library, 1932); hereafter cited as *TS*.

28. For an exhaustive examination of the theme of the machine in all Dos Passos's fiction, see Brantley, *Fiction of Dos Passos*.

29. JDP to McComb, February [1920], John Dos Passos Papers, Alderman Library, University of Virginia, Charlottesville (collection cited hereafter as JDP Papers, Virginia).

30. Apparently in order to ensure the reader's ironic distance from Fuselli, Dos Passos disrupts the formal pattern of *Three Soldiers*. Parts 1 and 2 are narrated from Fuselli's viewpoint, part 3 from Chrisfield's, and parts 4, 5, and 6 from Andrews's. However, twelve pages into part 1, Dos Passos inserts two chapters from Andrews's point of view. These serve to distance us from Fuselli, particularly since Andrews's appealing sensibility represents a criticism of the degraded mediocrity of Fuselli's.

31. Malcolm Cowley, "The Poet and the World," *New Republic* 70 (27 April 1932): 303, 304.

32. Henry Seidel Canby, review of *Three Soldiers*, *New York Evening Post Book Review*, 8 October 1921, p. 67.

33. George D. Snell, *Shapers of American Fiction, 1789–1947* (New York: Dutton, 1947), p. 250; John Peale Bishop, *The Collected Essays of John Peale Bishop*, ed. Edmund Wilson (New York: Scribners, 1948), pp. 233, 232; A. Hamilton Gibbs, review of *Three Soldiers*, *Freeman* 4 (30 November 1921): 283; W. C. Blum, review of *Three Soldiers*, *Dial* 71 (November 1921): 608.

34. Coningsby Dawson, review of *Three Soldiers*, *New York Times*, 2 October 1921, sec. 3, quotes on p. 17 and p. 1; "Another War Book—and the Worst," *New York Times*, 3 October 1921, p. 12; "An American Soldier on 'Three Soldiers,'" *New York Times*, 15 October 1921, p. 15; Harold Norman Denny, re-

view of *Three Soldiers*, *New York Times*, 16 October 1921, sec. 3, p. 1; "Mr. Denny's Record," *New York Times*, 23 October 1921, sec. 3, p. 30. Denny seems to have wanted very badly to make his joke about the yellow dust jacket of *Three Soldiers*. Jack Potter calls the jacket "orange," in *A Bibliography of John Dos Passos* (Chicago: Normandie House, 1950), p. 19 (hereafter cited as Potter). Reviewing *Three Soldiers* in the official VFW magazine, Norman Shannon Hall—who served in the army too, and "didn't whine"—wrote that Dos Passos himself "should be locked up" ("John Dos Passos Lies!" *Foreign Service* 10 [November 1921]: 11).

35. "His Defense Far From Adequate," *New York Times*, 2 March 1922, p. 20 (this editorial statement quotes Dos Passos's responses); JDP to Rumsey Marvin, June 1917, in *TFC*, p. 75.

36. JDP, "America and the Pursuit of Happiness," *Nation 111* (29 December 1920): 777. On 1919 and the Palmer Raids, see David A. Shannon, *Between the Wars: America, 1919–1941* (Boston: Houghton Mifflin, 1965), pp. 26–29; and Landsberg, *Dos Passos' Path*, pp. 79–83.

37. JDP to Marvin, November 1920, in *TFC*, p. 306; JDP to Marvin, April–May 1921, in *TFC*, p. 309.

38. JDP, "America and the Pursuit of Happiness," pp. 777–78.

39. JDP, *Rosinante to the Road Again* (New York: George H. Doran, 1922); hereafter cited as *RRA*.

40. See, for example, Edmund Wilson, *The Twenties: From Notebooks and Diaries of the Period*, ed. Leon Edel (New York: Farrar, Straus and Giroux, 1975), p. 207. Dos Passos, with a friend, did watch Pastora Imperio in Madrid and then try to walk to Toledo. See *TCO*, pp. 105–6.

41. JDP, "Barcelona of the Bombs," [1920], p. 4, JDP Papers, Virginia. On Dos Passos as anarchist, see David Sanders, "The 'Anarchism' of John Dos Passos," *South Atlantic Quarterly* 60 (Winter 1961): 44–55.

42. JDP to Thomas P. Cope, January 1922, in *TFC*, p. 344; Michael Gold sees a very strong escapist impulse behind Dos Passos's perpetual traveling. Dos Passos, he writes, "devoured oceans and continents searching for heart's-ease. Tourism was a spiritual malady that beset literary youth everywhere after the war. It was the beating of singed wings, a longing for escape from tremendous social realities" ("The Education of John Dos Passos," *English Journal* 22 [February 1933]: 92). As Ludington sees it, "travel was a palliative; Dos Passos tried to mask his inhibitions by traveling—or probably it was that he hoped to overcome them" (*TCO*, p. 184). Wagner sees Dos Passos's travel (and travel writing) in this period as perhaps "one way of avoiding a direct confrontation with the serious fiction that somehow managed, he then felt, to elude him" (*Dos Passos*, p. 32).

43. JDP to McComb, 27 August 1921, quoted in Landsberg, *Dos Passos' Path*, p. 95; JDP to Robert Hillyer, 10 January 1922, in *TFC*, p. 346; JDP to Stewart Mitchell, 10 December 1921, in *TFC*, p. 331; JDP to Rumsey Marvin, 5 November 1921, in *TFC*, p. 324.

44. JDP, *Orient Express* (New York: Harper and Brothers, 1927; reprint ed., New York: Jonathan Cape and Harrison Smith, 1930); hereafter cited as

151

OE. Quotes from *OE* in text are from sections originally published in 1921 or 1922, unless otherwise indicated.

45. Elsie Weil, review of *Orient Express, New York Herald Tribune Books*, 1 May 1927, p. 19.

46. JDP, "The Caucasus Under the Soviets," *Liberator* 5 (August 1922): 5–8. Quotes from pp. 8, 7.

47. Davis, *John Dos Passos*, p. 14; Becker, *John Dos Passos*, p. 33.

48. JDP, *A Pushcart at the Curb* (New York: George H. Doran, 1922), pp. 42, 116, 195. For a more detailed discussion of Dos Passos's poetry, see Wagner, *Dos Passos*, pp. 3–10.

49. *TCO*, p. 202; JDP to Robert Hillyer, February–March 1923, in *TFC*, p. 354. Dos Passos's art was exhibited in January, 1923. He also did paintings and sketches for several books, including *A Pushcart at the Curb, Orient Express, The Garbage Man, Manhattan Transfer*, a 1923 translation of *The Quest* by Pío Baroja, and his own translation of Blaise Cendrars's *Panama; or, The Adventures of My Seven Uncles* (New York: Harper and Brothers, 1931).

50. Frederick J. Hoffman, *The Twenties: American Writing in the Postwar Decade*, rev. ed. (New York: Free Press, 1962), pp. 39–40; Malcolm Cowley, *Exile's Return: A Literary Odyssey of the 1920's* (1934; rev. ed., New York: Viking Press, 1951), pp. 61–62.

51. John P. Diggins, *The American Left in the Twentieth Century* (New York: Harcourt Brace Jovanovich, 1973), p. 73; Floyd Dell, *Homecoming* (New York, 1930), p. 251, quoted in Diggins, *American Left*, p. 80; Malcolm Cowley, *Exile's Return*, quoted in Hoffman, *The Twenties*, p. 37. On the isolation of radical intellectuals, see Christopher Lasch, *The Agony of the American Left* (New York: Alfred A. Knopf, 1969), pp. 43–47.

52. Hoffman, *The Twenties*, p. 43.

53. Bruce Barton, *The Man Nobody Knows* (Indianapolis: Bobbs-Merrill, 1925), from preface, "How it Came to Be Written," [n.p.].

54. *Best Times*, p. 135; JDP, review of *The Enormous Room* by E. E. Cummings, in *Philadelphia Ledger*, 27 May 1922, quoted in Landsberg, *Dos Passos' Path*, p. 242 n. 32; JDP, review of *The Enormous Room* by E. E. Cummings, in *Dial* 73 (July 1922): 98; JDP to Rumsey Marvin, 2 August [1919] in *TFC*, p. 257. On Dos Passos's inhibitions, see also *TCO*, pp. 218–20.

55. See JDP to John Howard Lawson, 11 October 1920, in *TFC*, p. 301.

56. JDP, *The Garbage Man: A Parade with Shouting* (New York: Harper and Brothers, 1926); reprinted in JDP, *Three Plays* (New York: Harcourt, Brace, 1934); hereafter cited as *TP*. An earlier manuscript version is titled "The Garbage Man: A Ballet of Shouting" (JDP Papers, Virginia). Quote from Wilson, *The Twenties*, p. 323.

57. JDP, *The Garbage Man*, p. 159.

58. Terry Eagleton, *Marxism and Literary Criticism* (Berkeley: University of California Press, 1976), pp. 25, 26.

59. Karl Marx, *Capital*, trans. Samuel Moore and Edward Aveling (1889; reprint ed., New York: International Publishers, 1947), p. 216. Landsberg, *Dos Passos' Path*, p. 150, mentions that Dos Passos read *Capital* after the war.

NOTES (pp. 38–43)

60. According to Shannon, *Between the Wars*, p. 85, in the postwar depression year of 1921, 4,750,000 were unemployed.

61. JDP, *Streets of Night* (New York: George H. Doran, 1923), pp. 155, 149 (hereafter cited as *SON*). Edwards, "Dos Passos Divided," p. 28, observes that "the voluminous letters to [Rumsey] Marvin are colored with the tones and imagery of a no doubt theoretical and literary homoeroticism" and that a 1919 letter to Marvin "seems to reflect strong anxiety about sex and physical manliness ('kisses and fighting') in his early life." Fanshaw is also the forerunner of several quite stereotyped homosexual characters, male and female, to appear in Dos Passos's novels: the Communist villains, for example, in *The Grand Design*, and Oglethorpe, Ellen's first husband, in *Manhattan Transfer*.

62. JDP quoted in Edmund Wilson to F. Scott Fitzgerald, 26 May 1922, in Edmund Wilson, *Letters on Literature and Politics 1912–1972*, ed. Elena Wilson (New York: Farrar, Straus and Giroux, 1977), p. 85.

63. David L. Vanderwerken, in "Dos Passos' *Streets of Night*: A Reconsideration," *Markham Review* 4 (October 1974): 61, points to an "id" figure for each major character that complements these "superego" figures: Wenny for Fanshaw, Whitey the hobo for Wenny, and Mabel Worthington, the adventurous fellow Fadette, for Nan.

64. See JDP to Edmund Wilson, 12 January 1924, in *TFC*, p. 355.

65. JDP, *The Theme is Freedom* (New York: Dodd, Mead, 1956; reprint ed., Freeport, New York: Books for Libraries Press, 1970), p. 41 (hereafter cited as *TF*). Dos Passos mentions, among others, the following influences on *Manhattan Transfer*: the Italian futurists, Rimbaud, Blaise Cendrars, Pío Baroja, and Emile Verhaeren. See Landsberg, *Dos Passos' Path*, pp. 113, 117; David Sanders, "The Art of Fiction XLIV" (interview with JDP), *Paris Review* 46 (Spring 1969): 155; JDP, "Contemporary Chronicles," *Carleton Miscellany* 2 (Spring 1961): 26; Jules Chametzky, "Reflections on *U.S.A.* as Novel and Play," *Massachusetts Review* 1 (Winter 1960): 392–94; and Charles F. Madden, ed., *Talks with Authors* (Carbondale: Southern Illinois University Press, 1968), p. 4.

66. Gold, "The Education of John Dos Passos," p. 93.

67. Colley, *Fiction of Despair*, p. 49.

68. Quote from Allen Belkind, ed., *Dos Passos, the Critics, and the Writer's Intention* (Carbondale: Southern Illinois University Press, 1971), p. xxxiv. Joseph Warren Beach, *American Fiction: 1920–1940* (New York: MacMillan, 1941), p. 50, sees in the novel "not a story in the traditional sense . . . [but] an abstract composition of story elements made to develop a series of themes." On the form of *Manhattan Transfer*, see also Blanche H. Gelfant, *The American City Novel* (Norman: University of Oklahoma Press, 1954), pp. 133–74; and E. D. Lowry, "The Lively Art of *Manhattan Transfer*," *PMLA* 84 (October 1969): 1628–38.

69. Gelfant, *American City Novel*, p. 160. For a discussion of the influence of *The Waste Land* on *Manhattan Transfer*, see E. D. Lowry, *Manhattan Transfer*: Dos Passos' Wasteland," *University Review* (Kansas City) 30 (October 1963): 47–52.

153

70. JDP, *Manhattan Transfer* (1925; reprint ed., Boston: Houghton Mifflin, 1953), p. 10 (hereafter cited as *MT*).

71. Eugene Arden, *"Manhattan Transfer*: An Experiment in Technique," *University of Kansas City Review* 22 (Winter 1955): 154.

72. D. H. Lawrence, review of *Manhattan Transfer*, in *The Portable D. H. Lawrence*, ed. Diana Trilling (New York: Viking, 1947), p. 643. In a letter to John Peale Bishop, 15 January 1924, Edmund Wilson writes that Dos Passos is "from the rumors I hear, experimenting with the amorous pastimes and entanglements from which he has withheld, I should say, all too long" (Wilson, *Letters*, p. 119).

73. Dos Passos seems to have found this image of nonconformity compelling: he also uses it in *The Garbage Man* (*TP*, p. 70).

74. Charles Child Walcutt, *American Literary Naturalism, A Divided Stream* (Minneapolis: University of Minnesota Press, 1956), pp. 280–89, argues the novel's naturalism most strongly. Quote from Paul Elmer More, *The Demon of the Absolute* (Princeton: Princeton University Press, 1928), p. 63. On the symbolism in *Manhattan Transfer*, see Gelfant, *American City Novel*, pp. 152–59. For an extended discussion of the novel's imagery, see Sharon Fusselman Mizener, *Manhattan Transients* (Hicksville, N.Y.: Exposition Press, 1977), pp. 23–38.

75. Beach, *American Fiction*, p. 41.

76. For the opposite view, see Becker, *John Dos Passos*, p. 53; and Gelfant, *American City Novel*, p. 148.

77. In Deming Brown, *Soviet Attitudes Toward American Writing* (Princeton: Princeton University Press, 1962), p. 84; Astre, *John Dos Passos*, p. 141 (my translation); Michael Millgate, *American Social Fiction: James to Cozzens* (Edinburgh: Oliver and Boyd, 1964), p. 140; H. Seebuhr, "Writer Too Shy to Speak in Public," *Brooklyn Sunday Eagle Magazine*, 19 September 1926, quoted in Donnell, "John Dos Passos," p. 847 n. 7; Edmund Wilson, "Dos Passos and the Social Revolution," *New Republic* (17 April 1929), reprinted in Edmund Wilson, *A Literary Chronicle: 1920–1950* (Garden City, N. Y.: Doubleday, 1956), p. 130.

78. Mason Wade, "Novelist of America: John Dos Passos," *North American Review* 244 (Winter 1937–38): 355.

Chapter Two

1. JDP to Robert Cantwell, September 1934, in *TFC*, p. 442.

2. JDP, "Abd El Krim," *New Masses* 1 (July 1926): 21; JDP, *Best Times*, p. 163.

3. JDP, "300 N.Y. Agitators Reach Passaic," *New Masses* 1 (June 1926): 8.

4. JDP, "The New Masses I'd Like," *New Masses* 1 (June 1926): 20; Michael Gold, "Let It Be Really New!" *New Masses* 1 (June 1926): 20.

5. Cowley, *Exile's Return*, p. 223. Dos Passos is listed as an executive board member from the first issue through the issue of 2 January 1934. See Potter, p. 90.

6. See Daniel Aaron, *Writers on the Left: Episodes in American Literary Communism* (New York: Harcourt, Brace and World, 1961), pp. 96–102, esp. p. 100; and Joseph Freeman, *An American Testament: A Narrative of Rebels and Romantics* (New York: Farrar and Rinehart, 1936), pp. 378–82.

7. JDP, "The Pit and the Pendulum," *New Masses* 1 (August 1926): 10–11, 30; JDP, *Facing the Chair: Story of the Americanization of Two Foreignborn Workmen* (Boston: Sacco-Vanzetti Defense Committee, 1927) (hereafter cited as *FTC*); Nicola Sacco to Leonard Abbott, 1 April 1927, in *The Letters of Sacco and Vanzetti*, ed. Marion Denman Frankfurter and Gardner Jackson (New York: Viking, 1928), p. 50.

8. See Felix Frankfurter, *The Case of Sacco and Vanzetti* (1927; reprint ed., New York: Grosset and Dunlap, 1962); Herbert B. Ehrmann, *The Case That Will Not Die: Commonwealth vs. Sacco & Vanzetti* (Boston: Little, Brown, 1969).

9. JDP, *U.S.A.: The Big Money* (New York: Modern Library, [1939]), p. 462. Hasty composition of *FTC* is suggested by a comparison of pages 64 and 69, where Dos Passos virtually repeats himself, twice reusing material from "The Pit and the Pendulum."

10. "An Open Letter to President Lowell," *Nation* 125 (24 August 1927): 176; "Foreword," in *Walled in This Tomb: Questions Left Unanswered by the Lowell Committee in the Sacco-Vanzetti Case And Their Pertinence in Understanding the Conflicts Sweeping the World at This Hour: For Especial Consideration by the Alumni of Harvard University During Its Tercentenary Celebration* (Boston: Excelsior Press, [1936]), pp. 3–5; signed by twenty-eight Harvard alumni, including Dos Passos.

11. Frederick Lewis Allen, *Only Yesterday: An Informal History of the 1920s* (1931; reprint ed., New York: Harper and Row, 1964), p. 70; JDP to Edmund Wilson, 19 September 1927, in *TFC*, p. 371. John D. Baker summarizes the rather confusing *New York Times* accounts of Dos Passos's arrests in "Italian Anarchism and the American Dream—The View of John Dos Passos," in *Italian American Radicalism—Old World Origins and New World Developments* (Proceedings of the Fifth Annual Conference of the American Italian Historical Association, November 11, 1972), p. 33.

12. JDP, "Sacco and Vanzetti," *New Masses* 3 (November 1927): 25; JDP to Germaine Lucas-Championnière, April 1928, quoted in *TCO*, p. 265. See also Dos Passos's poem on Sacco and Vanzetti, "They Are Dead Now," *New Masses* 3 (October 1927): 7.

13. JDP, *Airways, Inc.* (New York: Macaulay, 1928); hereafter cited as *AI*. A somewhat revised version appears in *Three Plays*. For a detailed history of the New Playwrights Theatre, see Knox and Stahl, *Dos Passos*.

14. See JDP, "The Misadventures of 'Deburau,' " *Freeman* 2 (2 February 1921): 498; and also his Foreword to John Howard Lawson, *Roger Bloomer: A Play in Three Acts* (New York: Thomas J. Seltzer, 1923), pp. v–viii.

15. Production "Note" to JDP, *The Garbage Man: A Parade with Shouting* (New York: Harper and Brothers, 1926), p. 159; JDP, "Is the 'Realistic' Theatre Obsolete?" *Vanity Fair* 24 (May 1925): 64; Knox and Stahl, *Dos Passos*, p. 67.

16. Knox and Stahl, *Dos Passos*, p. 31 (see also pp. 16–20); JDP, "They Want Ritzy Art," *New Masses* 4 (June 1928): 8; JDP, "Propaganda in the Theatre," *Daily Worker*, 30 April 1927, quoted in Thomas Richard Gorman, "Words and Deeds: A Study of the Political Attitudes of John Dos Passos" (Ph.D. diss., University of Pennsylvania, 1960), p. 63; JDP, "They Want Ritzy Art"; JDP, "Towards a Revolutionary Theatre," *New Masses* 3 (December 1927): 20. See also Dos Passos's letters to the editor of the *Daily Worker*, 20 January 1928, p. 4, and 28 January 1928, p. 6.

17. Landsberg, *Dos Passos' Path*, p. 150.

18. JDP, "The New Masses I'd Like," p. 20.

19. JDP, *Three Plays*, p. 158.

20. JDP, *Three Plays*, p. 158; JDP to Germaine Lucas-Championnière, April 1929, quoted in *TCO*, p. 276; Richard Watts, Jr., review of production of *Airways, Inc.*, *New York Herald Tribune*, 21 February 1929, p. 19; Knox and Stahl, *Dos Passos*, pp. 174–75; advertisement for "Daily Worker Benefit Performances" on February 21, 22, and 23, *Daily Worker*, 21 February 1929; A. B. Magil, " 'Airways,' Inc. [*sic*] Is Best Play Produced by New Playwrights," *Daily Worker*, 23 February 1929, p. 4; Michael Gold, "The Education of John Dos Passos," p. 95; Edmund Wilson, "Dos Passos and the Social Revolution," in *Literary Chronicle*, pp. 128–29.

21. *TCO*, p. 277; JDP to John Howard Lawson and Francis Edward Faragoh, March 1929, in *TFC*, p. 390. Edmund Wilson relates Dos Passos's breaking with the New Playwrights Theatre to their "trying to high-hat him by giving him to understand that *Airways* was insufficiently social-revolutionary, while he on his part had certainly made a supreme effort to be as social-revolutionary as possible!" Edmund Wilson to John Peale Bishop, 7 August 1929, in Wilson, *Letters*, p. 167.

22. JDP, "Did the New Playwrights Theatre Fail?" *New Masses* 5 (August 1929): 13; JDP, "American Theatre: 1930–31," *New Republic* 66 (1 April 1931): 175; JDP, reply to a questionnaire, in "Prospects for the American Theatre," *New Theatre* (New York) 1 (February 1934): 13; JDP, "Did the New Playwrights Theatre Fail?" p. 13.

23. JDP, "Inside Watching Out," *New Masses* 2 (February 1927): 27; JDP, "A Great American," *New Masses* 3 (December 1927): 26; JDP, "Told by a Believer," *New Masses* 2 (March 1927): 30; JDP, "Snarling Diplomats," *New Masses* 1 (September 1926): 24; JDP, "Paint the Revolution," *New Masses* 2 (March 1927): 15; JDP, "Zapata's Ghost Walks," *New Masses* 3 (September 1927): 11–12, in JDP, *In All Countries* (New York: Harcourt, Brace, 1934), pp. 80–90 (hereafter cited as *IAC*); JDP, "Relief Map of Mexico," *New Masses* 2 (April 1927): 24, in *IAC*, p. 78.

24. Lincoln Steffens quoted in Theodore Draper, *The Roots of American Communism* (New York: Viking, 1963), p. 115.

25. JDP, "Rainy Days in Leningrad," *New Masses* 4 (February 1929): 3–5, in *IAC*, pp. 21–30; "New Theater in Russia," *New Republic* 62 (16 April 1930): 236–40, in *IAC*, pp. 58–67; JDP, notebook labeled "In All Countries," JDP Papers, Virginia; *TF*, p. 67. See also *IAC*, pp. 64–67.

26. Carleton Beals, quoted in *TCO*, p. 294; Edmund Wilson to F. Scott Fitzgerald, 8 August 1930, in Wilson, *Letters*, p. 202.

27. JDP to Edmund Wilson, 14 January 1931, in *TFC*, p. 398. See "To All Revolutionary Writers of the World," *Literature of the World Revolution* (Moscow) 1 (June 1931): 127–28; and JDP, "An Appeal for Aid," *New Republic* 67 (5 August 1931): 318.

28. JDP, "Back to Red Hysteria!" *New Republic* 63 (2 July 1930): 168–69; JDP, Introduction to *Story of the Imperial Valley*, by Frank Spector, International Labor Defense Pamphlet no. 3 [1930], pp. 3–4.

29. JDP, "The Making of a Writer," *New Masses* 4 (March 1929): 23; JDP, "Whom Can We Appeal To?" *New Masses* 6 (August 1930): 8; JDP, "Wanted: An Ivy Lee for Liberals," *New Republic* 63 (13 August 1930): 371.

30. JDP, "Back to Red Hysteria!" See, for example, *TFC*, pp. 382–83. In *TCO*, however, Ludington acknowledges that the term may be "misleading" (p. 291), but later (p. 311) he takes "middle-class liberal" at face value.

31. JDP quoted by Edmund Wilson in "The Literary Consequences of the Crash" (1932), in *The Shores of Light* (New York: Farrar, Straus and Giroux, 1952), p. 498; JDP, "Back to Red Hysteria!"

32. National Committee for the Defense of Political Prisoners, *Harlan Miners Speak* (New York: Harcourt, Brace [1932]). Dos Passos contributed some "Explanatory Paragraphs" to a chapter entitled "The Miners Speak For Themselves" (pp. 91–98), which quoted more testimony and described his experiences. Most of the descriptive passages originally appeared as "Free Speech Speakin's," *Student Review* 1 (January–February 1932): 5–6. See also, "Harlan: Working Under the Gun," *New Republic* 69 (2 December 1931): 62–67, reprinted in *IAC*, pp. 190–98. Matthew Josephson discusses the two committees in *Infidel in the Temple: A Memoir of the Nineteen-Thirties* (New York: Alfred A. Knopf, 1967), pp. 110–13. Quote from p. 112.

33. Irving Bernstein, *The Lean Years: A History of the American Worker* 1920–1933 (Boston: Houghton Mifflin, 1960), p. 364. See also Landsberg, *Dos Passos' Path*, 164, 166.

34. *Best Times*, p. 206; open letter from JDP, January 1932, in *TFC*, p. 401; *IAC*, p. 195.

35. See Landsberg, *Dos Passos' Path*, p. 169; Josephson, *Infidel in the Temple*, pp. 110–13; *Best Times*, p. 208. On the policies of the "Third Period" (1927–35), see James Weinstein, *Ambiguous Legacy: The Left in American Politics* (New York: New Viewpoints, 1975), pp. 43–56.

36. *TF*, p. 73.

37. JDP, "Whither the American Writer?" *Modern Quarterly* 6 (Summer 1932): 11–12 (a reply to a questionnaire); JDP, "Detroit: City of Leisure," *New Republic* 71 (13 July 1932): 280–82, in *IAC*, pp. 199–206; JDP to Katharine Smith Dos Passos, 25 June 1932, in *TFC*, p. 412.

38. JDP, "Red Day on Capitol Hill," *New Republic* 69 (23 December 1931): 153–55, in *IAC*, pp. 213–22.

39. JDP, Foreword to *Veterans on the March*, by Jack Douglas (New York: Workers Library, 1934), pp. v–vi; JDP, "Washington and Chicago, Part I:

The Veterans Come Home to Roost," *New Republic* 71 (29 June 1932): 177–79, in *IAC*, pp. 222–28.

40. "Washington and Chicago, Part II: Spotlights and Microphones," *New Republic* 71 (29 June 1932): 177–79, in *IAC*, pp. 229–31, covers the Republican convention. "Out of the Red with Roosevelt," *New Republic* 71 (13 July 1932): 230–32, in *IAC*, pp. 231–37, covers the Democratic convention. On Hoover and Roosevelt, see also *IAC*, pp. 237–48, passim.

41. *Culture and the Crisis: An Open Letter to the Writers, Artists, Teachers, Physicians, Engineers, Scientists and Other Professional Workers of America* (New York: League of Professional Groups for Foster and Ford, 1932), p. 31.

42. JDP, "Help the Scottsboro Boys," *New Republic* 72 (24 August 1932): 49 (Dos Passos writes as a treasurer of a defense fund); and "An Appeal," *Student Review* 2 (October 1932): 21 (Dos Passos is one of fourteen signers). For criticism of Communist ideology, see, for example, JDP, "Whither the American Writer?"

43. Katharine Smith Dos Passos to Edmund Wilson, 12 April 1933, Edmund Wilson Papers, Beinecke Library, Yale University, New Haven, Conn. (her letter is dated "Wednesday, *Black April* 1933"); Carlos Baker, *Ernest Hemingway: A Life Story* (New York: Scribners, 1969), p. 240; JDP to Ernest Hemingway, 18 May 1933, in *TFC*, p. 431.

44. D. Mirsky, "Dos Passos in Two Soviet Productions," *International Literature* (July 1934): 152-54. The movie is discussed in two letters, JDP to Theodore Dreiser, one postmarked 8 February 1934, the other undated, but probably written February or March 1934. Theodore Dreiser Papers, Van Pelt Library, University of Pennsylvania, Philadelphia.

45. JDP, *Fortune Heights*, in *Three Plays*, p. 178 (hereafter cited as *TP*). Owen Hunter's name, obviously, is suggestive. Whether this hunter for wealth will eventually *own* his business or always be *owin'* money to creditors is what the audience is waiting to find out.

46. John Howard Lawson to JDP, 24 January [1934], JDP Papers, Virginia; Mirsky, "Dos Passos in Two Soviet Productions," p. 152.

47. JDP to Ernest Hemingway, 25 May 1933, in *TFC*, p. 432.

48. *TCO*, p. 351.

49. Marion Hammet Smith, "Recollections of Dos," *Connecticut Review* 8 (April 1975): 22; "Note by Cantwell on Dos Passos" [ca. 1950], Robert Cantwell Papers, University of Oregon Library, Eugene; "Private Historian," *Time* 28 (10 August 1936): 52. See also Dan Wakefield, "Dos, Which Side Are You On?" *Esquire* 59 (April 1963): 118.

50. JDP to Ernest Hemingway, 27 July 1934, in *TFC*, p. 437; JDP to C. A. Pearce, 18 September 1934, in *TFC*, p. 442; JDP to E. E. Cummings, 20 September [1934], Houghton Library, Harvard University, Cambridge, Mass.; JDP to Edmund Wilson, 24 September 1934, in *TFC*, p. 443.

51. JDP, "World's Iron, Our Blood and Their Profits," *Student Outlook* 3 (October 1934): 17–18; JDP, Preface to *Terror in Cuba*, by Arthur Pincus (New York: Workers Defense League, [1936]), p. 3. On capitalism and war, see also JDP, "Two Views of the Student Strike," *Student Outlook* 3 (April 1935): 5.

52. "Thank You, Mr. Hitler," *Common Sense* 1 (27 April 1933): 13; JDP to Stewart Mitchell, 27 March 1935, in *TFC*, p. 469; JDP to Robert Cantwell, September 1934, in *TFC*, p. 441; JDP to F. Scott Fitzgerald, September 1936, in *TFC*, p. 488.

53. The entire debate, including the "Open Letter" and both replies, is in "To John Dos Passos," *New Masses* 10 (6 March 1934): 8–9; and "Unintelligent Fanaticism," *New Masses* 10 (27 March 1934): 6, 8. For a detailed summary of the *New York Times* account of the rally incident, see Landsberg, *Dos Passos' Path*, p. 180.

54. Edmund Wilson to JDP, 11 January 1935, in Wilson, *Letters*, p. 255; JDP to Edmund Wilson, 23 December 1934, in *TFC*, p. 459; JDP to Edmund Wilson, January 1935, in *TFC*, p. 461. See also *TFC*, pp. 465–68.

55. See JDP to Edmund Wilson, 5 February 1935, in *TFC*, p. 465.

56. Malcolm Cowley, in Daniel Aaron, moderator, "Thirty Years Later: Memories of the First American Writers Congress," *American Scholar* 35 (Summer 1966): 498. For a discussion of the Communists' Popular Front strategy, see Weinstein, *Ambiguous Legacy*, pp. 56–86.

57. Most of this reporting originally appeared in *New Masses, Common Sense,* and *New Republic* in early 1934. See *IAC*, pp. 249–73. Quotes from postcard, JDP to Edmund Wilson, [winter-spring 1934], Edmund Wilson Papers, Beinecke Library, Yale University, New Haven, Conn.; *IAC*, 270–72; and JDP to Ernest Hemingway, 18 May 1933, in *TFC*, p. 431. "Delano the Magician" is probably an allusion to Thomas Mann's story about Italian fascism, "Mario and the Magician."

58. "Whither the American Writer?" p. 12; JDP to Theodore Dreiser, 8 July 1936, Theodore Dreiser Papers, Van Pelt Library, University of Pennsylvania, Philadelphia; JDP, "A Case of Conscience," *Common Sense* 4 (May 1935): 16. See George R. Rawick, "Common Sense," in Joseph R. Conlin, ed., *The American Radical Press, 1880–1960*, 2 vols. (Westport, Conn.: Greenwood Press, 1974), 1:450.

59. JDP to Edmund Wilson, 14 January 1931, in *TFC*, p. 397; JDP to Edmund Wilson, May 1932, in *TFC*, p. 409; JDP, Introduction to *Three Soldiers*, p. vii; Granville Hicks, "The Crisis in American Criticism" (from *New Masses*, February 1933), in *Granville Hicks in the New Masses*, ed. Jack Alan Robbins (Port Washington, N.Y.: Kennikat Press, 1974), pp. 11–12. For Marx's views on literature, and for a criticism of Hicks, see Edmund Wilson, "Marxism and Literature," in his *Triple Thinkers*, pp. 197–212. On American Communist literary theory, see Aaron, *Writers on the Left*, passim; and James Burkhart Gilbert, *Writers and Partisans* (New York: John Wiley and Sons, 1968), pp. 73–87.

60. JDP to Edmund Wilson, 27 March 1935, in *TFC*, p. 468; JDP, "The Writer as Technician," in Henry Hart, ed., *American Writers Congress* (New York: International Publishers, 1935), pp. 78–82. For a detailed discussion of the first American Writers Congress, see Aaron, *Writers on the Left*, pp. 280–308.

61. JDP, "Statement of Belief," *Bookman* 68 (September 1928): 26; JDP to Robert Cantwell, 25 January 1935, in *TFC*, p. 463; JDP, Introduction to *Three Soldiers*, pp. vii–viii.

62. JDP, *U.S.A.: 1. The 42nd Parallel: 2. Nineteen Nineteen: 3. The Big Money* (1938; reprint ed., New York: Modern Library, [1939]); individual novels of the trilogy hereafter cited as *FSP, NN,* and *BM.* The trilogy as a whole, including for the first time the sketch "U.S.A.," was published 27 January 1938, although 1937 is the latest date to appear in the original Harcourt, Brace edition. See Potter, pp. 46–47. Quote from David Sanders, "Interview with John Dos Passos," *Claremont Quarterly* 11 (Spring 1964): 97.

63. For a discussion of the technique of the biographies, see George Knox, "Voice in the *U.S.A.* Biographies," *Texas Studies in Literature and Language* 4 (Spring 1962): 109–16. On the role of historical fact in *U.S.A.*, see Barbara Foley, "From *U.S.A.* to *Ragtime*: Notes on the Forms of Historical Consciousness in Modern Fiction," *American Literature* 50 (March 1978): 85–105.

64. On the "Art Novel," see "The Artist as Rebel: *Three Soldiers*," in chapter 1, above. For Cowley's evolving views on the Camera Eye, see his "The Poet and the World"; and his "Afterthoughts on Dos Passos," *New Republic* 88 (9 September 1936): 134. On the Camera Eye as autobiography, see James N. Westerhoven, "Autobiographical Elements in the Camera Eye," *American Literature* 48 (November 1976): 341–64.

65. On Dos Passos's acknowledged debt to Eisenstein, see Chametzky, "Reflections on *U.S.A.*," p. 394, which quotes from a 1956 radio interview with Dos Passos. See also his response to a questionnaire in *Cahiers du Cinema* 185 (December 1966), p. 89. For a discussion of Dos Passos's relationship to film, see Edward Murray, *The Cinematic Imagination: Writers and the Motion Pictures* (New York: Frederick Ungar, 1972), pp. 168–78.

66. In a 1934 book review, Dos Passos writes that there are few "living and rounded characters" in recent American fiction because "the whole direction of American life tends so towards emphasis on the function of a person or event rather than on the person or on the event" ("The Business of a Novelist," *New Republic* 78 [4 April 1934]: 220). On Dos Passos's characters, see also Anthony Winner, "The Characters of John Dos Passos," *Literatur in Wissenschaft und Unterricht* 2 (1969): 1–19.

67. JDP to Edmund Wilson, 27 July 1939, in *TFC*, p. 522.

68. Upton Sinclair to JDP, 9 September 1936, JDP Papers, Virginia. The 1942 University of Texas incident, which contributed to the eventual firing of Homer Price Rainy as president, is described on pp. 22–24 of a brochure advertising the publication (21 November 1946), by Houghton Mifflin, of a three-volume edition of *U.S.A.* illustrated by Reginald Marsh.

69. On imperialism, see, for example, the biography of Minor C. Keith, founder of the United Fruit Company (*FSP*, pp. 241–44). Joe Williams later witnesses United Fruit machinations in the Caribbean. See *NN*, pp. 154–57.

70. Charley Anderson is discussed in somewhat similar terms in Richard H. Pells, *Radical Visions and American Dreams: Culture and Social Thought in the Depression Years* (New York: Harper and Row, 1973), pp. 234–35; and in Diggins, *Communism*, pp. 112–13.

71. JDP, Draft of Henry Ford biography in *The Big Money*, from crossed out section of p. 6, Philip Kaplan Collection, Morris Library, Southern Illinois University, Carbondale (my interpolation). For Dos Passos's views on

NOTES (pp. 84–91)

technology, see also "Theodore Dreiser—John Dos Passos: A Conversation," *Direction* 1 (January 1938): 28; and JDP, "Edison and Steinmetz: Medicine Men," *New Republic* 61 (18 December 1929): 103–4. For an excellent discussion of the significance of Taylor's work, see Harry Braverman, *Labor and Monopoly Capital: The Degradation of Work in the Twentieth Century* (New York: Monthly Review Press, 1974), pp. 85–138.

72. Joe and Janey are discussed in more or less similar terms in Landsberg, *Dos Passos' Path*, pp. 211–12; and in Brantley, *Fiction of Dos Passos*, p. 63.

73. David E. E. Sloane, "The Black Experience in Dos Passos' *U.S.A.*," *CEA Critic* 36 (March 1974): 22–23.

74. Quoted in Manning Marable, "A. Philip Randolph and the Foundations of Black American Socialism," *Radical America* 14 (March–April 1980): 7.

75. Lalli, *John Dos Passos*, p. 63; Eleanor Widmer, "The Lost Girls of *U.S.A.*: Dos Passos' 30s Movie," in Warren French, ed., *The Thirties: Fiction, Poetry, Drama* (Deland, Florida: Everett Edwards, 1967), pp. 11–19.

76. Quotes from T. K. Whipple, *Study Out the Land* (Berkeley: University of California Press, 1943), p. 90; and Richard Horchler, "Prophet Without Hope," *Commonweal* 75 (29 September 1961): 15. Lionel Trilling also argues that *U.S.A.* demands social change, in "The America of John Dos Passos," *Partisan Review* 4 (April 1938): 26–32. Of the major characters in *U.S.A.*, Jean-Paul Sartre writes: "In capitalist society, men do not have lives, they have only destinies. [Dos Passos] never says this, but he makes it felt throughout. He expresses it discreetly, cautiously, until we feel like smashing our destinies. We have become rebels; he has achieved his purpose" (*Literary and Philosophical Essays* [London: Rider and Company, 1955], p. 91).

77. Arthur Mizener, *The Sense of Life in the Modern Novel* (Boston: Houghton Mifflin, 1964), p. 130.

78. On the theme of language in *U.S.A.*, cf. John Lydenberg, "Dos Passos's *U.S.A.*: The Words of the Hollow Men," in Sydney J. Krause, ed., *Essays on Determinism in American Literature*, Kent Studies in English, no. 1 (Kent, Ohio: Kent State University Press, 1964), pp. 97–107; and David L. Vanderwerken, "*U.S.A.*: Dos Passos and the 'Old Words,' " *Twentieth Century Literature* 23 (May 1977): 195–228.

79. Davis, *John Dos Passos*, pp. 28–30 argues similarly.

80. JDP to Malcolm Cowley, February 1932, in *TFC*, p. 404.

81. Granville Hicks, "Dos Passos' Gifts," *New Republic* 67 (24 June 1931): 158; V. F. Calverton, *The Liberation of American Literature* (New York: Scribners, 1932), p. 462; Gold, "The Education of John Dos Passos," p. 97; Granville Hicks, "John Dos Passos," *Bookman* 75 (April 1932): 42; Michael Gold, "Change the World," *Daily Worker*, 26 February 1938, p. 7.

82. "Soviet Literature and Dos Passos," *International Literature* 5 (1933–34): 103–12; Brown, *Soviet Attitudes*, pp. 326, 105, see also pp. 83, 98–108. For a recent, rather negative Soviet view, see Y. Zasursky, "Dos Passos' Experimental Novel," in *20th Century American Literature: A Soviet View* (Moscow: Progress Publishers, 1976), pp. 331–50.

83. Sartre, *Essays*, p. 96; Herbert Marshall McLuhan, "John Dos Passos:

NOTES (pp. 91–94)

Technique vs. Sensibility," in Harold C. Gardner, S. J., ed., *Fifty Years of the American Novel: A Christian Appraisal* (New York: Scribners, 1951), pp. 152, 156; Alfred Kazin, *On Native Grounds* (Garden City, N.Y.: Doubleday, Anchor Books, 1956), pp. 241, 269, 281. See also Jean-Paul Sartre, "American Novelists in French Eyes," *Atlantic Monthly* 178 (August 1946): 117. French critic Claude-Edmonde Magny calls the "technique" of *U.S.A.* "so profoundly original that it has a posterity instead of an ancestry" (*The Age of the American Novel: The Film Aesthetic of Fiction Between the Two Wars*, trans. Eleanor Hochman [New York: Frederick Ungar, 1972], p. 111). For an overview of Dos Passos's critical reception in France, see Thelma M. Smith and Ward L. Miner, *Transatlantic Migration: The Contemporary American Novel in France* (Durham: Duke University Press, 1955), pp. 87–98, 217–21.

84. Max Eastman, "Motive-Patterns of Socialism," *Modern Quarterly* 11 (Fall 1939): 45.

85. Ibid., p. 46. See, for example, JDP to John Howard Lawson, October 1934, in *TFC*, p. 447.

86. On the "comrats," see, for example, JDP to John Howard Lawson, October 1934, in *TFC*, p. 447.

87. On the Socialist party, see Dos Passos, "Whither the American Writer?" p. 11; and JDP to Fredricka Field, 29 November 1932, in *TFC*, p. 413. On Trotskyists, see JDP to Edmund Wilson, January 1935, in *TFC*, p. 461. A. J. Muste's American Worker's party he considered just "emasculated communists." JDP to John Howard Lawson, October, 1934, in *TFC*, p. 447. Quote in text from JDP to Thomas Chilton Wheeler [n.d.], in Wheeler, "The Political Philosophy of John Dos Passos" (Undergraduate Honors Thesis, Harvard College, 1951), Appendix, p. 3. Dos Passos calls himself "libertarian" in JDP to John Howard Lawson, Fall 1937, in *TFC*, p. 515; and in JDP to Bernard Kollenberg, 18 September 1938, in *TFC*, p. 521.

88. JDP, "The Communist Party and the War Spirit," *Common Sense* 6 (December 1937): 13; George Orwell, *Homage to Catalonia* (1938; reprint ed., New York: Harcourt, Brace, and World, 1952), p. 109; JDP to E. E. Cummings, 23 August 1937, in *TFC*, p. 508. For a defense of the Spanish anarchists, see Daniel Guérin, *Anarchism: From Theory to Practice*, trans. Mary Klopper (New York: Monthly Review Press, 1970), pp. 114–43.

89. See Baker, *Life Story*, pp. 305–6; and Carlos Baker, *Hemingway: The Writer As Artist* (Princeton: Princeton University Press, 1963), p. 233.

90. *TCO*, p. 333. In 1938, Hemingway wrote a mocking, unfair account of a tall man "with strips of blond hair pasted carefully across a flat-topped bald head" (no doubt Dos Passos) who stupidly insisted without evidence that the Spanish government was creating "a terror" (Ernest Hemingway, "Fresh Air on an Inside Story," *Ken*, 22 September 1938, reprinted in *By Line: Ernest Hemingway: Selected Articles and Dispatches of Four Decades*, ed. William White [New York: Scribners, 1967], pp. 294–97). And Hemingway was quite vicious in a letter to his former friend, referring to Dos Passos's writings on Spain as "attacking, for money, the side that you were always supposed to be on," and calling him the kind of friend who would "knife you in the back for a dime"

162

(Photostat of letter Ernest Hemingway to JDP [1938], JDP Papers, Virginia).

91. JDP, "Death of José Robles," *New Republic* 99 (19 July 1939): 309, a letter to the editor, reprinted in *TFC*, pp. 527–29. For a more detailed account of the Robles incident, see *TCO*, pp. 366–74, passim. See also Malcolm Cowley, "Disillusionment" (review of *Adventures of a Young Man*), *New Republic* 99 (14 June 1939): 163; and Josephine Herbst, "The Starched Blue Sky of Spain," *noble savage* 1 (1960): 76–117. Herbst, a novelist and a close friend of Dos Passos's, was also in Spain in 1937. For a bitter fictionalized version of Dos Passos's experiences, see his last novel, unfinished at his death, *Century's Ebb* (Boston: Gambit, 1975), pp. 35–56, 67–99.

92. The *Esquire* articles appeared in December, 1937 and January, 1938. *The Villages Are the Heart of Spain* (Chicago: Esquire-Coronet, 1938), published in January, appeared as an article in *Esquire*, the following month (hereafter cited as *VHS*). On Dos Passos's uncertainty, see *TF*, p. 130. Dos Passos also writes of Spain in his *Journeys Between Wars* (New York: Harcourt, Brace, 1938), pp. 375–81. The rest of the book reprints previously published material.

93. JDP, "Farewell to Europe," *Common Sense* 6 (July 1937): 10; JDP to Claude Bowers, 5 September 1937, Claude Bowers Papers, Lilly Library, Indiana University, Bloomington; JDP, "Farewell to Europe," p. 11.

94. JDP, *Adventures of a Young Man* (New York: Harcourt, Brace, 1939); hereafter cited as *AYM*. In 1952, Dos Passos published *Adventures of a Young Man* as part of a trilogy, *District of Columbia*. The italicized sermons on history and freedom that appear there between chapters of *Adventures of a Young Man* date from 1952, not 1939.

95. Dos Passos himself refers to the novel's "behavioristic satirical narrative style" in JDP to Selden Rodman [1939], Selden Rodman Collection, Archive of Contemporary History, University of Wyoming, Laramie. And Ludington (*TFC*, p. 499) alludes to "the satire Dos Passos intended," though he finds it "hard to recognize" because effective satire requires "a sense of distance between the narrator and the narrative." For an attempt to see the whole *District of Columbia* trilogy as comedy, in the tradition of Jonson and Swift, see Arthur Mizener, Introduction to JDP, *District of Columbia* (Boston: Houghton, Mifflin, 1952), pp. vii–xii. For a general discussion of Dos Passos as satirist, see Charles T. Ludington, Jr., "The Neglected Satires of John Dos Passos," *Satire Newsletter* (Oneonta, N.Y.) 7 (Spring 1970): 127–36. Townsend Ludington's biography, *TCO*, incorporates this view when, in passing, he discusses Dos Passos's novels.

96. Georg Lukács, "The Intellectual Physiognomy in Characterization," in *Writer & Critic, and Other Essays*, trans. Arthur D. Kahn (New York: Grossett and Dunlap, 1971), pp. 149–88.

97. For a defense of the novel and a partisan survey of other (mostly negative) criticism, see James T. Farrell, "Dos Passos and the Critics," *American Mercury* 47 (August 1939): 489–94.

98. JDP to Eugene Lyons [ca. 1939], Max Eastman Papers, Lilly Library, Indiana University, Bloomington.

Chapter Three

1. JDP to Max Eastman, 25 December 1953, in *TFC*, p. 605.

2. JDP to James T. Farrell, 2 April [1941], James T. Farrell Papers, Van Pelt Library, University of Pennsylvania, Philadelphia.

3. JDP, "Tom Paine's 'Common Sense,'" *Common Sense* 8 (September 1939): 3; JDP, "Tom Paine's 'Rights of Man,'" *Common Sense* 8 (October 1939): 13. This two-part essay also appears in Alfred O. Mendel, ed., *The Living Thoughts of Tom Paine: Presented by John Dos Passos* (New York: Longmans, Green, 1940), pp. 1–52.

4. JDP, *The Ground We Stand On: Some Examples from the History of a Political Creed* (New York: Harcourt, Brace, 1941), p. 8; hereafter cited as *GWSO*.

5. JDP, *Number One* (Boston: Houghton, Mifflin, 1943); hereafter cited as *NO*.

6. John Lydenberg sees "gross sentimentalism" in Dos Passos's treatment of the subjects of these portraits as "the fount of all virtue" ("Dos Passos and the Ruined Words," *Pacific Spectator* 5 [Summer 1951]: 320).

7. Cf. Colley, *Fiction of Despair*, p. 128: "One reads with horror and disappointment the platitudes that Dos Passos evidently means to be accepted as the moral conclusion of his book."

8. The dust jacket of *Number One* contains a statement by Dos Passos telling readers to buy war bonds. See Potter, p. 55.

9. JDP, "'Las Palmeras,'" *Socialist Call* 7 (12 April 1941): 2; and JDP, "Refugees Still Suffering," *New York Times*, 3 December 1940, p. 24. Both are letters to the editor. Concerning civil liberties, see Sidney Hook, *et. al.*, "Statement of the Committee for Cultural Freedom," *American Mercury* 47 (July 1939): 375–76 (signed by Dos Passos and twenty-two others); and Donnell, "John Dos Passos," p. 910 n. 20.

10. "JOHN DOS PASSOS / PROJECT OF WORK," undated carbon of application for Guggenheim grant (support for writing *The Ground We Stand On*), Edmund Wilson Papers, Beinecke Library, Yale University, New Haven, Conn.; JDP, "To a Liberal in Office," *Nation* 153 (6 September 1941): 197.

11. JDP to Robert Hillyer, 24 February 1943, in *TFC*, p. 536; JDP, *State of the Nation* (Boston: Houghton, Mifflin, 1944); hereafter cited as *SN*.

12. JDP, "England in the Great Lull," *Harpers* 184 (February 1942): 237; JDP, *Tour of Duty* (Boston: Houghton, Mifflin, 1946), p. 140; hereafter cited as *TD*. This volume collects most of Dos Passos's war reporting.

13. JDP to Gerald and Sara Murphy, 21 February 1945, in *TFC*, p. 550; JDP to Katharine Smith Dos Passos, 7 January [1945], JDP Papers, Virginia. Dos Passos seems to have forgotten the hatred of racial and ethnic slurs he once expressed in *U.S.A.*, in his pamphlet defending Sacco and Vanzetti, and elsewhere. In *Tour of Duty*, he writes of a "mongrel yellow boy" in Waikiki and calls the "Jap[s]" or "little Nips" a "small stubby people with slow ungraceful movements" and "an outlandish dusty little people with wooden faces" (*TD*, pp. 6, 99, 64, 65). Elsewhere, he calls the Japanese "really . . . a horrid little people" (JDP to Katharine Smith Dos Passos, 9 February [1945], JDP Papers, Virginia).

14. JDP to Katharine Smith Dos Passos, 7 January 1945, JDP Papers, Virginia; Henry R. Luce, *The American Century* (New York: Farrar and Rinehart [1941]).

15. JDP to Edmund Wilson, 18 May 1945, in *TFC*, p. 552; Brown spiral notebook labeled "Berlin 1945" [p. 5], JDP Papers, Virginia.

16. JDP, quoted in advertisement for *The Gallery*, by John Horne Burns, *New York Times Book Review*, 13 July 1947, p. 16; JDP "There is ONLY One Freedom," '47 1 (April 1947): 76.

17. For example, Dos Passos told a reporter: "It's no secret that the most active force in the world today is Communism. . . . The Kremlin is taking over mighty fast, from the looks of things" (Paul F. Kneeland, "This Country Needs 'A Free and Vigorous Society,'" *Boston Globe*, 16 January 1949, p. A-21). For a description of the Tresca incident, see *TCO*, pp. 416–17. For Dos Passos's tributes to Tresca, see JDP, Foreword to *Who Killed Carlo Tresca?* (Tresca Memorial Committee, n.d.), pp. 4–6; and JDP, "Carlo Tresca," *Nation* 156 (23 January 1943): 123–24. A version of the *Nation* article appears in the magazine Tresca edited, *Il Martello* 28 (28 March 1943): 2.

18. JDP quoted in John L. Brown, "The Gallic Literary Scene: A Report from Paris," *New York Times Book Review*, 16 March 1947, p. 37.

19. JDP, "Britain's Dim Dictatorship," *Life* 23 (29 September 1947): 120–22.

20. JDP, "The Failure of Marxism," *Life* 24 (19 January 1948): 96–98; hereafter cited as FM.

21. "The Established Order," JDP Papers, Virginia.

22. Norman Thomas, "Casual Reflections of a Random Rover," *New York Herald Tribune Book Review*, 5 November 1950, p. 4 (review of *The Prospect Before Us*, which reuses material from "The Failure of Marxism"); Granville Hicks, "The Politics of John Dos Passos," *Antioch Review* 10 (March 1950): 97–98; Philip Rahv, "Disillusionment and Partial Answers," *Partisan Review* 15 (May 1948): p. 523.

23. Under the Control of Engagements Order, only "29 individuals were directed to take new employment and 688 . . . required to remain in agriculture or coal mining" (Alfred F. Havighurst, *Twentieth Century Britain, 2nd ed.* [New York: Harper and Row, 1962], p. 402.)

24. A historian not entirely unsympathetic to Dos Passos's abandonment of his radical views finds this analogy particularly wrong-headed, deriving "from many assumptions characteristic of Old Left thinkers who knew too much Stalinism and not enough Marxism" (Diggins, *Communism*, p. 235).

25. One reader made the following criticisms of "The Failure of Marxism" in a letter to *Life*: that the USSR is not socialism but state capitalism; that Britain's nationalizations were no more than the purchase of faltering industries at inflated prices; and that Britain was simply a "statified capitalist" nation. *Life* gave the letter to Dos Passos and he sent it to Wilson, commenting on its author: "I think he's bats but he's consistent" (JDP to Edmund Wilson, n.d., Edmund Wilson Papers, Beinecke Library, Yale University, New Haven, Conn.).

26. JDP, "project for a possible libertarian pamphlet," undated one-page outline, JDP Papers, Virginia.

27. JDP to Claude Bowers, 7 April 1939, Claude Bowers Papers, Lilly Library, Indiana University, Bloomington; *TF* (1956), p. 161; JDP, *The Grand Design* (Boston: Houghton, Mifflin, 1949) (hereafter cited as *GD*). Dos Passos also discusses his voting in Wheeler, "Political Philosophy," Appendix. For a quite uncharacteristically favorable discussion of Roosevelt, see the narrative sections signed by Dos Passos in *Life's Picture History of World War II* (New York: Time, Inc., 1950), especially p. 267.

28. See Wrenn, *John Dos Passos*, p. 173; Joseph Blotner, *The Modern American Political Novel* (Austin: University of Texas Press, 1966), p. 313; and Donnell, "John Dos Passos," p. 951, n. 54.

29. Dos Passos describes a visit to Bob Garst and other farmers in "Revolution on the Farm," *Life* 25 (23 August 1948): 95–98.

30. See, for example, Howard Zinn, "The Limits of the New Deal," in his *The Politics of History* (Boston: Beacon, 1970), pp. 118–36; and Ronald Radosh, "The Myth of the New Deal," in Ronald Radosh and Murray N. Rothbard, eds., *A New History of Leviathan: Essays on the Rise of the American Corporate State* (New York: E. P. Dutton, 1972), pp. 146–87.

31. Irving Howe, "John Dos Passos: The Loss of Passion," *Tomorrow* 8 (March 1949): 57. Malcolm Cowley summarizes some of the reviews of *The Grand Design* in " Dos Passos and His Critics," *New Republic* 120 (28 February 1949): 21–23.

32. *TCO*, p. 432; JDP to Sara Murphy, 7 November 1948, in *TFC*, p. 586; JDP to Stewart Mitchell, 21 May 1950, in *TFC*, p. 590.

33. *TCO*, p. 441.

34. JDP to Edmund Wilson, 15 September 1951, in *TFC*, p. 596.

35. JDP, *The Prospect Before Us* (Boston: Houghton, Mifflin, 1950) (hereafter cited as *PBU*); JDP to Edmund Wilson, 24 January 1950, in Edmund Wilson Papers, Beinecke Library, Yale University, New Haven, Conn.

36. James Burnham, "Is Democracy Possible?" in Irving DeWitt Talmadge, *Whose Revolution?: A Study of the Future Course of Liberalism in the United States* (New York: Howell, Siskin, 1941), p. 188. For a discussion of Burnham's book, *The Managerial Revolution* (1941), see Diggins, *Communism*, pp. 189–98.

37. JDP, *Chosen Country* (Boston: Houghton, Mifflin, 1951); hereafter cited as *CC*.

38. Brantley, *Fiction of Dos Passos*, p. 103.

39. As Brantley (ibid., p. 108) points out, Dos Passos in fact borrows directly from his earlier work. For example, descriptions of Jay's travels to Beirut after the war are "lifted verbatim" from *Orient Express*. For a richly suggestive psychoanalytic interpretation of *Chosen Country*, see Gelfant, "Search for Identity."

40. Granville Hicks writes that Dos Passos "attempted to compress into a few years an intellectual process that in his own life had taken decades, and consequently either the foreground or the background was constantly out of focus" (see "Dos Passos: The Fruits of Disillusionment," *New Republic* 131 [27 September 1954]: 18).

41. JDP, "Mr. Chambers' Descent into Hell," *Saturday Review* 35 (24 May 1952): 11; JDP to Upton Sinclair, 4 May 1949, in *TFC*, p. 588; JDP, "Mr. Chambers' Descent into Hell," p. 11; JDP, Introduction to *Up From Liberalism*, by William F. Buckley, Jr. (New York: McDowell, Obolensky, 1959), p. ix; JDP, "Mr. Chambers' Descent into Hell," p. 11.

42. JDP to William Rose Benét, 12 January 1948, in *TFC*, p. 581; Richard Whalen, "A Conversation with Dos Passos," *New Leader* 42 (23 February 1959): 21. Dos Passos's *Century's Ebb* includes a long, rather heroic biographical portrait of McCarthy, entitled "Bogey" (see pp. 151–65).

43. Issac Deutscher, "The Ex-Communist's Conscience," in his *Russia in Transition and Other Essays* (New York: Coward-McCann, 1957), p. 209.

44. *TF*, pp. 247–48. See also *PBU*, pp. 5–7. In 1961, Dos Passos told a Newsweek reporter: "What the Russians are spreading is nothing but a less plausible version of what we already have here. Add a secret police to the combined AFL-CIO and you couldn't tell the difference" ("Out of the Past," *Newsweek* 57 [27 February 1961]: 93).

45. *TF*, p. 262; JDP to Arthur Schlesinger, Jr., 13 April 1958, in *TFC*, p. 616; Norman Mailer, in "Our Country and Our Culture: A Symposium," *Partisan Review* 19 (May–June, 1952): 299.

46. JDP, *Most Likely To Succeed* (New York: Prentice-Hall, 1954); hereafter cited as *ML*.

47. Dos Passos wrote Wilson: "I was certainly pleased that you found a few things to laugh at in Most Likely. Such criticism as I saw took it with depressing seriousness" (JDP to Edmund Wilson, 6 November 1954, in *TFC*, p. 607). But in an eight-page Prentice-Hall promotional brochure for *Most Likely To Succeed*, Dos Passos reveals the central impulse behind the novel: "Books are written to get something off the man's chest. For many years now, I've been watching with a sort of horrified obsession the development of political delusions in the minds of certain men and women who started out as sane and up-and-coming young people and potential good citizens, but whose lives have by these delusions been thoroughly warped, and the good in them, in my opinion, just about destroyed" (Max Eastman et al., *John Dos Passos: An Appreciation*, 1954).

48. JDP to Edmund Wilson, 17 June 1955, in Edmund Wilson Papers, Beinecke Library, Yale University, New Haven, Conn. According to Diggins, *Communism*, p. 267, only Allan Nevins among professional historians took "a keen interest" in Dos Passos's historical writings. Others "have dismissed his narratives as a mountain of pious Americana."

49. JDP, *The Head and Heart of Thomas Jefferson* (Garden City, N.Y.: Doubleday, 1954); hereafter cited as *TJ*. Irving Howe, "The Perils of Americana," *New Republic* 130 (25 January 1954): 16.

50. JDP to Arthur K. McComb, 26 August 1916, quoted in Landsberg, *Dos Passos' Path*, p. 48.

51. Diggins, *Communism*, pp. 256, 265. For a general discussion, by a historian, of Dos Passos's qualities as a history writer, see Diggins, *Communism*, pp. 254–68.

52. See, for example, *TJ*, pp. 204–05. On Jefferson's views of blacks, see

Jesse Lemisch, "The American Revolution Seen From the Bottom Up," in Barton J. Bernstein, ed., *Towards A New Past: Dissenting Essays in American History* (New York: Pantheon, 1968), p. 11 and p. 36 n. 48.

53. Lemisch, "The American Revolution," p. 6; "U.S.A.," in JDP, *U.S.A.*, p. vii; Lee Grove, "New Liberalism Needed: 'Static Liberalism' Bothers Dos Passos," *Washington Post*, 20 January 1949, quoted in Donnell, "John Dos Passos," p. 915 n. 38.

54. See, for example, Staughton Lynd, "Beyond Beard," in Bernstein, *Towards a New Past*, pp. 47–49.

55. Dos Passos quoted in John K. Hutchens, "On the Books," *New York Herald Tribune Weekly Book Review*, 30 January 1949, p. 10. Dos Passos also writes: "the great formulations of the generation of 1776 [are] as valid as ever" ("A Question of Elbow Room" [1958], in JDP, *Occasions and Protests* [Chicago: Henry Regnery, 1964], p. 64).

56. Dos Passos also published a study of a twentieth-century failure to follow Jeffersonian principles, *Mr. Wilson's War* (Garden City, N.Y.: Doubleday, 1962).

57. JDP, *The Great Days* (New York: Sagamore Press, 1958); hereafter cited as *TGD*.

58. See Gelfant, "Search for Identity," p. 149.

59. Davis, *John Dos Passos*, p. 38. For a defense of the novel, see James T. Farrell, "How Should We Rate Dos Passos?" *New Republic* 138 (28 April 1958): 17–18; and Brantley, *Fiction of Dos Passos*, pp. 114–22.

60. See, for example, Dos Passos's talk of "*selfgovernment*" in describing his views and activities in the 1920s (*TF*, pp. 3–4), or his description of his negative reaction to people leaving a "*protest meeting*" (*TF*, p. 6). In general, he tends throughout to make other leftists seem more rigid and himself more uncertain than his original writings of the period indicate.

61. His editing of "The Failure of Marxism," for example, cuts out (among other things) his analysis of the specific historical reasons why the Russian Revolution developed as it did, leaving a much stronger impression that socialism is inherently totalitarian. See *TF*, pp. 236–45.

62. Dos Passos makes this explicit in his "Looking Back on 'U.S.A.,' " *New York Times*, 25 October 1959, sec. 2, p. 5; in Phil Casey, "Dos Passos Speeds Up His Pen After 4 Decades of Writing," *Washington Post*, 16 July 1959, p. B-1; and in Kneeland, "This Country Needs," p. A-21.

63. JDP, "Statement of Belief" (1928), p. 26; Frank Gado, ed., *First Person: Conversations on Writers and Writing* (Schenectady, N.Y.: Union College Press, 1973), p. 41 (interview took place in 1968).

64. "Contemporary Chronicles," pp. 25–29; "Acceptance by John Dos Passos," *Proceedings of the American Academy of Arts and Letters and the National Institute of Arts and Letters*, 2nd ser., no. 8 (New York, 1958), p. 193; "Out of the Past," *Newsweek* 57 (27 February 1961): 93. Dos Passos also discusses his role as writer in "What Makes a Novelist," *National Review* 20 (16 January 1968); 29–32. For a brief discussion of Dos Passos's method as "not satiric but analytic," see Becker, *John Dos Passos*, pp. 115–16. For an opposing view, see Belkind, *Dos Passos*, pp. xxxvii–xlii. On the very deradicalized 1959 stage version

NOTES (pp. 132–36)

(by Dos Passos and Paul Shyre) of *U.S.A.*, see Chametzky "Reflections on U.S.A." The play is Paul Shyre and JDP, *U.S.A.: A Dramatic Review* (New York: Samuel French, 1963).

65. Wakefield, "Dos, Which Side Are You On?" p. 117, mentions the Taft committee; JDP, "Adlai Stevenson: Patrician with a Mission," part 2, *National Review* 2 (3 November 1956): 13.

66. JDP, "Speech at a dinner for Bill Buckley," 11 November 1965, JDP Papers, Virginia; JDP, Introduction to *Up From Liberalism;* JDP, Foreword to *The American Cause* by Russell Kirk (Chicago: Henry Regnery, 1966), pp. v–xv (the foreword also appeared, with only minor differences, as JDP, "The New Left, A Spook Out of the Past," *National Review* 18 [18 October 1966]: 1037–39); JDP to The Committee on Admissions of The Century Association, 17 July 1970, in *TFC*, p. 644. On Goldwater, see JDP, "The Battle of San Francisco," *National Review* 16 (28 July 1964): 640; and JDP, "What Hope for Maintaining a Conservative Opposition?" *National Review* 16 (20 October 1964): 907–9.

67. Allen Guttmann, *The Conservative Tradition in America* (New York: Oxford University Press, 1967), pp. 3–13; "The Magazine's Credenda," *National Review* 1 (19 November 1955): 6; Guttmann, *The Conservative Tradition*, p. 168.

68. On ethics and Christianity, see, for example, *TF*, pp. 259, 260. The Buckley quote is from his *Up From Liberalism*, p. 193. Dos Passos told Dan Wakefield he differed "from Buckley and the *National Review* boys" in that he did not "have the confidence in capitalism *per se* that they have" (Wakefield, "Dos, Which Side Are You On?" p. 118).

69. JDP, "A Question of Elbow Room," in *Occasions and Protests*, p. 64; JDP, "Adlai Stevenson: Patrician with a Mission," part 1, *National Review* 2 (27 October 1956): 14; Diggins, *Communism*, p. 350.

70. "Tract for the Times," *Liberation* 1 (March 1956): 3–6. Quotes from pp. 4, 5. Another journal, *Dissent*, begun two years earlier, sought to "reassert the libertarian values of the socialist ideal" (see *Dissent* 1 [Winter 1954]: 3). Dos Passos refers to the "*Abominable Snowmen*" in *TF*, p. 148.

71. William F. Buckley, Jr., "Publisher's Statement," *National Review* 1 (19 November 1955): 5; Whalen, "A Conversation with Dos Passos," p. 21. Eisenhower quoted in Lawrence S. Wittner, *Cold War America: From Hiroshima to Watergate* (New York: Praeger, 1974), p. 118.

72. Buckley, *Up From Liberalism*, p. 202.

73. Dos Passos uses the phrase in a letter to LeBaron Barker, 16 August 1960, Houghton Library, Harvard University, Cambridge, Mass. Noam Chomsky, Introduction to *Anarchism: From Theory to Practice*, by Daniel Guérin, p. xii. In the first quote, Chomsky is paraphrasing the anarchist historian Rudolf Rocker. Dos Passos uses the term "humanitarian socialism" to describe his views during the 1920s in Wheeler, "Political Philosophy," p. 1 (1951).

74. JDP, *Midcentury* (Boston: Houghton, Mifflin, 1961); hereafter cited as *MC*.

75. JDP to Robert Hillyer, 24 November 1959, in *TFC*, p. 621.

76. See JDP, "What Union Members Have Been Writing Senator McClellan," *Readers Digest* 73 (September 1958): 25–32. The expression

NOTES (pp. 138–43)

"hair-raising" is from John Dos Passos, "APPLICATION FOR GRANT-IN-AID" [ca. 1958], JDP Papers, Virginia.

77. See Astre, *John Dos Passos*, p. 481.

78. See, for example, Harry T. Moore, "Proud Men in an Age of Conformity," *New York Times Book Review*, 26 February 1961, p. 1.

79. See, for example, *PBU*, pp. 296–324, on General Mills; pp. 336–57, on the rubber worker's union; and pp. 329–33, for the cake mix episode which appears on pp. 310–12 in *Midcentury*.

80. Moore, "Proud Men," p. 1.

81. Edmund Wilson to JDP, 26 November 1966, in Wilson, *Letters*, p. 666. For comments by James T. Farrell, Josephine Herbst, and others, see Wakefield, "Dos, Which Side Are You On?"

82. JDP to Robert Cantwell, 25 January 1935, in *TFC*, p. 464; JDP, "What Hope for Maintaining a Conservative Opposition?" p. 908; JDP, "Please Mr. Rip Van Winkle, Wake Up Some More," *National Reveiw* 16 (28 January 1964): 72 (a review of Wilson's *The Cold War and the Income Tax: A Protest*, 1963); Edmund Wilson to JDP, 1 February 1964, in Wilson, *Letters*, p. 643; JDP, "The New Left, A Spook Out of the Past," p. 1038; JDP, "Cogitations in a Roman Theatre," in *Occasions and Protests*, p. 284; JDP to Lois Hazell, 24 June 1970, in *TFC*, p. 642.

83. There is innuendo to this effect in JDP, "The Battle of San Francisco," p. 640.

84. "An Important Statement by the Writers of the New Leader," *New Leader* 33 (26 August 1950): 32 (back cover) (Dos Passos was one of many signers); *San Jose Mercury*, 12 November 1964; *San Jose Mercury* 15 May 1964; *San Jose Mercury*, 12 November 1964. A biography of Malcolm X appears in *Century's Ebb*, pp. 443–56. On racial issues, see also *SN* (1944), pp. 98–99, 166–69, 176, and passim.

85. Tom Hayden et al., Introduction to the *Port Huron Statement* (1962), in Loren Baritz, ed., *The American Left: Radical Political Thought in the Twentieth Century* (New York: Basic Books, 1971), p. 394 (the Port Huron Statement was the founding statement of Students for a Democratic Society); JDP, "The New Left, A Spook Out of the Past," p. 1039; Gado, *First Person*, p. 32; JDP to Lucy Dos Passos, 23 May 1970, in *TFC*, p. 639.

86. JDP to Harold and Faith Weston, 25 June 1970, in *TFC*, p. 643; JDP, "Please Mr. Rip Van Winkle, Wake Up Some More," pp. 71–74; Gado, *First Person*, p. 47; JDP, " '1968,' " *National Review* 20 (13 August 1968): 799, 793. On the New Deal, see, for example, JDP, " '1968,' " p. 793.

87. " '1968,' " p. 799; JDP to Lucy Dos Passos, 23 May 1970, in *TFC* p. 640; JDP, "On the Way to the Moon Shot," *National Review* 23 (9 February 1971): 135–36; JDP, "Pavlovian Society Dinner," address, 6 September 1968, JDP Papers, Virginia.

88. JDP, *Brazil on the Move* (Garden City, N.Y.: Doubleday, 1963); JDP, *The Portugal Story: Three Centuries of Exploration and Discovery* (Garden City, N. Y.: Doubleday, 1969); JDP, *Easter Island: Island of Enigmas* (Garden City, N. Y.: Doubleday, 1971); JDP, *Thomas Jefferson—The Making of a President* (Boston: Houghton, Mifflin, 1964); JDP, *Occasions and Protests* (1964); JDP,

World in a Glass: A View of Our Century (Boston: Houghton, Mifflin, 1966); JDP, *The Best Times* (1966).

89. JDP to Harold and Faith Weston, 25 June 1970, in *TFC*, p. 643; Davis, *John Dos Passos*, p. 5. Among the other subjects of biographical portraits in *Century's Ebb* are George Orwell, John Dewey, Joseph McCarthy, Henry Wallace, Robert H. Goddard, and Lee Harvey Oswald. *Century's Ebb* is composite in form, like *Midcentury*, but probably—even if finished and revised—would have remained far less coherent than the earlier novel. For a very favorable discussion of *Century's Ebb*, see Wagner, *Dos Passos*, pp. 159–76, passim.

90. Quotes are from JDP, *RRA*, p. 93; and from Malcolm Cowley, review of *Century's Ebb* and of *Thornton Wilder* by Richard H. Goldstone, *New York Times Book Review*, 9 November 1975, p. 6.

SELECTED BIBLIOGRAPHY

The following is by no means a complete list of works by and about Dos Passos, or even of all works used in this study. It simply gives all works by Dos Passos cited in the text or notes and includes those secondary sources which have been cited in short form at least once in the notes or are otherwise important. For a more complete listing of material by or about Dos Passos, see the following bibliographies: Jack Potter, *A Bibliography of John Dos Passos* (Chicago: Normandie House, 1950); William White, "John Dos Passos and his Reviewers," *Bulletin of Bibliography* 20 (May–August 1950): 45–57 (contains over 200 items not in Potter); William White, "More Dos Passos: Bibliographical Addenda," *Papers of the Bibliographic Society of America* 45 (1951): 156–58; and Virginia S. Reinhart, "John Dos Passos 1950–1966: Bibliography," *Twentieth Century Literature* 13 (1967): 167–78.

Works by Dos Passos

Books and Pamphlets

One Man's Initiation—1917. London: Allen and Unwin, 1920. Reprint ed. Ithaca: Cornell University Press, 1969.
Three Soldiers. New York: George H. Doran Co., 1921. Reprint ed. New York: Modern Library, 1932.
Rosinante to the Road Again. New York: George H. Doran Co., 1922.
A Pushcart at the Curb. New York: George H. Doran Co., 1922.
Streets of Night. New York: George H. Doran Co., 1923.

SELECTED BIBLIOGRAPHY

Manhattan Transfer. New York: Harper and Brothers, 1925. Reprint ed. Boston: Houghton, Mifflin Co., Sentry edition, 1953.

The Garbage Man: A Parade with Shouting. New York: Harper and Brothers, 1926.

Orient Express. New York: Harper and Brothers, 1927. Reprint ed. New York: Jonathan Cape and Harrison Smith, 1930.

Facing the Chair: Story of the Americanization of Two Foreignborn Workmen. Boston: Sacco-Vanzetti Defense Committee, 1927. Facsimile reprint ed. New York: Oriole Chapbooks, n.d.

Airways, Inc. New York: Macaulay Co., 1928.

The 42nd Parallel. New York: Harper and Brothers, 1930.

1919. New York: Harcourt, Brace and Co., 1932.

In All Countries. New York: Harcourt, Brace and Co., 1934.

Three Plays: The Garbage Man, Airways, Inc., Fortune Heights. New York: Harcourt, Brace and Co., 1934.

The Big Money. New York: Harcourt, Brace and Co., 1936.

The Villages Are the Heart of Spain. Chicago: Esquire-Coronet, Inc., 1938.

U.S.A.: 1. The 42nd Parallel; 2. Nineteen Nineteen; 3. The Big Money. New York: Harcourt, Brace and Co., 1938. Reprint ed. New York: Modern Library [1939].

Journeys Between Wars. New York: Harcourt, Brace and Co., 1938.

Adventures of a Young Man. New York: Harcourt, Brace and Co., 1939.

The Ground We Stand On: Some Examples from the History of a Political Creed. New York: Harcourt, Brace and Co., 1941.

Number One. Boston: Houghton, Mifflin Co., 1943.

State of the Nation. Boston: Houghton, Mifflin Co., 1944.

Tour of Duty. Boston: Houghton, Mifflin Co., 1946.

The Grand Design. Boston: Houghton, Mifflin Co., 1949.

The Prospect Before Us. Boston: Houghton, Mifflin Co., 1950.

Chosen Country. Boston: Houghton, Mifflin Co., 1951.

District of Columbia. Boston: Houghton, Mifflin Co., 1952. Reprints as a trilogy *Adventures of a Young Man, Number One,* and *The Grand Design.*

The Head and Heart of Thomas Jefferson. Garden City, N.Y.: Doubleday and Co., 1954.

Most Likely to Succeed. New York: Prentice-Hall, Inc., 1954.

The Theme Is Freedom. New York: Dodd, Mead and Co., 1956. Reprint ed. Freeport, New York: Books for Libraries Press, 1970.

The Men Who Made the Nation. Garden City, N.Y.: Doubleday and Co., 1957.

The Great Days. New York: Sagamore Press, 1958.

Prospects of a Golden Age. Englewood Cliffs, N.J.: Prentice-Hall, Inc., 1959.

Midcentury. Boston: Houghton, Mifflin Co., 1961.

Mr. Wilson's War. Garden City, N.Y.: Doubleday and Co., 1962.

Brazil on the Move. Garden City, N.Y.: Doubleday and Co., 1963.

With Paul Shyre. *U.S.A.: A Dramatic Review.* New York: Samuel French, Inc., 1963.

Thomas Jefferson—The Making of a President. Boston: Houghton, Mifflin Co., 1964.

174

Occasions and Protests. Chicago: Henry Regnery Co., 1964.
The Best Times: An Informal Memoir. New York: New American Library, 1966.
World in a Glass: A View of Our Century. Boston: Houghton, Mifflin Co., 1966.
The Shackles of Power: Three Jeffersonian Decades. Garden City, N.Y.: Doubleday and Co., 1966.
The Portugal Story: Three Centuries of Exploration and Discovery. Garden City, N.Y.: Doubleday and Co., 1966.
Easter Island: Island of Enigmas. Garden City, N.Y.: Doubleday and Co., 1971.
The Fourteenth Chronicle: Letters and Diaries of John Dos Passos. Edited and with a biographical narrative by Townsend Ludington. Boston: Gambit, Inc., 1973.
Century's Ebb. Boston: Gambit, Inc., 1975.

Material in Periodicals and Contributions to Books and Pamphlets

Review of *Insurgent Mexico*, by Jack Reed. *Harvard Monthly* 59 (November 1914):67–68
"The World Decision." *Harvard Monthy* 62 (March 1916):23–24.
"A Humble Protest." *Harvard Monthly* 62 (June 1916):115–20.
"A Conference on Foreign Relations." *Harvard Monthly* 62 (June 1916):126–27.
Review of *The War in Eastern Europe*, by Jack Reed. *Harvard Monthly* 62 (July 1916):148–49.
"Against American Literature." *New Republic* 8 (14 October 1916):269–71.
"Young Spain." *Seven Arts* 2 (August 1917):473–88.
"In Portugal." *Liberator* 3 (April 1920):25.
"America and the Pursuit of Happiness." *Nation* 111 (29 December 1920):777–78.
"The Misadventures of 'Deburau.'" *Freeman* 2 (2 February 1921):497–98.
Review of *The Enormous Room*, by E. E. Cummings. *Dial* 73 (July 1922):97–102.
"The Caucasus Under the Soviets." *Liberator* 5 (August 1922):5–8.
Foreword to *Roger Bloomer*, by John Howard Lawson. New York: Thomas J. Seltzer, 1923.
"Is the 'Realistic' Theatre Obsolete?" *Vanity Fair* 24 (May 1925):64.
"300 N.Y. Agitators Reach Passaic." *New Masses* 1 (June 1926):8.
"The New Masses I'd Like." *New Masses* 1 (June 1926):20.
"Abd El Krim" *New Masses* 1 (July 1926):21.
"The Pit and the Pendulum." *New Masses* 1 (August 1926):10–11.
"Snarling Diplomats." *New Masses* 1 (September 1926):24.
"Inside Watching Out." *New Masses* 2 (February 1927):27.
"Paint the Revolution." *New Masses* 2 (March 1927):15.
"Told By a Believer." *New Masses* 2 (March 1927):30.
"An Open Letter to President Lowell." *Nation* 125 (24 August 1927):176.

175

"They Are Dead Now." *New Maseses* 3 (October 1927):7.
"Sacco and Vanzetti." *New Masses* 3 (November 1927):25.
"Towards a Revolutionary Theatre." *New Masses* 3 (December 1927):20.
"A Great American." *New Masses* 3 (December 1927):26.
"They Want Ritzy Art." *New Masses* 4 (June 1928):8.
"Statement of Belief." *Bookman* 68 (September 1928):26.
"The Making of a Writer." *New Masses* 4 (March 1929):23.
"Did the New Playwrights Theatre Fail?" *New Masses* 5 (August 1929):13.
"Edison and Steinmetz: Medicine Men." *New Republic* 61 (18 December 1929):103–4.
Introduction to *Story of the Imperial Valley*, by Frank Spector. International Labor Defense Pamphlet no. 3 [1930].
"Un Grande Journaliste: John Reed." *Le Monde*, 18 January 1930, p. 3.
"Back to Red Hysteria!" *New Republic* 63 (2 July 1930): 168–69.
"Whom Can We Appeal To?" *New Masses* 6 (August 1930):8.
"Wanted: An Ivy Lee for Liberals." *New Republic* 63 (13 August 1930):371–72.
"American Theatre: 1930–31." *New Republic* 66 (1 April 1931):171–75.
"An Appeal for Aid." *New Republic* 67 (5 August 1931):318.
Introduction to *Three Soldiers*, by John Dos Passos. New York: Modern Library, 1932.
"The Miners Speak for Themselves" and "The Free Speech Speakin's." In *Harlan Miners Speak*, National Committee for the Defense of Political Prisoners, pp. 91–198, 277–97. New York: Harcourt, Brace and Company, 1932. Editorial comment by Dos Passos.
"Whither the American Writer?" *Modern Quarterly* 6 (Summer 1932):11–12.
"Help the Scottsboro Boys." *New Republic* 72 (24 August 1932):49.
"Thank You, Mr. Hitler." *Common Sense* 1 (27 April 1933):13.
Foreword to *Veterans on the March*, by Jack Douglas. New York: Workers Library, 1934.
Reply to a questionnaire, in "Prospects for the American Theatre." *New Theatre* 1 (February 1934):13.
"The Business of a Novelist." *New Republic* 78 (4 April 1934):220.
"World's Iron, Our Blood, and Their Profits." *Student Outlook* 3 (October 1934):17–18.
"The Writer as Technician." In *American Writers Congress*, edited by Henry Hart, pp. 78–82. New York: International Publishers, 1935.
"Two Views of the Student Strike." *Student Outlook* 3 (April 1935):5.
"A Case of Conscience." *Common Sense* 4 (May 1935):16–19.
Preface to *Terror in Cuba*, by Arthur Pincus. New York: Workers Defense League [1936].
"Farewell to Europe." *Common Sense* 6 (July 1937):9–11.
"The Communist Party and the War Spirit." *Common Sense* 6 (December 1937):11–14.
With Theodore Dreiser. "Theodore Dreiser—John Dos Passos: A Conversation." *Direction* 1 (January 1938):2–3.
"Death of José Robles." *New Republic* 99 (19 July 1939):308–9.

"Tom Paine's 'Common Sense.' " *Common Sense* 8 (September 1939):3–6.
"Tom Paine's 'Rights of Man.' " *Common Sense* 8 (October 1939):12–15.
"To a Liberal in Office." *Nation* 153 (6 September 1941):195–97.
"England in the Great Lull." *Harpers* 184 (February 1942):235–44.
"Carlo Tresca." *Nation* 156 (23 January 1943):123–24.
Foreword to *Who Killed Carlo Tresca?* Tresca Memorial Committee, n.d., pp. 4–6.
"There is ONLY One Freedom." *'47* 1 (April 1947):74–76.
"Britain's Dim Dictatorship." *Life* 23 (29 September 1947):120–22.
"The Failure of Marxism." *Life* 24 (19 January 1948):96–98.
"Revolution on the Farm." *Life* 25 (23 August 1948):95–98.
Life's Picture History of World War II. New York: Time, Inc., 1950. Text by Dos Passos and others.
"The General." *Modern Millwheel* 14 (January 1950 through June 1950). A six-part article.
"Mr. Chambers' Descent Into Hell." *Saturday Review* 35 (24 May 1952):11.
"Adlai Stevenson: Patrician with a Mission." *National Review* 2 (27 October 1956):11–15 and (3 November 1956):13–15.
"P.S. to Dean Briggs." In *College in a Yard: Minutes by Thirty-Nine Harvard Men*, edited by Brooks Atkinson, pp. 63–67. Cambridge: Harvard University Press, 1957.
"Acceptance by John Dos Passos." *Proceedings of the American Academy of Arts and Letters and the National Institute of Arts and Letters*, 2d ser., no. 8 (N.Y., 1958):193.
"A Question of Elbow Room." In *Essays in Individuality*, edited by Felix Morley. Philadelphia: University of Pennsylvania Press, 1958. Reprinted in *Occasions and Protests*, by John Dos Passos, pp. 52–76. Chicago: Henry Regnery Co., 1964.
"What Union Members Have Been Writing Senator McClellan." *Reader's Digest* 73 (September 1958):25–32.
Introduction to *Up From Liberalism*, by William F. Buckley, Jr. New York: McDowell, Obolensky, 1959.
"Looking Back on 'U.S.A.' " *New York Times*, 25 October 1959, sec. 2, p. 5.
"Contemporary Chronicles." *Carleton Miscellany* 2 (Spring 1961):25–29.
"Cogitations in a Roman Theatre." In *Occasions and Protests*, by John Dos Passos, pp. 278–90. Chicago: Henry Regnery Co., 1964.
"Please Mr. Rip Van Winkle, Wake Up Some More." *National Review* 16 (28 January 1964):71–74.
"The Battle of San Francisco." *National Review* 16 (28 July 1964): 640.
"What Hope for Maintaining a Conservative Opposition?" *National Review* 16 (20 October 1964):907–9.
"The New Left, A Spook Out of the Past." *National Review* 18 (18 October 1966):1037–39.
"What Makes a Novelist." *National Review* 20 (16 January 1968):29–32.
" '1968.' " *National Review* 20 (13 August 1968):793–94.
"On the Way to the Moon Shot." *National Review* 23 (9 February 1971):135–36.

Manuscript Collection

Austin, Texas. Humanities Research Center, University of Texas.
Bloomington, Indiana. Lilly Library, Indiana University. Claude Bowers papers and Max Eastman papers.
Cambridge, Massachusetts. Houghton Library, Harvard University.
Carbondale, Illinois. Morris Library, Southern Illinois University. Philip Kaplan collection.
Charlottesville, Virginia. Alderman Library, University of Virginia. John Dos Passos papers.
Eugene, Oregon. University of Oregon Library. Robert Cantwell papers.
Laramie, Wyoming. Archive of Contemporary History, University of Wyoming. Selden Rodman collection.
New Haven, Connecticut. Beinecke Library, Yale University. Edmund Wilson papers.
Philadelphia, Pennsylvania. Van Pelt Library, University of Pennsylvania. Theodore Dreiser papers and James T. Farrell papers.

Critical and Historical Works

Aaron, Daniel. *Writers on the Left: Episodes in American Literary Communism*. New York: Harcourt, Brace and World, 1961.
———. "The Riddle of John Dos Passos." *Harpers* 224 (March 1962):55–60.
Aldridge, John W. *After the Lost Generation: A Critical Study of the Writers of Two Wars*. New York: McGraw-Hill, 1951.
Arden, Eugene. "*Manhattan Transfer*: An Experiment in Technique." *University of Kansas City Review* 22 (Winter 1955):153–58.
Astre, Georges-Albert. *John Dos Passos: de "L'Initiation d'un homme à 'U.S.A..' "* 1956–58. Reprint. Paris: Lettres Modernes, 1974.
Baker, Carlos. *Hemingway: The Writer as Artist*. Princeton: Princeton University Press, 1963.
———. *Ernest Hemingway: A Life Story*. New York: Charles Scribner's Sons, 1969.
Baker, John D. "Italian Anarchism and the American Dream—The View of John Dos Passos." In *Italian American Radicalism—Old World Origins and New World Developments: Proceedings of the Fifth Annual Conference of the American Italian Historical Association*. (Boston, November 11, 1972).
Beach, Joseph Warren. *American Fiction: 1920–1940*. New York: MacMillan, 1941.
Becker, George J. *John Dos Passos*. New York: Frederick Ungar Publishing Co., 1974.
Belkind, Allen, ed. *Dos Passos, the Critics, and the Writer's Intention*. Carbondale: Southern Illinois University Press, 1971. Includes some of the articles and reviews listed here.
Bernardin, Charles W. "Dos Passos' Harvard Years." *New England Quarterly* 27 (March 1954):3–26.

Bernstein, Barton J., ed. *Towards a New Past: Dissenting Essays in American History.* New York: Pantheon, 1968.

Bernstein, Irving. *The Lean Years: A History of the American Worker 1920–1933.* Boston: Houghton Mifflin, 1960.

Brantley, John D. *The Fiction of John Dos Passos.* Studies in American Literature, no. 16. The Hague: Mouton, 1968.

Brown, Deming. *Soviet Attitudes Toward American Writing.* Princeton: Princeton University Press, 1962.

Buckley, William F., Jr. *Up From Liberalism.* New York: McDowell, Obolensky, 1959.

Canby, Henry Seidel. Review of *Three Soldiers. New York Evening Post Book Review,* 8 October 1921, p. 67.

Casey, Phil. "Dos Passos Speeds Up His Pen After 4 Decades of Writing." *Washington Post,* 16 July 1959, p. B-1.

Chamberlain, John. "John Dos Passos." *Saturday Review of Literature* 20 (3 June 1939):3–4.

Chametzky, Jules. "Reflections on *U.S.A.* as Novel and Play." *Massachusetts Review* 1 (Winter 1960):391–99.

Colley, Iain. *Dos Passos and the Fiction of Despair.* Totowa, N.J.: Rowman and Littlefield, 1978.

Conlin, Joseph R., ed. *The American Radical Press 1880–1960.* 2 vols. Westport, Connecticut: Greenwood Press, 1974.

Cooperman, Stanley. *World War I and the American Novel.* Baltimore: The Johns Hopkins Press, 1967.

Cowley, Malcolm. "The Poet and the World." *New Republic* 70 (27 April 1932):303–5.

———. *Exile's Return: A Literary Odyssey of the 1920's.* New York: W. W. Norton, 1934. Reprint ed. New York: Viking Press, 1951.

———. "Afterthoughts on Dos Passos." *New Republic* 88 (9 September 1936):134.

———. "Dos Passos and His Critics." *New Republic* 120 (28 February 1949): 21–23.

Culture and the Crisis: An Open Letter to the Writers, Artists, Teachers, Physicians, Engineers, Scientists and Other Professional Workers of America. New York: League of Professional Groups for Foster and Ford, 1932. Dos Passos is one of fifty-two signers of a political statement on pp. 31–32, of this pamphlet.

Davis, Robert Gorham. *John Dos Passos.* University of Minnesota Pamphlets on American Literature, no. 20. Minneapolis: University of Minnesota Press, 1962.

Deutscher, Isaac. *Russia in Transition and Other Essays.* New York: Coward-McCann, 1957.

Diggins, John P. *The American Left in the Twentieth Century.* New York: Harcourt, Brace, Jovanovich, 1973.

———. *Up From Communism: Conservative Odysseys in American Intellectual History.* New York: Harper and Row, 1975.

SELECTED BIBLIOGRAPHY

Dommerques, Pierre. "John Dos Passos: An Old Dream Behind the Mask of Rebellion." *St. Andrews Review* 2 (Fall–Winter 1972):56–59.

Donnell, Richard Stover. "John Dos Passos: Satirical Historian of American Morality." 2 vols. Ph.D. dissertation, Harvard University, 1960.

Eastman, Max. "Motive-Patterns of Socialism. *Modern Quarterly* 11 (Fall 1939):45–55.

——— et al. *John Dos Passos: An Appreciation.* New York: Prentice-Hall, 1954. Eight page publicity brochure for release of *Most Likely To Succeed.*

Edwards, Thomas R. "Dos Passos Divided." *New York Review of Books*, 29 November 1973, pp. 28–30.

Farrell, James T. "Dos Passos and the Critics." *American Mercury* 47 (August 1939):489–94.

———. "How Should We Rate Dos Passos?" *New Republic* 138 (28 April 1958):17–18.

Freeman, Joseph. *An American Testament: A Narrative of Rebels and Romantics.* New York: Farrar and Rinehart, 1936.

French, Warren, ed. *The Thirties: Fiction, Poetry, Drama.* Deland, Florida: Everett Edwards, 1967.

Gado, Frank, ed. *First Person: Conversations on Writers and Writing.* Schenectady, New York: Union College Press, 1973. The interview with Dos Passos is from 1968.

Geismar, Maxwell. *Writers in Crisis.* Boston: Houghton, Mifflin Company, 1942.

———. *American Moderns: From Rebellion to Conformity.* New York: Hill and Wang 1958.

Gelfant, Blanche H. *The American City Novel.* Norman: University of Oklahoma Press, 1954.

———. "The Search for Identity in the Novels of John Dos Passos." *PMLA* 76 (March 1961):133–49.

Gilbert, James Burkhart. *Writers and Partisans: A History of Literary Radicalism in America.* New York: John Wiley and Sons, 1968.

Gold, Michael. "Let It Be Really New." *New Masses* 1 (June 1926):20.

———. "The Education of John Dos Passos." *English Journal* 22 (February 1933):87–97.

———. "Change the World." *Daily Worker*, 26 February 1938, p. 7.

Gorman, Thomas Richard. "Words and Deeds: A Study of the Political Attitudes of John Dos Passos." Ph.D. dissertation, University of Pennsylvania, 1960.

Guttmann, Allen. *The Conservative Tradition in America.* New York: Oxford University Press, 1967.

Havighurst, Alfred F. *Twentieth Century Britain.* 2nd ed. New York: Harper and Row, 1962.

Herbst, Josephine. "The Starched Blue Sky of Spain." *noble savage* 1 (1960):76–117.

Hicks, Granville, "The Politics of John Dos Passos." *Antioch Review* 10 (March 1950):85–98.

———. "Dos Passos: The Fruits of Disillusionment." *New Republic* 131 (27 September 1954):17–18.

Hoffman, Frederick. *The Twenties: American Writing in the Postwar Decade.* New York: Free Press, 1965.

Hook, Andrew, ed. *Dos Passos: A Collection of Critical Essays.* Twentieth Century Views Series. Englewood Cliffs, N.J.: Prentice-Hall, Inc., 1974. Includes some of the articles and reviews listed here.

Horchler, Richard. "Prophet Without Hope." *Commonweal* 75 (29 September 1961):13–16.

Hutchens, John K. "On the Books." *New York Herald Tribune Weekly Book Review,* 30 January 1949, p. 10.

Huthmacher, J. Joseph. *Trial by War and Depression: 1917–1941.* Boston: Allyn and Bacon, Inc., 1973.

Josephson, Matthew. *Infidel in the Temple: A Memoir of the Nineteen-Thirties.* New York: Alfred A. Knopf, 1967.

Kallich, Martin. "John Dos Passos: Liberty and the Father-Image." *Antioch Review* 10 (March 1950):99–106.

———. "John Dos Passos Fellow Traveler: A Dossier with Commentary." *Twentieth Century Literature* 1 (January 1956):173–90.

Kazin, Alfred. *On Native Grounds.* New York: Harcourt, Brace and World, Inc., 1942. Reprint ed. Garden City, New York: Doubleday and Co., 1956.

Kneeland, Paul F. "This Country Needs 'A Free and Vigorous Society.' " *Boston Sun Globe,* 16 January 1949, p. A-21. Report of an interview with Dos Passos.

Knox, George. "Voice in the *U.S.A.* Biographies." *Texas Studies in Literature and Language* 4 (Spring 1962):109–16.

Knox, George A., and Stahl, Herbert M. *Dos Passos and "The Revolting Playwrights."* Uppsala, Sweden: Uppsala University Press, 1964.

Krause, Sydney J., ed. *Essays on Determinism in American Literature.* Kent Studies in English, no. 1. Kent, Ohio: Kent State University Press, 1964.

Lalli, Bianca Tedeschini. *Dos Passos. Il castoro* series, no. 21. Florence: La Nuova Italia, 1974.

Landsberg, Melvin. *Dos Passos' Path to "U.S.A.": A Political Biography 1912–1936.* Boulder: Colorado Associated University Press, 1972.

Lasch, Christopher. *The Agony of the American Left.* New York: Alfred A. Knopf, 1969.

Lemisch, Jesse. "The American Revolution Seen From the Bottom Up." In *Towards A New Past: Dissenting Essays in American History,* edited by Barton J. Bernstein, pp. 3–45. New York: Pantheon, 1968.

Lewis, Sinclair. *John Dos Passos' "Manhattan Transfer."* New York: Harper and Brothers, 1926.

Lowry, E. D. "*Manhattan Transfer*: Dos Passos' Wasteland." *University Review* (Kansas City) 30 (October 1963):47–52.

———. "The Lively Art of *Manhattan Transfer*." *PMLA* 84 (October 1969): 1628–38.

Ludington, Charles T., Jr. "The Neglected Satires of John Dos Passos." *Satire Newsletter* 7 (Spring 1970):127–36.

Ludington, Townsend, ed. *The Fourteenth Chronicle: Letters and Diaries of John Dos Passos*. Boston: Gambit, 1973.

———. *John Dos Passos: A Twentieth Century Odyssey*. New York: E. P. Dutton, 1980.

McLuhan, Herbert Marshall. "John Dos Passos: Technique vs. Sensibility." In *Fifty Years of the American Novel: A Christian Appraisal*, edited by Harold C. Gardiner, S. J., pp. 151–64. New York: Charles Scribner's Sons, 1951.

Madden, Charles F., ed. *Talks with Authors*. Carbondale: Southern Illinois University Press, 1968.

Millgate, Michael. *American Social Fiction: James to Cozzens*. Edinburgh: Oliver and Boyd, 1964.

Mirsky, D. "Dos Passos in Two Soviet Productions." *International Literature*, July 1934, pp. 152–54.

Mizener, Sharon Fusselman. *Manhattan Transients*. Hicksville, N.Y.: Exposition Press, 1977.

Moore, Harry T. "Proud Men in An Age of Conformity." *New York Times Book Review*, 26 February 1961, p. 1.

Murray, Edward. *The Cinematic Imagination: Writers and the Motion Pictures*. New York: Frederick Ungar, 1972.

Pells, Richard H. *Radical Visions and American Dreams: Culture and Social Thought in the Depression Years*. New York: Harper and Row, 1973.

Rahv, Philip. "Proletarian Literature: A Political Autopsy." *Southern Review* 4 (Winter 1939):616–28.

———. "Disillusionment and Partial Answers." *Partisan Review* 15 (May 1948):519–29.

Robbins, Jack Alan, ed. *Granville Hicks in the New Masses*. Port Washington, N.Y.: Kennikat Press, 1974.

Sanders, David. "The 'Anarchism' of John Dos Passos." *South Atlantic Quarterly* 60 (Winter 1961):44–55.

———. "Interview with John Dos Passos." *Claremont Quarterly* 11 (Spring 1964):89–100.

———. "The Art of Fiction XLIV." *Paris Review* 46 (Spring 1969):147–72. Interview with Dos Passos.

———, ed. *Studies in "U.S.A."* Merrill Studies Series. Columbus, Ohio: Charles E. Merrill, 1971.

Sartre, Jean-Paul. *Literary and Philosophical Essays*. London: Rider and Co., 1955.

———. "American Novelists in French Eyes." *Atlantic Monthly* 178 (August 1946):114–18.

Shannon, David A. *Between the Wars: America, 1919–1941*. Boston: Houghton, Mifflin Co., 1965.

Sloane, David E. E. "The Black Experience in Dos Passos' *U.S.A.*" *CEA Critic* 36 (March 1974):22–23.

Smith, Marion Hammett. "Recollections of Dos." *Connecticut Review* 8 (April 1975):21–24.

Snell, George D. *Shapers of American Fiction*, 1789–1947. New York: Dutton, 1947.

Solow, Herbert. "Minutiae of Left-Wing Literary History." *Partisan Review* 4 (March 1938):59–62.

——. "Substitution at Left Tackle, Hemingway for Dos Passos." *Partisan Review* 4–5 (April 1938):63–64.

"Soviet Literature and Dos Passos." *International Literature* 5 (1933–34):103–12.

Stade, George. "The Two Faces of Dos Passos." *Partisan Review* 41 (1974):476–83.

Thorp, Willard. "American Writers on the Left." In *Socialism and American Life*, edited by Donald Drew Egbert and Stow Persons, vol. 1, pp. 599–620. 2 vols. Princeton: Princeton University Press, 1952.

"To John Dos Passos." *New Masses* 10 (6 March 1934):8–9.

"Tract for the Times." *Liberation* 1 (March 1956):3–6.

Trilling, Lionel. "The America of John Dos Passos." *Partisan Review* 4 (April 1938):26–32.

"Unintelligent Fanaticism." *New Masses* 10 (27 March 1934):6, 8.

"U.S.A." Thirty-six page publicity brochure for November 21, 1946 publication of three-volume edition of *U.S.A.* illustrated by Reginald Marsh.

Vanderwerken, David L. "Dos Passos' *Streets of Night*: A Reconsideration." *Markham Review* 4 (October 1974):61–65.

——. "*U.S.A.*: Dos Passos and the 'Old Words.' " *Twentieth Century Literature* 23 (May 1977):195–228.

Wagner, Linda W. *Dos Passos: Artist as American*. Austin: University of Texas Press, 1979.

Wakefield, Dan. "Dos, Which Side Are You On?" *Esquire* 59 (April 1963):112–14.

Walcutt, Charles Child. *American Literary Naturalism, A Divided Stream*. Minneapolis: University of Minnesota Press, 1956.

Wald, Alan M. *James T. Farrell: The Revolutionary Socialist Years*. New York: New York University Press, 1978.

Walled In This Tomb: Questions Left Unanswered by the Lowell Committee in the Sacco-Vanzetti Case and Their Pertinence in Understanding the Conflicts Sweeping the World at This Hour: For Especial Consideration by the Alumni of Harvard University During Its Tercentenary Celebration. Boston: Excelsior Press [1936]. Foreword signed by twenty-eight Harvard alumni, including Dos Passos.

Weinstein, James. *Ambiguous Legacy: The Left in American Politics*. New York: New Viewpoints, 1975.

Westerhoven, James N. "Autobiographical Elements in the Camera Eye." *American Literature* 48 (November 1976):341–64.

Whalen, Richard. "A Conversation with Dos Passos." *New Leader* 42 (23 February 1959):20–21.

Wheeler, Thomas Chilton. "The Political Philosophy of John Dos Passos." Undergraduate Honors Thesis, Harvard College, 1951. Appendix contains a long letter from Dos Passos, a reply to a questionnaire.

183

Whipple, T. K. *Study Out the Land.* Berkeley: University of California Press, 1943.

Wilson, Edmund. *The Triple Thinkers: Twelve Essays on Literary Subjects.* New York: Oxford University Press, 1948.

―――. *Shores of Light.* New York: Farrar, Straus and Giroux, 1952.

―――. *A Literary Chronicle: 1920–1950.* Garden City, N.Y.: Doubleday and Company, 1956.

―――. *The Twenties: From Notebooks and Diaries of the Period.* Edited with an introduction by Leon Edel. New York: Farrar, Straus and Giroux, 1975.

―――. *Letters on Literature and Politics 1912–1972.* Edited by Elena Wilson. New York: Farrar, Straus and Giroux, 1977.

Winner, Anthony. "The Characters of John Dos Passos." *Literatur in Wissenschaft und Unterricht* 2 (1969):1–19.

Wittner, Lawrence S. *Cold War America: From Hiroshima to Watergate.* New York: Praeger Publishers, 1974.

Wrenn, John H. *John Dos Passos.* Twayne's United States Authors Series. New Haven: College and University Press, 1961.

Zasursky, Y. "Dos Passos' Experimental Novel." In *20th Century American Literature: A Soviet View*, pp. 331–50. Moscow: Progress Publishers, 1976.

INDEX

185

INDEX

Press, 8, 14, 25, 65–66, 85, 86. See also
New York Times
Progressive party, 41
Prospect Before Us, The, 117–18, 130, 139,
140, 141
Prospects of a Golden Age, 128
Puritanism, 32, 33, 34, 39–40, 54, 138. See
also Dos Passos, John, and sexuality
Pushcart at the Curb, A, 32, 152 n. 49

Quest, The (Baroja), 152 n. 49
Quixote, Don, 27

Racism, 66, 84, 142–43, 164 n. 13
Rahv, Philip, 109
Rainy, Homer Price, 160 n. 68
Randolph, A. Philip, 84
Reagan, Ronald, 143
Realism, 16, 60, 72
Red Cross, 8, 13
Reed, John, 5, 83
Religion, 4, 27, 31, 61, 133, 138
Republican party, 70, 71, 111, 132
Reuther, Walter, 137
Rimbaud, Arthur, 10, 153 n. 65
Robles, José, 94, 107, 122
Rockwell, Norman, 114
Roosevelt, Eleanor (Mrs. Franklin D.),
94, 136
Roosevelt, Franklin D.: criticism of in
Grand Design, The, 111–15; Dos Passos's
views on, 76–77, 111, 143, 159 n. 57;
open letter to, 104; mentioned, 70, 94,
95, 126, 128, 135. See also New Deal
Rosenberg, Ethel and Julius, 142
Rosinante to the Road Again, 26–29, 30, 34,
36, 40, 48, 54, 62, 82, 95, 114, 125
Russia. See Soviet Union
Russian Revolution, 31–32, 33, 62–64,
89, 92–93, 99–100. See also Soviet
Union
Rustin, Bayard, 134

Sacco-Vanzetti case, 52–56; in Dos Passos's fiction, 57, 87, 88, 89, 118; mentioned, 59, 78, 93
Sacco-Vanzetti Defense Committee, 49,
52, 61
Sanger, Margaret, 85
Sartre, Jean-Paul, 91, 161 n. 76
Satire: in Dos Passos's fiction, 37, 39, 58,
97, 124, 132, 163 n. 95, 167 n. 47;

mentioned, 5, 6
Schlesinger, Arthur, Jr., 134
Science, 5. See also Industrialism; Tech-
nology
Scottsboro defense, 71
Seven Times Round the Walls of Jericho (Dos
Passos and Hillyer), 149 n. 19
Sexism, 84–85
Shackles of Power, The, 128
Sinclair, Upton, 81, 86
Slavery, 126
Smith, Adam, 44
Smith, Katharine. See Dos Passos, Katha-
rine Smith
Smith Act, 104
Socialism: Dos Passos's views on, 76,
91–93, 95, 107–10; mentioned, 5, 7,
134, 135
Socialist party, 34, 70, 71, 75–76, 92
Socialist Realism, 91
Socialist Workers party, 104
Sorbonne, 13, 18
Soviet Union: critics from on U.S.A.,
90–91; Dos Passos's views on, 14, 76,
107, 110, 122; Dos Passos's visits to,
31–32, 62–64; mentioned, 41, 68, 72,
73, 93
Spain, 6–7, 14, 26–29, 93, 96, 125; civil
war in, 93–96, 162 n. 90
Stalin, Joseph, 63, 76, 92
Standard Oil, 76
Stars and Stripes, 106
State, Department of, 75
State of the Nation, 104–5, 107, 111
Steffens, Lincoln, 62
Stein, Gertrude, 41
Steinmetz, Charles Proteus, 82
Stevenson, Adlai, 134
Story of the Imperial Valley, 66
Streets of Night, 32, 38–41, 42, 45, 54, 59,
92, 138, 153 n. 63
Strikes, 14, 24, 28, 51, 55, 65, 67–68; in
Dos Passos's fiction, 22, 57–60 passim,
86, 88, 96, 137. See also Labor unions
Sugar Trust, 3

Taylor, Frederick Winslow, 79–80, 83,
92, 105, 140
Tcheka, 31
Technology, 10, 82–83, 105, 106. See also
Industrialism
Texas, University of, 81, 160 n. 68

190

"Thank You, Mr. Hitler," 75
Thayer, Webster, 54, 55
Theater: American, Dos Passos on, 35, 56–57, 61, 63; Russian, Dos Passos on, 63, 64. *See also* New Playwrights Theatre
Theme Is Freedom, The, 130–31, 168 n. 60, 168 n. 61
Thomas, J. Parnell, 122
Thomas, Norman, 108
Thoreau, Henry David, 134
Three Soldiers, 15–23, 150 n. 30; reviews of, 23–24, 151 n. 34; mentioned, 14, 34, 36, 39, 42, 46, 85
Thurmond, Strom, 133
Tobin, Dan, 137
Tour of Duty, 130, 164 n. 12
Tresca, Carlo, 107
Truman Doctrine, 107

Ulysses (Joyce), 41
Unamuno, Miguel, 28
Unemployed Councils, 76
Unions. *See* Labor unions
United Fruit Company, 76, 160 n. 69
United Mine Workers of America (UMWA), 67–68
Up from Liberalism (Buckley), 132
U.S.A., 78–91; biographies in, 79–80, 82–83, 84–85, 86, 136, 141; Camera Eye in, 42, 78, 80, 86–87, 90, 91–92, 136, 141; comparison of three volumes of, 89–90; critics on, 90–91, 161 n. 76, 162 n. 83; *Midcentury* compared to, 136, 139, 140–41; Newsreels in, 79, 80, 86, 87, 136, 141; stage version of, 168 n. 64; mentioned, 16, 17, 29, 41, 48, 49, 50, 56, 64, 73, 74, 96, 103, 110, 112, 113, 114, 115, 119, 120, 126, 127, 132, 144, 145. See also, *Big Money, The; 42nd Parallel, The; 1919*

Valentino, Rudolph, 85

Vanzetti, Bartolomeo. *See* Sacco-Vanzetti case
Veblen, Thorstein, 5, 83, 86, 89, 112
Verhaeren, Emile, 153 n. 65
Versailles Peace Conference, 25, 80
Villages Are the Heart of Spain, The, 94–95
Von Sternberg, Josef, 74
Voting, by Dos Passos, 24, 41, 71, 111, 132, 133

Wagner, Linda, 151 n. 42
Wallace, Henry, 171 n. 89
War, 75, 82, 105–6. *See also* World War I; World War II; Spain, civil war in
War Production Board, 105
Watts, Richard, Jr., 60
Wayne, John, 133
Whitman, Walt, 6, 143
Widmer, Eleanor, 84
Williams, Roger, 100
Wilson, Edmund: Dos Passos's letters to, 55, 65, 76, 116; quoted, 35, 48, 60, 65, 76, 142, 154 n. 72; mentioned 32, 71, 74
Wilson, Woodrow, 7, 25, 61, 84; in *U.S.A.,* 79, 80, 83, 87, 88, 89
Wobblies. *See* Industrial Workers of the World
Woodstock, 143
World War I: domestic repression during and after, 7–8, 24, 33, 53, 65, 70, 77; Dos Passos in 8–9, 13–14; Dos Passos on, 5–9, 24–25; in Dos Passos's fiction, 10–13, 15–23, 82
World War II, 103, 110; Dos Passos's reporting on, 104–6
Wright, Orville and Wilbur, 83

Young Americans for Freedom, 133
"Young Spain," 6–7, 27

Zapata, Emiliano, 61
Zola, Emile, 10